W9-AON-722

Discover Cape Cod

AMC's Guide to the Best Hiking, Biking, and Paddling

MICHAEL O'CONNOR

Appalachian Mountain Club Books
Boston, Massachusetts

The AMC is a nonprofit organization and sales of AMC books fund our mission of protecting the Northeast outdoors. If you appreciate our efforts and would like to make a donation to the AMC, contact us at Appalachian Mountain Club, 5 Joy Street, Boston, MA 02108.

http://www.outdoors.org/publications/books/

Distributed by The Globe Pequot Press, Guilford, Connecticut.

Front cover images: (top l–r) © Jerry and Marcy Monkman, © Veer Incorporated, © iStock, (bottom) © Pixtal / BrightQube
Back cover images: (l–r) © Aditi Wagh, © Juice Images, © Jerry and Marcy Monkman
Book design by Eric Edstam
Maps by Ken Dumas, © Appalachian Mountain Club
All interior photographs © Michael O'Connor except for those on pages: 7, 11, 26, 38, 61, 75, 83, 88, 155, 158, 229 © William DeSousa-Mauk; i, 149, 172 © Massachusetts Office of Travel and Tourism/Kindra Clineff; 19, 23 © Jacqueline Miller; 48, 124, 203 Cape Cod Chamber of Commerce; 106 © Massachusetts Office of Travel & Tourism; 64, 102, 184 © Jerry and Marcy Monkman; 97 © Kim Hojackni; 166, 191 © Paul Rezendez

Library of Congress Cataloging-in-Publication Data
O'Connor, Michael (Michael Patrick), 1952–
  Discover Cape Cod : AMC's guide to the best hiking, biking, and paddling / Michael O'Connor.
    p. cm.
  Includes index.
  ISBN 978-1-934028-17-9
1. Outdoor recreation—Massachusetts—Cape Cod—Guidebooks. 2. Cape Cod (Mass.)—Guidebooks. I. Appalachian Mountain Club. II. Title.
  GV191.42.M4O36 2009
  917.44'92—dc22
                    2009006724

The paper used in this publication meets the minimum requirements of the American National Standard for Information Sciences-Permanence of Paper for Printed Library Materials, ANSI Z39.48-1984. ∞

Outdoor recreation activities by their very nature are potentially hazardous. This book is not a substitute for good personal judgment and training in outdoor skills. Due to changes in conditions, use of the information in this book is at the sole risk of the user. The author and the Appalachian Mountain Club assume no liability for accidents happening to, or injuries sustained by, readers who engage in the activities described in this book.

Printed in the United States of America.

Printed on paper that contains 30 percent post-consumer recycled fiber, using soy-based inks.

10 9 8 7 6 5 4 3 2 1   09 10 11 12 13 14 15 16

Locator Map

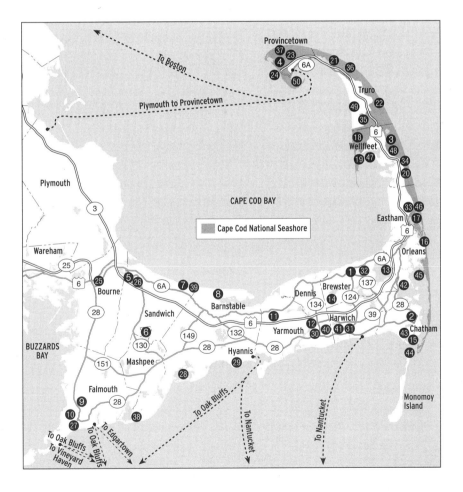

Contents

Nature and History Essays

Appendices

Index

At-a-Glance Trip Planner

Trip	Page	Location (town)	Distance	Difficulty
HIKES				
1 Brewster Town Walk	5	Brewster	2 mi	Easy
2 Chatham Town Walk	9	Chatham	3 mi	Easy
3 Wellfleet Town Walk	13	Wellfleet	3 mi	Easy
4 Provincetown Walk	17	Provincetown	2.5 mi	Easy
5 Shawme-Crowell State Forest	24	Sandwich	3 mi	Easy to moderate
6 Lowell Holly Reservation	29	Mashpee/Sandwich	4 mi	Easy to moderate
7 Murkwood	33	Sandwich	1.5 mi	Easy
8 Sandy Neck	36	Barnstable	6 mi	Moderate
9 Long Pond Conservation Area	42	Falmouth	5 mi	Easy to moderate
10 Beebe Woods/Peterson Farm	46	Falmouth	4 mi	Moderate

Estimated time	Fee	Good for kids	Dogs allowed	Swimming allowed	Trip highlights
3 hrs		✓	✓	✓	Country store, ice cream, and beach
4 hrs		✓	✓	✓	Quintessential Cape village
2 hrs		✓	✓		Galleries, gift shops, and a scenic harbor
3 hrs			✓		A grand carnival at the tip of the Cape
2 hrs		✓	✓		A family-friendly campground
3 hrs	$	✓	✓	✓	Peninsula between two glacial ponds
1 hr		✓	✓		Short, lovely loop with great salt marsh views
4 hrs	$		✓	✓	Barrier beach, dunes, and a salt marsh
3 hrs		✓	✓	✓	Loop trail through a forest and around a pond
3 hrs		✓	✓	✓	A pretty pond and a former farm

Estimated time	Fee	Good for kids	Dogs allowed	Swimming allowed	Trip highlights
1 hr		✓	✓		A lesson on local history and a trip around a pond
1 hr			✓		A trip from Town Hall to the scenic Bass River
3 hrs		✓	✓	✓	The Cape's largest state park
3 hrs		✓	✓		"Forgotten" woodlands on old roads
2 hrs		✓	✓	✓	Variety of animals, including deer, shorebirds, and seals
6 hrs	$		✓	✓	Scenic barrier beach
4 hrs				✓	A tidal marsh and beach
2 hrs		✓	✓	✓	Colonial house and Cape Cod Bay beach
4 hrs		✓		✓	Barrier beach on Cape Cod Bay
2 hrs		✓			Forest of Atlantic white cedars
3 hrs		✓			Swamp and vistas
1.5 hrs		✓		✓	Uplands, dunes, and beach
3 hrs			✓	✓	Dunes and an iconic lighthouse
2 hrs			✓	✓	A quiet shoreline walk to an historic lighthouse
4 hrs		✓			Views of boats traveling a scenic waterway

Estimated time	Fee	Good for kids	Dogs allowed	Swimming allowed	Trip highlights
4 hrs		✓			Campground, historic houses, colonial-era grist mill
4 hrs		✓			One of the Cape's loveliest paths
3 hrs				✓	Leisurely ride to a conservation area
3 hrs				✓	A visit to Kennedy country
4 hrs		✓		✓	Woodlands, cranberry bogs, and lovely ponds
6 hrs		✓			A scenic ride through the center of Harwich into the heart of Chatham
6 hrs				✓	Kettle hole ponds, cranberry bogs, and the beach
1 hr		✓		✓	Wooded uplands, a salt marsh, and the Atlantic
4 hrs				✓	A ride past the ocean and ponds to the bay
4 hrs				✓	Country roads, an old railroad bed, and Truro Harbor
4 hrs	$	✓			An old salt meadow and a lighthouse
3 hrs				✓	A paved route through seashore wilds
4 hrs				✓	Scenic bay to a lovely barrier island
3 hrs		✓			A tidal waterway leading through a scenic marsh
2 hrs		✓		✓	An under-appreciated river gem
3 hrs		✓			Marshlands, birds, and tall grasses

Estimated time	Fee	Good for kids	Dogs allowed	Swimming allowed	Trip highlights
4 hrs	$				Bay and tidal creeks
4 hrs				🏊	Tidal creek, small bay, and a lovely beach
5 hrs				🏊	A memorable coastal environment
3 hrs	$			🏊	A world of open water, islands, and creeks
3 hrs	$			🏊	History and ecology meet in this marsh
2 hrs	$			🏊	One of the Cape's prettiest harbors
1.5 hrs	$	🚶		🏊	A large pond and a pair of smaller ones
4 hrs				🏊	Meandering river to Cape Cod Bay
4 hrs	$			🏊	A paddle from the upper harbor to a quiet beach

Preface

MORE THAN 5 MILLION VISITORS ENJOY CAPE COD EACH YEAR, most of them from Memorial Day through mid-October. That's a lot of people to put on a skinny, coastal peninsula—especially one attached to Massachusetts, a state with one of the highest population densities in the nation. Yet even at the height of a Cape summer, it's surprisingly easy to wander a quiet stretch of beach, pedal through a pine-oak forest and see no one in either direction, or paddle a tidal marsh shared with seemingly only a great blue heron.

That this 60-mile spit of sand and upland can still introduce visitors to its natural wonders through such pristine experiences is one of the Cape's finest qualities—and the primary reason I love it. Despite an annual tourist glut, the resultant traffic snarls, the exposure of locals' "secret" places, and continued development, I still believe Cape Cod is for sharing with others. Indeed, it was my Massachusetts-born wife (to whom this guide is dedicated) who years ago introduced her new, non-native husband to this cornucopia of the outdoors.

My wife and I biked along the Cape Cod Canal and soon thereafter along the Cape Cod Rail Trail, when it first pushed east from Dennis, past the cranberry bogs and glacial ponds of Harwich and Brewster. We paddled our canoe down the Swan Pond River and right into Nantucket Sound (where we got dual lessons from wind and wave—and eventually made the switch to kayaks). And we hiked, hiked, hiked the Cape Cod National Seashore, from Chatham's Monomoy Islands to Long Point in Provincetown, and across most of the woodlands and wetlands in between.

It's always been about the beauty of the place.

A chief goal of this guide is to share that beauty with visitors—families and friends, couples and individuals—who would like to make outdoor recreation part of their Cape Cod experience. Many visitors, especially vacationers, have only so much time in which to enjoy lots of activities—while keeping everyone in their group happy. The trips in this guide are designed to occupy only part of a day, not all of it. Many are located close to towns that offer their own attractions and amenities. Tired hikers can revive themselves with a cold beverage on a restaurant patio; paddlers can later peruse an art gallery's offerings. And almost all the trips are designed for those of novice or moderate ability, to serve as welcoming introductions to the natural world and thus encourage participants to keep coming back for more.

I still keep coming back, more than a quarter century after first stepping out of a car east of the canal, and I hope you will too.

Acknowledgments

THIS GUIDE HAS BEEN INSPIRED BY a desire to show many more people how they can easily enjoy these habitats by foot, bike, and kayak or canoe. Thus, I am grateful to the Appalachian Mountain Club, which since 1876 has recognized the importance of conservation and recreation in the Northeast. Thanks go to former senior editor Vanessa Torrado for suggesting this project. Publisher Heather Stephenson was understanding and supportive throughout and kept me on track. Particular acknowledgement goes to editor Dan Eisner, whose professionalism, calm demeanor, and encouragement have made all the difference. Thank you, Dan.

The following members of the Southeastern Massachusetts Chapter of the AMC were also helpful: Cape Hiking Chair John Gould, Biking Chair Joe Tavilla, and former Kayaking Chair Bob Zani. I am also grateful to Sue Moynihan, Chief of Interpretation and Cultural Resources Management at the Cape Cod National Seashore, as well as the rest of the interpretive staff.

Although neither my mother nor late father, Eleanor and Edward O'Connor, were outdoors types, they both were early and constant supporters of my explorations in the natural world, from Rock Creek Park and Sleeping Giant, to Mount Washington and the Pamet River.

And finally, I must acknowledge my wife and steadfast outdoors companion, Jacqueline Perry O'Connor, the only guide I'll ever need.

Stewardship and Conservation

Protect the Resource!

With so many people enjoying the Cape, everyone needs to learn and adhere to Leave No Trace principles. These principles were developed and are updated regularly by the Leave No Trace Center for Outdoor Ethics to promote and inspire responsible outdoor recreation. How we use this spectacular place now determines what the Cape will be like in the future. Whether you are hiking, biking, or paddling, follow these principles:

Plan Ahead and Prepare

Plan a trip that you know everyone in your group can finish. Be prepared for unexpected events by having extra food, water, and clothing. Paddlers need to know tides and currents. Bicyclists need to know how to change a flat. Hikers need to be prepared for blisters. Keep your group size to ten or less and split into smaller groups if necessary. Try to avoid travel in wet and muddy conditions. Planning ahead also means confirming that you are going to be recreating in areas where it is legal to do so.

Travel on durable surfaces. When hiking, try to stay on trails and rocks. Stay in the center of the trail, even when it is wet and muddy. Use your boots! Trails are hardened sites where use should be concentrated. Avoid contributing to the widening of trails and their erosion. When hiking within the National Seashore or similar coastal landscapes, respect signs about erosion threats and the destruction of dunes and dune vegetation, and stay on marked trails and established sand routes.

When biking, always stay on the trail. Cape soils are thin and thus especially vulnerable to erosion and wear.

Dispose of Waste Properly

Pack out *all* that you bring in—including any and all food you might drop while eating. Urinate at least 200 yards from any water source and pack out your used toilet paper. To dispose of solid human waste in the outdoors where toilets are not available, dig an individual "cat hole" at least 200 yards from a trail or water source. Organic topsoil is preferable to sandy mineral soil. Dig a hole 4 to 8 inches deep and about 6 inches in diameter. After use, mix some soil into the cat hole with a stick and cover with the remainder of the soil. Disguise the hole by covering it with leaves or other brush. Pack out your toilet paper in a Ziploc bag. You need to be especially careful not to pollute near any watercourse, because it probably leads to a campground or town water source.

Leave What You Find

Leave all natural and historical items as you find them. Cape Cod has long been a treasure trove of pre-colonial and colonial-era archaeological and cultural artifacts. Do not disturb items, and contact local historical groups or the National Seashore at 508-771-2144. The Cape has much human history that should be left for future visitors to enjoy. Natural delights: Before picking any wild edibles, consider the number of other people who might be using the area and decide if you might negatively affect an important food source for wildlife.

Minimize Campfire Impacts

If you plan to build a fire on the beach, you must first obtain a permit from the National Seashore or local municipalities. If you are granted a permit, try to keep a fire small, and make sure it is completely extinguished before you leave.

Respect Wildlife

Remain reasonably quiet while in the Cape's open spaces, and give animals enough space so that they feel secure. When you are watching wildlife, if you notice them changing their behavior, you are most likely too close. In that case, back off and give the animals space. Avoid nesting or calving sites and *never* attempt to feed any wildlife, even sunning seals. Shorebird species including piping plovers and certain terns are endangered, and harassing them or destroying their nests is a crime. For low-impact, wildlife-watching tips, visit Watchable Wildlife's website, www.watchablewildlife.org.

Be Considerate of Other Visitors
Refrain from using cell phones and radios. When hiking or cycling, take rests on the side of the trail so that other hikers do not have to walk around you. When on the water, remember that sound carries a long, long way. Dogs are allowed on some trails and beaches within the National Seashore, but must be kept on leash. In other areas, always keep dogs within sight and under voice control.

You can learn more about the Leave No Trace program by visiting their website, www.lnt.org, or by writing them at Leave No Trace, P.O. Box 997, Boulder, CO 80306.

Introduction to Cape Cod

IN ONE IMPORTANT WAY, THE CAPE IS A MICROCOSM of the New England outdoors: You can experience multiple natural environments within a short distance. Only 60 miles long from the Canal to Provincetown's Herring Cove at the terminus of Route 6, the peninsula is but 20 miles across at its widest point, and a mere one mile of land separates ocean from bay in Eastham.

Do the mileage math: You can paddle up a tidal stream, haul your boat where you have your bike stashed, and pedal to a trailhead for a 2.0-mile hike through the Cape Cod National Seashore to the Atlantic Ocean, and be done by noon, ready for whatever the rest of your day on the Cape holds.

Whether you're a day-tripper with a bike on your vehicle or a bird book in your pack, a vacationing family that wants more than just movies and malls to remember of the Cape, or a weekending couple who loves both remote landscapes and in-town rewards, you can find much of what you seek in these pages.

Hikes that lead through forests and dunes to spectacular ocean views; bike routes that follow quiet lanes and pass through cranberry country; paddling excursions along protected coastlines, bays, and secluded salt ponds; and any adventure within the 44,000-acre Cape Cod National Seashore— these are the sorts of recreational adventures that create lasting memories and bond you to this magical corner of New England.

The following sections provide both newcomers and experienced outdoors people with descriptions of hiking, biking, and paddling forays from Falmouth to Provincetown, from one-hour trips to half-day adventures. The rest of this introductory chapter provides some basic information you can use to get started on your visit to Cape Cod.

Maps

Most Cape towns offer street maps of their communities, as well as information on municipal open spaces, boat ramps, etc. Towns along the Cape Cod Rail Trail provide maps of the bikeway. For Rail Trail maps, you can also visit www.mass.gov/dcr/parks/southeast/ccrt.htm.

For maps of the Cape's state parks and forests, contact Scusset State Beach Reservation (508-888-0859) and Shawme-Crowell State Forest (508-888-0351) in Sandwich, and Nickerson State Park (508-896-3491). The material includes campsite clusters, as well as hiking and biking routes. You can also visit the Massachusetts Department of Conservation and Recreation website at www.mass.gov/dcr/forparks.htm.

The Cape Cod National Seashore offers a variety of maps to its landscapes and attractions—including hiking and biking trails—at the Salt Pond Visitor Center in Eastham, National Seashore headquarters in Wellfleet, and at the Province Lands Visitor Center in Provincetown. Or you can visit www.nps.gov/caco.

Maps for the Monomoy National Wildlife Refuge can be obtained weekdays at the refuge office on Morris Island in South Chatham or by visiting www.fws.gov/northeast/monomoy/. (Paddlers: Be advised of continuing shoaling and other impacts on coastal geology within the refuge, including re-connection between South Beach and South Monomoy Island and changes to the Southway channel.)

Topographic maps produced by the United States Geological Survey (USGS) are excellent overall reference charts for suggesting where (and by what route) you might want to go on Cape Cod. Because they include contour lines that denote elevation, myriad natural features, and dotted lines that indicate dirt tracks and footpaths, "topo" maps are an outdoorsperson's great friend. They can be purchased at outdoors stores, outfitters, fishing/hunting shops, and general stores on the Cape or by visiting topomaps.usgs.gov.

Climate

Cape Cod has a maritime climate and has temperatures that are generally more moderate that those found in the rest of the state. Because it is surrounded on three sides by Cape Cod Bay and the Atlantic Ocean, temperatures on the Cape tend to be a few degrees warmer in the winter and a few degrees colder in the summer than elsewhere in Massachusetts. Occasionally, Cape Cod is clipped by hurricanes or tropical storms as they pass to the east. The shore can be pounded by large waves, making swimming, surfing, and paddling dangerous.

The area receives less than 40 inches of rainfall per year, 42 to 46 inches less than the remainder of New England receives. In winter, 24 inches of snow falls, much lower than the 42 inches that falls in Boston. Nevertheless, powerful snowstorms, or "nor'easters," can cause much destruction in winter. Because of the frigid water temperatures, spring starts late on Cape Cod, but if you travel there in the fall, you find that season longer than it is in other parts of the state. You can find swimming—even on the ocean side— quite delightful, even in mid-September.

Getting There

Cape Cod is easily accessible by vehicle. The most well-traveled access route is MA 3, which connects metropolitan Boston with the Sagamore Bridge that spans the Cape Cod Canal. Many out-of-staters take I-195 or I-495 to Route 25, which crosses onto the Cape at the Bourne Bridge. Bus service is provided by several companies, including Peter Pan, Bonanza, and Plymouth and Brockton Street Railway Company. The Bay State Cruise Company and Boston Harbor Cruises provide seasonal ferry service to Provincetown from Boston, as does Capt. John Boats from Plymouth.

Lodging and Camping

You find literally hundreds of choices for lodging on Cape Cod. They range from basic campgrounds to very expensive, luxurious hotels and inns. Cape Cod is home to numerous private and public campgrounds, ranging from beach-side RV parks to semi-remote tent sites in the woods. For a list of private campgrounds on the Cape, I've found the following website to be helpful: www.capelinks.com/cape-cod/main/entry/cape-cod-campgrounds-and-camping-areas/. Also, search *camping* on the Cape Cod Chamber of Commerce site, www.capecodchamber.org.

Three state campgrounds serve Cape visitors: Scusset State Beach Reservation (508-888-0859) and Shawme-Crowell State Forest (508-888-0351) located on either side of the Cape Cod Canal in Sandwich; and Nickerson State Park (508-896-3491). Scusset is located on Cape Cod Bay and attracts mostly RV and motor homes, with an accent on enjoying the Cape Cod Bay beach and saltwater angling. Shawme-Crowell, located within a state forest, is a more traditional campground with almost 300 sites. Nickerson, at 1900 acres and more than 420 sites, dominates the southeast corner of Brewster and is the Cape's largest campground.

Alcoholic beverages are prohibited in all Massachusetts campgrounds.

General rules include:
- Quiet hours are 10 P.M. to 7 A.M. Please, no unnecessary or disturbing noise at any time.
- Confine campfires to designated fireplaces. Never leave fires unattended. Extinguish fires by midnight.
- Please keep your campsite clean. Don't wash dishes in the bathroom sink or at public faucets. Use dishwashing stations where available. Never dispose of human food or pet food in the area around your campsite.
- Children 16 years old and younger must wear a helmet when bicycling.
- Equipment is limited to two tents or one camping vehicle and one small tent per site. Tents are limited to 300 square feet of combined floor space.

Occupancy and Registration
- Check-in time is 1 P.M.
- Campsites should be occupied the first night and must not be left unoccupied for a period of more than 12 hours. Please call the park if you are going to arrive late. Failure to contact the park can result in your campsite being reassigned to another customer.
- Visitors are required to pay the park's day use fee to visit in the campground from 8 A.M. to 8 P.M.
- Check-out time is 11 A.M. Please notify staff on duty at the contact station when you leave.
- Rates are $15 per night for Massachusetts residents; $17 per night for out-of-state residents. For reservations call 1-877-I-CAMP-MA or 1-877-422-6762.

Private campgrounds near the National Seashore include Maurice's Campground (508-349-2029) in Wellfleet; Horton's Camping Resort (508-487-1220) and North of Highland Campground (508-487-1191) in North Truro; and Dune's Edge (508-487-9815) in Provincetown.

Cape Cod National Seashore Information

Many of the trips in this book are located within the Cape Cod National Seashore, which is managed and supervised by the National Park Service. Its website (www.nps.gov/caco) includes very helpful information and maps. Contact the park headquarters in Wellfleet at 508-349-3785. The Salt Pond Visitor Center in Eastham can be reached at 508-255-3421. You can call the Province Lands Visitor Center in Provincetown at 508-487-1256.

Fees

Enjoyment of the Cape Cod National Seashore is free, except for seasonal parking fees at National Seashore beaches. Cape municipalities also charge seasonally for beach parking, and some require stickers. Contact town halls for updated information.

Emergencies

In an emergency situation, you should call 911; operators can contact local or state police, National Seashore rangers and rescue personnel, and/or EMTs.

Choosing Your Trip

The 50 hiking, biking, and paddling trips in this book provide a variety of outdoor experiences, but most are connected to enjoyment of a coastal environment. Therefore, always be prepared for bright sun, and the possibility of interacting with water: ocean or bay, tidal stream, or glacial pond.

Before heading out, decide on the focus of your trip (paddling, ocean views, wildlife watching, etc.). You also need to decide how strenuous a trip you and your group can endure and complete. The trips described in this guide are geared to easy and moderate experiences, generally from one hour to a half-day. The trip highlights chart preceding this introduction has an easy-to-follow listing of all the trips, including their difficulty, length, and trip highlights. After you have narrowed down your choices, read the detailed trip descriptions in the individual hiking, biking, and paddling chapters to get a better idea of what the trip entails and what you might encounter.

Hunting Season

Hunting is allowed on Cape Cod, including the National Seashore. Hunting accidents are rare on the Cape, but everyone in your group, including dogs, should wear at least one piece of blaze-orange clothing during hunting season, particularly during November when deer hunters are allowed to hunt with rifles. Cape Cod hunting seasons, including deer, upland game birds, and coastal waterfowl, are set by the Massachusetts Division of Fisheries and Wildlife and Game Department and are posted on its website: www.mass.gov/dfwele/dfw/.

Don't Drink the Water

Do not drink water from Cape ponds, lakes, or streams. Even water bubbling up from a spring, or the most glistening of glacial ponds can contain bacteria, viruses, or protozoa that can cause illness. If you are just out for the day, the easiest thing to do is bring enough water with you.

1

Hiking Cape Cod

HISTORY HAS MADE MUCH OF WHAT MANY CONSIDER the Pilgrims' "first hike" in the New World: a desperate search across Truro for fresh water. Today you and your family or friends have much more to experience by foot—and at least your party can carry plenty of water!

Whether you have hundreds of miles under your Vibram soles or have never ventured down a trail, you can find hiking on the Cape enjoyable, and perhaps even enlightening or inspiring.

The 24 trips in this section invite you to cover some of the same terrain the Pilgrims walked four centuries ago, but also much more. To be sure, you can enjoy the broad vistas of East Bay and the shorefronts of the Atlantic Ocean and Cape Cod Bay, but you can also visit the re-forested uplands and working cranberry bogs of the interior. And some of these hikes pass through natural environments that barely existed in the 1600s, especially the wild dunescapes of the Province Lands.

Taking a path that emerges at one of the Cape's inviting "kettle hole" ponds is one of the most memorable experiences a hiker can have, especially a newcomer, but visitors and residents can also enjoy taking a leisurely stroll down Main Street in Chatham or experience a senses-expanding excursion along Provincetown's colorful Commercial Street. Perhaps most important is that you can use these decriptions as a primer for planning your own walks. You have as many Cape Cod ambles available as you want to create.

Hiking Times

Times are based on my experiences on the trails, as well as other published material. Your experiences will probably echo mine: Paved surfaces make for the quickest walking, followed by trails over bare ground, and dune and sand (slowest). Given the topography of the Cape, most routes described in this guide are flat or gently undulating, and thus not terribly demanding. However, hikes that take you through the sandy terrain of the dune lands of the National Seashore and along beaches in general are going to be more strenuous.

Your hiking times might be faster or slower, but always be prepared to spend more time than planned, either intentionally or because of unforeseen conditions. Always take into effect the potential for fatigue and the vagaries of weather.

Trip Ratings

Ratings vary in difficulty based on distance and trail conditions. *Easy* trips are suitable for first-time hikers, those of limited experience, and families with kids. *Moderate* hikes are longer and might entail more ups and downs and involve greater exposure to sun, wind, and tidal action that can affect a route. An example is Great Island in Wellfleet, an out-and-back 8.0-miler that features a couple of small hills and a sand strip that disappears as the tide rolls in. Energetic, older kids should have no problems on moderate-rated hikes.

Safety and Etiquette

With proper planning, each of the hikes offered in this section provides an enjoyable and safe experience. Before heading out for your hike, please consider the following tips:

- Select a trip that is appropriate for everyone in the group. Match the hike to the abilities of the least capable person in the group.
- Plan to return at or reasonably near the time noted for the hike. Determine a turnaround time and stick to it—even if you have not reached your goal for the day.
- Check the weather every time you head out for a hike. Know the forecast before you begin your hike, monitor the sky for changing conditions, and be prepared to alter your route or end your hike early.

Cape Cod weather from spring through fall is for the most part out-doors friendly: lots of sun; warm, light breezes off the ocean; and moderate rainfall. But bad storms can and do kick up, with dropping temperatures, rising winds, and torrential rainfall. With so much exposed land and open space, lightning strikes can also be a threat—take shelter if you hear thunder or see thunderstorms approaching. Pack a weatherproof outer layer as part of your hiking gear.

Warm, blue-sky weather can make for ideal hiking conditions, but the sun is not always your friend. Sun rays reflecting off water and sand surfaces can produce serious sunburn. Salt-laden coastal breezes can also do damage to skin. Apply sun block of 30 SPF or greater *before* your hike, and re-apply during the trip. Wear a billed cap or broad-brimmed hat. Use lip balm.

- Bring a pack with the following items:
  - ✓ Water: Two quarts per person is usually adequate, depending on the weather and length of the trip.
  - ✓ Food: Even for a short one-hour hike, bring some high-energy snacks like nuts, dried fruit, or snack bars. Bring a lunch for longer trips.
  - ✓ Map
  - ✓ Extra clothing: Rain gear, wool sweater or fleece, hat
  - ✓ Sunscreen
  - ✓ First-aid kit
  - ✓ Pocketknife
  - ✓ Binoculars for wildlife viewing (optional)
- Wear appropriate footwear and clothing. Wear wool or synthetic hiking socks and comfortable, waterproof hiking boots that provide good traction and ankle support. Avoid wearing cotton clothing, which absorbs sweat and rain, making for cold, damp hiking. Polypropylene, fleece, silk, and wool all do a good job of keeping moisture away from your body and keeping you warm in wet or cold conditions.

  In addition to practicing the Leave No Trace techniques described in the "Stewardship and Conservation" section, keep the following things in mind while hiking:
- Try not to disturb other hikers. While you might often feel alone in the wilderness, wild yelling or cell phone usage undoubtedly interferes with another person's quiet backcountry experience.

- When you are in front of the rest of your hiking group, wait at all trail junctions. This avoids confusion and keeps people in your group from getting lost or separated.
- If you see downed wood that appears to be purposely covering a trail, it probably means the trail is closed because of overuse or hazardous conditions.
- If a trail is muddy, walk through the mud or on rocks, never on tree roots or plants. Having waterproof boots keeps your feet comfortable, and by staying in the center of the trail you can keep the trail from eroding into a wide "hiking highway."
- If you decide to take an impromptu swim in a trailside stream or pond, be sure to wear sturdy sandals or old tennis shoes to protect your feet and give you traction on slippery surfaces. Also, wipe off sunscreen and bug spray to avoid polluting water on which animals and plants rely.
- Be aware of poison ivy. Most people suffer an allergic reaction when they come into contact with this plant. It is identifiable by its three almond-shaped leaves that are bunched together and connect to the stem. The leaves are green during the summer, but when the weather cools, they turn a dark, red wine color.
- Deer ticks, which transmit Lyme Disease, are a concern for hikers during the summer. Take precautions by using insect repellent, wearing light-colored long pants tucked into your socks, and frequently checking your clothing and skin.

By taking these precautions, you can spend your trip focusing on the pleasures of exploring Cape Cod. Most of the hikes in this book take you through multiple natural habitats, giving you the opportunity to see a variety of flora and fauna, from shorebirds and osprey to bearberry, pitch pine, and salt marsh cordgrass.

TRIP 1
BREWSTER TOWN WALK

Rating: Easy
Distance: 2.0 miles
Estimated Time: 3 hours

Experience the charm and ambience of a country store dating to the mid-1800s, then wander down a scenic byway to a Cape Cod Bay beach before returning to a lovely stretch of the "Old King's Highway."

Directions

From Route 6 east, take Exit 10, Route 124 north to Route 6A. Turn right and proceed east on 6A for about a half mile to public parking on right behind Town Hall.

Trip Description

Named in honor of William Brewster, a Pilgrim elder, this town on Cape Cod Bay was settled in 1656 and was originally part of Harwich. It was not incorporated as a separate town until 1803. Settlers first built homes around Stony Brook, site of the first water-powered grist and woolen mill in the country. Brewster soon developed a reputation for industriousness on land and at sea.

One look at the elegant Federal and Colonial style homes in town, built by men who made their fortunes on the ocean, and you can see why Brewster is sometimes called the "Sea Captains' Town." Many of these fine houses have been transformed into inns and galleries.

A massive bay-side mansion that is now part of the Ocean Edge Resort was once known as Fieldstone Hall and was the former home of nineteenth-century industrialist and railroad magnate Samuel Nickerson. (Other family connections also donated the land that is now Nickerson State Park at the southeast corner of Brewster.)

Many of the chief attractions and amenities of the town are located near Main Street, Route 6A. This secondary and much more scenic Cape thoroughfare traces its inside arc parallel to Cape Cod Bay. (And talk about

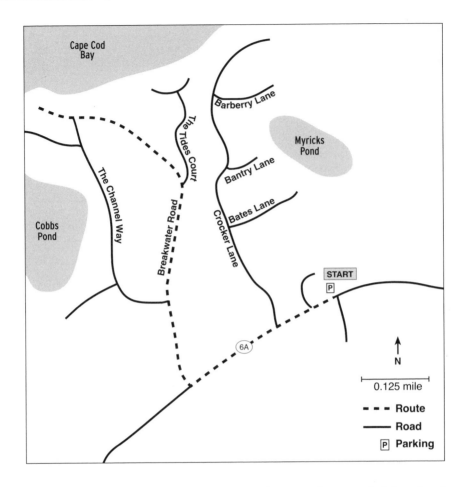

centrally situated: Brewster is located 31 miles from the Cape Cod Canal and 31 miles from Provincetown, at the Cape's tip.)

Park at the Town Hall complex at 2198 Main Street. The information and visitor's services office at the rear of the complex has plenty of brochures, activity listings, and other information, and the staff is helpful and knowledgeable. Head left on Main Street to one of the most popular and iconic destinations on Cape Cod, the Brewster General Store. Since its inception a decade before the Civil War, this store at Sears Square (where Route 124 meets Route 6A) has provided for and pleased locals and travelers alike.

From penny candy to geegaws, unique gifts, and ice cream, this classic emporium is a must-stop location. The original building was a two-story church, but a declining congregation prompted its sale. A store and post of-

The Brewster Flats are one of the widest expanses of tidal flats in North America.

fice soon took its place. The post office eventually moved out, and the store has survived the ups and downs of the intervening decades. In 1990, the emporium underwent a complete renovation, including restoration of the second-floor church windows.

Several years later, the rear shed was transformed into the Brewster Scoop, one of the most popular ice cream parlors on the Cape. (It is open from Memorial Day to Labor Day.)

Understandably, this emporium can be a busy spot in season, so if you want to escape the crowd for a while, follow the quiet lanes that lead down to the bay. I recommend walking the 0.5 mile down adjacent Breakwater Road to the beach of the same name. The town's shoreline on Cape Cod Bay is perhaps best known for showcasing the Brewster Flats, broad stretches of sand that extend more than 1.0 mile when the tide is low. In fact, this fun and inviting coastal environment extends from Dennis to Eastham (some claim these flats are the largest in the nation). This location can be a lovely habitat to explore, but you might want to bring along water shoes to avoid cuts from seashells and others protrusions. Also, be mindful of the tide, which can sneak up on oblivious explorers and beachcombers.

Named for the breakwaters and revetments built over the decades to repel storm waves, Breakwater Beach offers terrific swimming, especially for youngsters—you can find restrooms at the parking lot—and the flats provide perfect laboratories for up-close learning about shellfish and other marine life.

To the left of the beach are houses and condos that are part of the private Ocean Edge Resort, but beach walking is allowed. Make your way back along Breakwater Road to Main Street and consider your options.

Hungry? A good choice for those who crave tasty gifts of the sea is the Brewster Inn and Chowder House, just a short walk left on Main Street at 1993. Live entertainment takes places in the attached shed. Looking to dine especially well and spend a night or two? The Bramble Inn, a little farther up Main Street on the same side, has been a Brewster mainstay for more than 25 years.

Route 6A has been an "antique alley" for generations, and Main Street is home to its share of antique shops. Head across the street to Countryside Antiques (2052 Main Street), which features a broad array of European and American pieces. Continue east a short distance, and you arrive at the municipal lot.

TRIP 2
CHATHAM TOWN WALK

Rating: Easy
Distance: 3.0 miles
Estimated Time: 4 hours

From its Friday night band concerts just off a classic Main Street to an iconic lighthouse overlooking the Atlantic Ocean, Chatham is the epitome of a Cape Cod village. And true to its nature, Chatham also hosts one of the grandest Fourth of July parades on the Cape.

Directions

From Route 6 east, take Exit 11 (Route 137) south to terminus at Route 28. Take a left on Route 28 and proceed three miles, through rotary, to parking on left near library.

Trip Description

Walking this village is a treat. On Main Street, you pass gift shops and galleries, a candy-making emporium, ice cream parlors, and great dining spots. Attractions to the north include a golf course and railroad museum. To the south, you find scenic salt ponds, the famed Chatham Light guarding the grounds of a U.S. Coast Guard Station, and more beach and wild coastline than you might think possible.

Park in the public lot behind the information kiosk on Main Street and turn left to reach the rotary. Turn right onto Old Harbor Road (Route 28), and one block up, Depot Road enters from the left. Take Depot Road and look for the restored railroad depot on your right, now a museum that recounts the period when the town was served by a spur of the Old Colony line a century ago. The building, built in 1887, includes models, railroad paraphernalia and—a favorite of train buffs of all ages—a full size caboose that dates back to 1918.

Return to Old Harbor Road and continue north, to where Barcliff Road crosses. Take a right on Barcliff, which leads you to Shore Road and an amazing vista of Chatham Harbor and the long sand barrier of Nauset Beach,

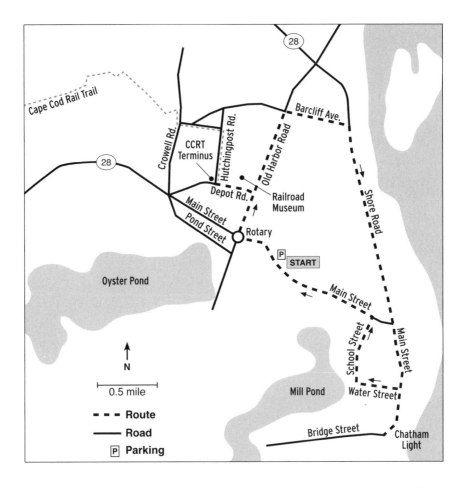

which extends for 7.0 miles from Orleans to Chatham. Turn right on Shore Road, and cross the street to the Chatham Fish Pier. Check out the visitors deck, from which you can watch fishing boats unloading their catch or gearing up to head on back to sea. You can also reserve space on a boat shuttle that can take to you to North and South Monomoy Islands.

Follow Shore Road south (watch the traffic), past its intersection with Main Street. In a few blocks, you reach a parking lot overlooking the famed Chatham sandbars and the tip of Nauset Beach, the scene of several dramatic breaks over the past two decades. Take a stairway down to Lighthouse Beach; because of erosional changes and storm, serious beachcombers can now walk south to reach shallows leading to the islands.

The Chatham Fish Pier is the center of the local commercial fishing industry.

On the right side of Shore Road stands the noble Chatham Light. Tours are scheduled May through October. Climb the 44 steps to the lens house to enjoy a spectacular view of this remarkable corner of Cape Cod.

Head back to Main Street and "downtown"—but not along Shore Road. Take this busy road for only a block or so and then turn left onto Water Street. You find yourself meandering through a lovely little neighborhood of narrow streets and classic Cape homes and cottages. At School Street, turn right, and follow School Street out to Main Street.

By this time you are likely to be hungry. Fortunately, you are close to the Chatham Squire, located in the heart of the village at 487 Main Street, a classic eatery, featuring two bars (one boisterous, the other quiet) and several dining areas. Here you can find good seafood and burgers and great local flavor.

Across the street, the Chatham Wayside Inn offers a more genteel atmosphere. Dine out on the terrace (terrific people watching) or in their elegant main restaurant. Around the corner on Chatham Bars Avenue is one of our favorites, the Impudent Oyster—fine homemade soups, fresh fish, and Portuguese specialties. The cozy bar features a huge stained glass figure that once occupied a window in a Maine church.

Between the restaurant and the golf course you see the Chatham Bandstand in Kate Gould Park, where live band music takes place every summer Friday night, beginning at 8:00 P.M. Bring chairs and come early—not only is this a town tradition, but also the concerts draw vacationers and music lovers from across the Cape.

Back on Main Street, watch some amazing confections being made by hand at the Chatham Candy Manor, an authentic chocolatier. On the same block, refine your artistic tastes at the Hearle Gallery (480 Main Street). Also, Wynne/Falconer Gallery at 492 Main Street features both established Cape painters and new talent.

Across the street stands a pair of businesses that seem almost threatened nowadays: a classic five-and-dime and a bookstore. The latter, the Yellow Umbrella, is a community fixture to be cherished, offering an array of literary classics and newer novels, national bestsellers, and offerings by local and regional writers. On the same side of the street, at 525 Main Street, stop in at Yankee Ingenuity. Here you find lots of reasons to browse or buy, from locally crafted jewelry and cool greeting cards to terrific photographs of coastal scenes and maritime subjects. As you continue west on Main Street, you see the information kiosk and parking lot directly ahead.

TRIP 3
WELLFLEET TOWN WALK

Rating: Easy
Distance: 3.0 miles
Estimated Time: 2 hours

This community is a study in contrasts: Wellfleet features both a wild, windswept ocean coast and a quiet bayside village, home to numerous art galleries, shops, and restaurants. The village proper comprises charming lanes that all seem to lead back to Main Street—or down to a bustling harbor.

Directions
From Route 6 east in Wellfleet, turn left at the sign for Wellfleet Center (traffic light) and proceed on Main Street a half-mile to parking on the right adjacent to Town Hall.

Trip Description
Located just about 100 miles from Boston, Wellfleet occupies 35 square miles on the outer Cape, right at the forearm of the 60-mile peninsula. Originally part of Eastham, it gained its independence a dozen years before the American Revolution began. Like most Cape towns, Wellfleet has been a fishing community since the first settlers entered its protected harbor in the seventeenth century. By the mid-1800s, it was also developing a reputation as a tourist destination.

And judging by the number of vacationers, weekenders, and day-trippers who walk Wellfleet's streets Memorial Day through Labor Day (and well into autumn), local tourism is healthier than ever, with inns and bed-and-breakfasts drawing visitors from around the world. They come for great seafood, to be sure, especially the shellfish for which Wellfleet has earned an international reputation.

The annual Wellfleet Oyster Festival, which takes place on the third weekend of October, has grown from a local effort to extend the tourist season to an international shellfish Woodstock. The festival literally takes over the town, with events and attractions taking place over three days from the

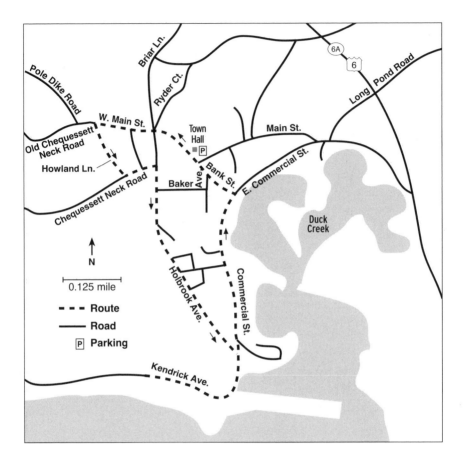

center of town to the harbor and beyond. Traffic and crowds have grown to the point where festival-goers park at the beaches and other outlying areas and take shuttle buses into town.

Throughout most of the year, visitors can also browse in almost two dozen galleries and crafts shops, dine at restaurants that offer both clam rolls and continental fare, and explore quiet lanes and byways.

Park at the town lot just off Main Street, across from a commercial block that includes Wellfleet Marketplace, a funky consignment shop, and a box office for the Wellfleet Harbor Actors Theater (W.H.A.T.). The theater was already a strong regional artistic voice when it expanded from semi-dilapidated digs on the harbor (hence its name) into a new, larger home next to the post office on Route 6.

Take a left on Main Street, and a few hundred feet up the street you reach a lovely former storefront (266 Main Street) that houses the Wellfleet Historical Society. You can know it by the small cannon that greets you on the lawn. In fact it's not a weapon of war at all, but rather a gun that coastal lifesavers fired to propel a line into the rigging of ships wrecked on the infamous Wellfleet shoals, thus beginning the dangerous process of rescuing the imperiled crew.

The museum recounts the town's renowned maritime history, as well as the origins of the United Fruit Company (started by a Wellfleet native in the 1870s and now famous for Chiquita bananas). And the historical society doesn't skimp on the exploits of radio pioneer Enrico Marconi, who built a station on the cliffs of what is now the National Seashore to send the first trans-Atlantic wireless message, from Wellfleet to Great Britain, in 1902.

Cross Main Street and loop back into the center of town. Pass a few gift shops until you reach a Wellfleet classic, the Lighthouse (317 Main Street), a popular eatery packed with families at breakfast and lunch and attracting a boisterous crowd at night. Across the street, Emack & Bolio's has been selling cones, dishes, and other ice cream confections for 20 years. Continue down Main Street to where the town library (full WiFi and lots of community information) sits on the left at the corner of Howland Lane. Take a left and follow Howland Lane up a rise that offers harbor views before it quickly meets Holbrook Avenue.

Follow Holbrook Avenue, which also offers pedestrian vistas across the harbor, to Commercial Street; turn right and walk a couple hundred yards to the harbor and marina. You can admire the boats of the small commercial fishing fleet or watch pleasure craft heading out into Cape Cod Bay. Here you can also try your own fishing luck on a charter boat, go on a cruise to Great Island, or rent your own small motor dinghy or sailboat.

Turn around and head up Commercial Street, following the upper harbor, and you soon meet a larger-than-life-size doryman, with fishing net in hand. The fisherman leans over the façade of Mac's Shack (91 Commercial Street), a longtime traditional seafood spot that now offers more sophisticated fare as well, including sushi.

Art galleries hug the upper harbor here, including the Left Bank (25 Commercial Street). Housed in a former veteran's hall/community center/roller rink, the spacious gallery features an outdoor sculpture garden overlooking the water. The harbor narrows into tidal Duck Creek, and a few steps farther up Commercial Street you arrive at Uncle Tim's Bridge, named for a nineteenth-century resident who operated a ship chandlery and supply shop when shipbuilding was still a thriving Wellfleet industry. Take the footbridge (rebuilt in 2008) across the tide creek to Hamblen Island, a wooded hill marked by a short loop trail that is ideal for children. From here, the views of the town and harbor are terrific.

Head back on Commercial Street a few steps to where Bank Street enters from the left. Check out the Blue Heron Gallery at 20 Bank Street before re-crossing the street to enter an authentic and elegant portal to Wellfleet's past: Jules Besch Stationers, housed in the former financial institution for which Bank Street is named. Each room is a delight.

Continue to climb Bank Street to its terminus at Main Street, and you find yourself only steps from the town parking lot. But first, more ice cream!

TRIP 4
PROVINCETOWN WALK

Rating: Easy
Distance: 2.5 miles
Estimated Time: 3 hours

Anchoring the tip of Cape Cod, Provincetown is a welcoming community that respects quirky individuality.

Directions
From Route 6 east in Provincetown, turn left at sign for Conwell Street (traffic light) and follow to terminus at Bradford Street. Turn right on Bradford to a large private lot on the right at the corner of Standish. Or proceed another block on Bradford to signs on the right leading to municipal parking (fee at all lots).

Trip Description
You want local characters, history and culture, cool bars and restaurants? Exquisite sunsets and extreme nightlife? Vintage shops and spectacular scenery? Arts and leisure in every form? You've come to the right place.

Commercial Street and Bradford Street run parallel a few blocks from each other and serve to frame the center of town. But it's Commercial, which traces the harbor from the East End to the West End, that is the Broadway of Provincetown. For two miles, you'll pass historic houses, art studios and galleries, semi-seedy bars and sublime restaurants, kitschy shops, drug stores, and drag shows. Provincetown has been a gay-friendly destination for decades, and the community prides itself on welcoming diversity. A "live and let live" attitude holds sway, and its manifestations can be outrageously entertaining, especially once night falls, when Commercial Street is transformed into a people-packed carnival.

There are public and private parking lots situated off Bradford Street, near the town center. Bradford is busy with vehicle traffic, while Commercial is more like a pedestrian mall, so that street should serve as your main artery. From your vehicle, walk east on Bradford Street (in the direction of

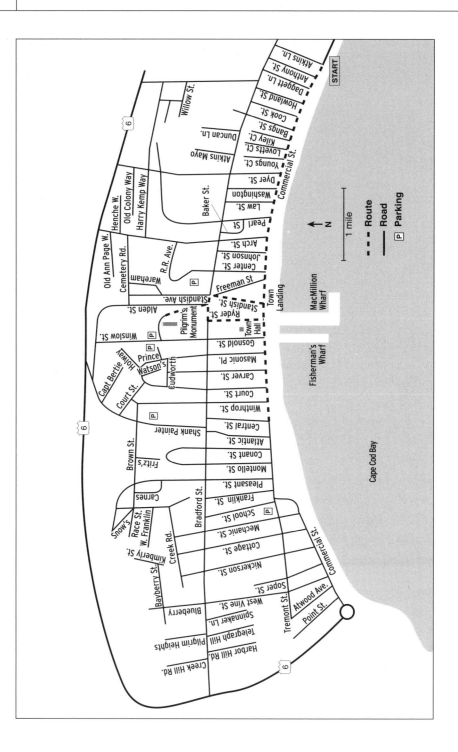

START

6

6

6

Atkins Ln.
Anthony St.
Daggett Ln.
Howland St.
Cook St.
Bangs St.
Kiley Ct.
Lovetts Ct.
Duncan Ln.
Youngs ct.
Atkins Mayo
Dyer St.
Washington
Law St.
Pearl St.
Arch St.
Johnson St.
Center St.
Wareham
Willow St.
Henche W.
Old Colony Way
Harry Kemp Way
Baker St.
Old Ann Page W.
Cemetery Rd.
R.R. Ave.
Commercial St.
Freeman St
Town Landing
Standish St.
Standish Ave.
Ryder St.
Pilgrim's Monument
Alden St.
Winslow St.
Prince
Watson's
Gudworth
Gosnold St.
Masonic Pl.
Carver St.
Court St.
Winthrop St.
Central St.
Atlantic St.
Conant St.
Montello St.
Pleasant St.
Franklin St.
School St.
Mechanic St.
Cottage St.
Nickerson St.
Soper St.
West Vine St.
Spinnaker Ln.
Telegraph Hill
Pilgrim Heights
Harbor Hill Rd.
Creek Hill Rd.
Blueberry
Bayberry St.
Kimberly St.
Creek Rd.
W. Franklin
Race St.
Snow's
Carnes
Bradford St.
Brown St.
Fritz's
Shank Painter
Court St.
Capt Bertie
Holway
Town Hall

Fisherman's Wharf
MacMillion Wharf

Cape Cod Bay

N
1 mile

Route
Road
P **Parking**

From Provincetown, memorable views of Cape Cod Bay abound.

Truro) a few blocks to Pearl Street. The walking on Bradford is difficult (as noted above) so take a right on Pearl to Commercial Street. Take a left and walk until you reach the 500 block. Turn around and begin your tour here.

The town's strong sense of community enjoys its most accessible manifestation in radio station WOMR ("Outer Most Radio"). This all-volunteer-DJ station, fittingly for the community it calls home, offers some of the most eclectic programming in New England. The station occupies the second floor of the Schoolhouse Gallery (494 Commercial), in a former, you guessed it, school house, and shares quarters with a first-floor gallery.

Across the street at 473 Commercial Street sits the Admiral MacMillan House, the former home of Arctic explorer Donald MacMillan (MacMillan Wharf in the center of town was named in his honor). Continuing west on Commercial, you enter the heart of Provincetown's arts district, with galleries festooning each block and both sides of the street. With its extraordinary natural light and unique play among sea, dune, and sky, Provincetown has been a mecca for painters and arts lovers for more than a century. Here, the landscape matters. Today, Simie Maryles (435 Commercial) paints unique cityscapes and her nighttime snow scenes of Provincetown streets are eye-catching. The Packard Gallery across the street at 418 features the large-format coastscapes of Anne Packard and the more esoteric work of her two daughters.

A few years ago, the Provincetown Art Association and Museum (PAAM) at 460 Commercial was expanded and renovated. Check it out for classic and cutting-edge works. The building itself is a statement.

At 379 Commercial Street, you will find The Wired Puppy, which features great coffees, baked goods and WiFi. Sit on the bench just outside to take a rest. Those visitors just seeking a funky bar with pub food should not pass up the Squealing Pig (335 Commercial). You find a solid selection of beers, a terrific juke box, and window-side tables that offer great perches for people watching.

Continue another few blocks on Commercial, then turn left onto massive MacMillan Wharf. Check out the active commercial fishing fleet (left side of the wharf) and the whale-watch and harbor cruise vessels (right side). At the far end of the wharf, consider a visit to the Expedition Whydah and Sea-Lab Center, where you'll learn the story of the eighteenth century pirate ship Whydah, her colorful captain, Black Jack Bellamy, and the bounty of coins, cannon, and other artifacts a determined treasure hunter found buried in sand off the Wellfleet shore more than two centuries later.

Return to Commercial Street and turn left, to reach one of the most unique army surplus stores in New England. A shopping universe in a warehouse setting, Marine Specialties has been wowing browsers and collectors for decades. The 235 Commercial Street icon features thousands of items, from traditional to quirky. Where else can you see a frogman's helmet, greeting cards, flip flops, and a Dutch airport security parka?

Return to the central intersection of Commercial and Ryder Street, and turn left up Ryder. The elegantly designed Town Hall, complete with a Pilgrim mural, is on your left and the immense Pilgrim Monument rises from a hill directly ahead.

At the corner of Bradford Street, across from Town Hall, the Center for Coastal Studies is located in a lovely former home. Stop here to bone up on your knowledge of whales, other marine mammals, and background on the natural habitats of Cape Cod. (You can also purchase T-shirts and other memorabilia.) This is the intrepid outfit often asked to engage in whale "rescues," by getting close enough to the leviathans to free them from fishing gear and other entanglements that threaten their lives. The center is the only organization on the East Coast federally authorized to perform this dangerous but important work.

Cross Bradford and take a quick left up High Pole Hill Road, which leads to the Pilgrim Monument, erected in honor of the intrepid band aboard the Mayflower who entered Provincetown Harbor in 1620. The tower's construction was a very big deal; President Teddy Roosevelt laid the cornerstone in 1907; three years later, President William Howard Taft presided at the dedication. During the original festivities, the harbor was clogged with U.S. naval vessels, steamships, and private yachts.

The monument complex also includes the Provincetown Museum (fee), which tells the story of the Pilgrims' five-week stay here, before venturing across Cape Cod Bay to Plymouth. The museum houses an impressive array of artifacts and collections. Over the past century, its mission has expanded to include the community's history as a fishing and whaling center, and as an early art and theater colony.

But many visitors want to climb to the top of the 252-foot tower, still the nation's tallest all-granite structure. After ascending 116 steps and 60 ramps, you are rewarded with unparalleled, 360-degree vistas of Provincetown, Cape Cod Bay, and the Atlantic. Don't miss this view!

Descend from the tower and museum and return to Bradford Street and your vehicle.

Pilgrim Landing

Signs of Cape Cod's most famous visitors, the Pilgrims, are everywhere on this coastal peninsula—even though they packed up and left for permanent digs at Plymouth only five weeks after making landfall here in November 1620.

At the far end of the 60-mile hook, the Pilgrim Monument rises 252 feet above Provincetown, epicenter of the Pilgrims' sojourn across the Outer Cape. At the upper end of the Cape, you find the Pilgrims Highway, the nickname for Route 3, a major artery leading down the Massachusetts mainland to the Sagamore Bridge and the Cape Cod Canal. The fifteen municipalities between the canal and Race Point boast more places with Pilgrim or Mayflower in their names than you can shake a buckled shoe at—not that these early European emigrants wore buckled shoes, or tall, broad-brimmed black hats, or even ate turkey.

Such popular appeal and commercial exploitation was no doubt inconceivable (and certainly sinful) to those aboard the Mayflower when it entered Provincetown Harbor on November 22, 1620. The ship's passengers comprised just more than 100, including seekers of religious freedom and their families (totaling fewer than 40) and others who were not devout and simply sought a new life in the New World. The Mayflower was a small, three-masted square rigger, about 90 feet long and 24 feet wide, and during months at sea, its occupants must have felt the ship get smaller, tighter, colder, and smellier by the day.

Finally, after 65 days, the crew spotted the high dune cliffs of what is now the National Seashore, probably at Truro. The Mayflower was much farther north than anyone had expected (and much closer to the enemy French in Canada and what is now northern New England). They immediately bore south, intent on reaching their original destination at the mouth of the Hudson River, but bad sea conditions forced a change in plans. After turning around, and following the curve of the Cape around such now-familiar coastal landmarks as Race Point, Herring Cove, and Wood End, they reached the entrance to the harbor on November 22nd.

Among the new arrivals' most immediate needs were water and food. Popular history points to Pilgrim Spring in North Truro, near the long, overgrown meadow that backs East Bay on the southeast, as the site where a parched exploration party from the Mayflower finally found fresh water; serious historians now doubt the tale and the site.

However, you find more general agreement that the Pilgrims uncovered and carried off a cache of corn on an upland just north of the Pamet River mouth. Today Corn Hill, marked by a plaque commemorating that discovery, is a popular Truro town beach. This advance band probed the bay coast aboard a shallop, a sail vessel that came with them, partially disassembled, aboard the Mayflower.

Continuing southward down the shore of Cape Cod Bay, the advance party, probably led by soldier Myles Standish, wandered as far as Eastham, where they skirmished with a small band of Americans Indians. Today, this place is also a well-known bayside swimming and sunning spot: First Encounter Beach.

The Pilgrims might have believed they could simply show up on the North American continent and appropriate what they chose. After all, they considered

The Pilgrim monument in Provincetown was built between 1907 and 1910.

themselves to be civilized men of God, and the indigenous people they met under both friendly and unfriendly circumstances to be heathen creatures. At best, the Europeans would accept the burden of civilizing the "savages"; at worst, they would eradicate them. With such attitudes, the colonists could easily adopt the rationale that they "owned" all the lands and resources they "discovered"—despite the reality that thriving Indian communities had been on the land for many centuries.

Indeed, when the Pilgrims endured even greater privations, disease, and death during the founding of Plymouth Colony, a local Wampanoag named Tisquantum, or Squanto, showed them the best hunting and fishing grounds and how to plant corn. The first Thanksgiving, in 1621, featured plenty of corn, and the feast, to which American Indian leaders were invited, might have been prompted by the Pilgrims' desire to "settle up" for having stolen corn from a storage pit the previous autumn.

TRIP 5
SHAWME-CROWELL STATE FOREST

Rating: Easy to moderate
Distance: 3.0 miles
Estimated Time: 2 hours
Location: Sandwich

Follow old farm tracks and foot trails that lead to the outer fringes of this popular Upper Cape campground, through woodlands and pine and oak, culminating in views of Cape Cod Bay.

Directions
Take Route 6 east to Exit 2, and follow Route 130 north into Sandwich for about three miles. The state forest campground entrance is on the left.

Trip Description
Once part of a much larger coastal landscape that emerged from a series of devastating fires in the early twentieth century, this mix of oak and pine forest and modest hillsides now features almost 300 campsites on 700 acres. One of the most popular campgrounds on Cape Cod, it's located within easy driving distance of local beaches, including Scusset Beach State Reservation, situated on the corner of land just north of the Cape Cod Canal (parking fees at the state reservation are included in your Shawme-Crowell camping permit).

You begin your hike by following the main campground road to where Bayview Road intersects just beyond the last of the "Area 1" campsites. Take a right on Bayview Road, which soon terminates at a gate; the road continues beyond as a dirt road. Wander though this scrubby terrain on a mild ascent, and note that you see few tall trees. The long-term impacts of fires that torched thousands of acres on this part of the Upper Cape in the mid-nineteenth century—including the state forest and what is now the Massachusetts Military Reservation just south of Route 6—are still being felt.

Continue up this track about a half mile, watching for signs on the right that designate the Mount Perry Trail. This trail is an easy loop that leads

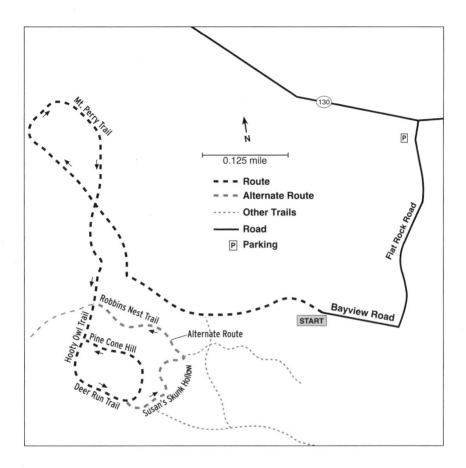

to the aforementioned views of the bay. You walk straight for .025 mile and reach an intersection of this trail, which loops like a ribbon. Continue straight, and you soon reach Mount Perry at the westernmost edge of the campground. You can survey the stretch of Cape Cod Bay fronting on Scusset Beach. It must be acknowledged that Mount Perry is not a mountain at all, but merely the highest point in the forest, only a few hundred feet above sea level.

In especially clear weather, later in the day when the sun is fully behind you, the outermost regions of the Cape might be visible, including Wellfleet, Truro, and Provincetown. If you can ignore the canal-side power plant in the middle distance, the view of the bay and shoreline is pretty interesting, if only because few places on the Upper Cape offer panoramic views from any serious elevation. As you continue along the loop, you cross the intersection

The Shawme-Crowell forest and campground are just a short distance from the salt marsh boardwalk.

you passed earlier in your hike and then reach Bayview Road. Turn left to head back toward your car.

You find more than a dozen trails south of Bayview Road. These trails are generally family friendly, with names like Deer Run, Hooty Owl, and Tilly's Turkey. As you might expect at the beginning of a 60.0-mile sand spit at the edge of the ocean, you encounter very little elevation gain.

You can create your own short loop routes by taking the Hooty Owl Trail to where it hooks left to become the Deer Run Trail. Follow Deer Run Trail to where the Pine Cone Hill Trail enters from the left. Turn here and follow this path, which loops back to Hooty Owl Trail, and then take a right at this junction and return to Bayview Road. Or you can continue on the Deer Run Trail a short distance beyond the turn onto Pine Cone Hill Trail to Susan's Skunk Hollow. What youngster would not want to explore this path? Turn left and follow this trail to where the Robbin's Nest Trail enters from the left. Turn left here and follow Robbins Nest Trail to where it meets Hooty Owl Trail. A right on Hooty Owl Trail brings you and your party back to Bayview Road.

If you want to explore the town of Sandwich, the area offers plenty of attractions for kids, from the miniature golf emporium alongside a tidal creek to an ice cream shop and fish hatchery (all on Route 6A). I can also recommend Heritage Museums and Gardens, not only for its beautiful de-signed spaces and museum displays, but also for its own network of trails. It also features a series of children's programs that run through the camping season.

Note: Shawme-Crowell welcomes pets, but they must be well behaved, never left unattended, and kept on leashes. Owners are also responsible for cleaning up after their pets and disposing of waste responsibly. As an owner of a dog that often accompanies my wife and me on the trail, I am often disappointed by the amount of dog droppings we see on pathways. Please re-member that trails are to be enjoyed by everyone. Make sure you always have sufficient water for your pet, and if the weather is hot and humid, consider postponing your hike for another day, out of respect for your four-footed hiking companions.

Coyotes on the Cape

My wife and I were following a path through the National Seashore and crested a rise, where we stopped to take in a panorama of the wild Outer Cape: white-capped ocean, wind-blasted dunes, hardscrabble pitch pine woodlands. Sud-denly, the scene grew immeasurably wilder. A chestnut-colored coyote the size of a German shepherd appeared in the mid-distance, as if rising from the sand itself.

This very substantial specimen of *Canis latrans* did not approach, but also did not hustle away. It did not stare at the pair of upright mammals who had gone stock-still, but rather seemed to observe us with only minor interest as we watched it intently. The coyote soon continued on its travels, following its nose and other sensory tools tied to its ancient genetics, and in a minute had disap-peared into its surroundings.

Such sightings of a healthy wild animal in a rugged habitat make for terrific memories. Although the colonists' fear and loathing of such predators resulted in the eventual extirpation of wolves from throughout New England, coyotes began to return to significant numbers on the Cape a generation ago. Now a protected game species that may be hunted only in limited seasons, the coyote faces threats from commercial and residential development, traffic, and sometimes dangerous interactions with humans.

Coyotes are primarily nocturnal and elusive. They're also smart and opportunistic. You actually have a greater chance of spotting one on a back road or golf course than you do in the backcountry, because they've found dependable food sources in trash cans, in dumpsters—and, unfortunately, among Cape Cod's small-pet population. (They also hunt more traditional prey, including rabbits, squirrels, and birds.)

Comparable to mid-sized dogs, coyotes have longer, thicker fur; they are 2 feet high, 4 feet to 5 feet long, have a black-tipped bushy tail, and weigh up to 50 pounds or more. The eastern coyote you see on the Cape is larger than its western cousin, having perhaps mated with dogs or wolves as it migrated from the Midwest and Canada. Its coloring ranges from the light-brown specimen we observed to gray, reddish-brown, and darker.

Coyotes most likely reached the Cape by crossing the Sagamore and Bourne bridges, though some might have swum the canal, overcoming its strong currents. However they arrived, they have taken up housekeeping in every community from Sandwich to Provincetown. Adults, which can mate for life, build dens in hillsides and typically have litters of four to eight pups in spring.

A coyote's call often starts as a few yips before extending into a long howl that is positively unearthly. When several vocalize together, they create one of nature's wildest choirs. As top animal predators, they are here to stay, wildlife officials believe. Coyote hunting season runs from early autumn through early winter. The coyote is a protected game species; they cannot be shot out of season, except by authorized officers, nor harassed in any way. If you see a coyote in the wild, observe it from a safe distance and leave the area immediately if it approaches you. If you spot one in a street or yard, recreation path, or other location that might restrict its movement, leave the area immediately. Coyotes are not especially aggressive toward people, but do respond if they feel threatened.

TRIP 6
LOWELL HOLLY RESERVATION

Rating: Easy to moderate
Distance: 4.0 miles
Estimated Time: 3 hours
Location: Mashpee and Sandwich

Follow carriage roads and footpaths along a 135-acre peninsula planted with many varieties of American holly and bordered by a pair of ponds.

Directions
From Route 6, take Exit 2 onto Route 130 south and follow for 1.5 miles. Turn left onto Cotuit Road and follow for 3.4 miles. Then turn right onto South Sandwich Road and follow for 0.2 mile to a free year-round parking area (6 cars) on the right or continue another 0.5 mile to an unmarked road on the right that leads to a seasonal parking area (20 cars), where you will have to pay a fee.

Trip Description
The peninsula, shaped somewhat like a wrist and hand with fingers and a thumb pointing in opposite directions, splits one large freshwater kettle hole into a pair of smaller ones. Enjoy expansive water views open to the north (Wakeby Pond) and south (Mashpee Pond). Almost immediately after reaching the peninsula, you have a choice: continue straight or veer right out past Conaumet Cove. I recommend continuing straight on a carriage road, heading southwest into the heart of the wooded landscape. Owned and cared for by The Trustees of Reservations since 1943, Lowell Holly was a fishing ground of the Wampanoag people for centuries. Anglers still fish the ponds, which sustain a natural population of smallmouth bass and other freshwater species. The Massachusetts Division of Fisheries and Wildlife also stocks the ponds each spring and fall with brown, brook, and rainbow trout. The ponds are also popular with power boaters; with a Trustees permit (visit www.thetrustees.org for information), they can land on the property and

explore the woodlands, climb the modest hillsides, and enjoy a shore-side picnic.

Hikers and nature lovers—especially those who appreciate uncommon flora—might not be the most numerous visitors, but they are going to be among the most satisfied at the end of a sojourn. That's because Lowell Holly, as the name suggests, was planted with some 50 varieties of American holly. These were introduced by Wilfred Wheeler, who served as the first Massachusetts Secretary of Agriculture from 1919–1920. Wheeler was continuing a tradition established by former Harvard University president Abbot Lawrence Lowell, for whom the property was named and who bequeathed it to the Trustees in 1942. Lowell, a scholar and amateur horticulturist, had planted lovely rosebay rhododendrons and mountain laurel earlier in the last century. In season, you can also see everything from pink lady's slipper in moister, shadier areas to patches of blueberries. And remember, poison ivy can be found in many of the "edge" areas, between woods and trail and paths and parking lots.

Once on the reservation proper, the main carriage road, part of the system designed by Lowell, meanders along a hillside; from its summit you can get a great view of the pond extending southward. On the south side of this hillside a second beach beckons, this one drawing boaters and anglers. It's a great spot for a swim (if the obligatory music emanating from a powerboat is not blasting, as it sometimes is).

Continue on the route inland, as it becomes the Wheeler Trail, and follow it for another 0.5 mile past mature stands of hardwoods and pines to where it terminates in a small loop near The Narrows, where the peninsula ends and a small passage links the ponds. On the not-so-far western shore, the Air National Guard base dominates this part of Mashpee; the fighter jets that once scrambled off the deck to chase Soviet bombers away from the U.S. coast are now based in western Massachusetts, but the runways still see plenty of military traffic, from jets and prop craft to Coast Guard helicopters. (Children are especially thrilled by the sight and sound of aircraft coming in low over the trees. Of course, so are plenty of adults.)

Retrace your steps along this spur until you return to the main stem, which now continues (briefly) north. Hike straight ahead and you can follow a loop back to the Conaumet Cove beach and the parking area. Bear left and you can maneuver along the narrow "thumb" leading to Conaumet Point, passing plenty of holly along the way. This 0.25-mile side trip offers ample

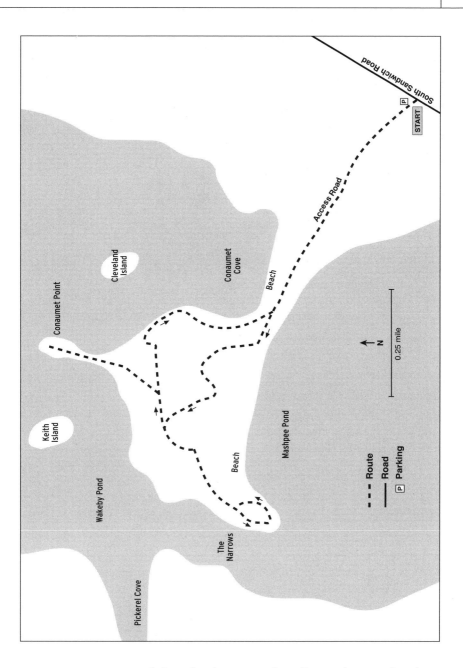

opportunities to swim, left and right, or to take off your shoes and wade in the water, but otherwise, it's a single-file walk to a dead end. (I have had the best osprey sightings at this northernmost tip of the reservation, however.)

Woods roads and footpaths lace Lowell Holly Reservation.

After again returning to the main trail, turn left as the pathway loops back to your starting point, with Conaumet Cove now on your left. In about four-tenths of a mile (with a modest climb and descent along the way), you'll find yourself back at the main beach, wondering if you have time for one last dip. If you've parked here and are tired, your vehicle is right where you want it. If you've parked out by South Sandwich Road, enjoy the leisurely walk back.

TRIP 7
MURKWOOD

Rating: Easy
Distance: 1.5 miles
Estimated Time: 1 hour
Location: East Sandwich

Enter a small, intimate coastal woodland that offers fine views of the Scorton Marsh and passes through a serene grove of red cedar before returning you back to busy Route 6A.

Directions

From Route 6 east take Exit 3 (Quaker Meetinghouse Road) north less than a mile to Route 6A. Take a right on Route 6A about 1.5 miles to the East Sandwich fire station on the right (where parking is available), just beyond where Old County Road enters from the right. The trailhead is located a few hundred feet farther east, on the north side of Route 6A, where you also find parking for several vehicles.

Trip Description

Murkwood is aptly named, with its thick, resurgent woodlands—you see lots of black and white oak and maple, with tupelo mixed in. The understory is full of tough, low-lying shrub and cat briar. Scorton Marsh spreads off to the east and north, to where meandering Scorton Creek eventually meets Cape Cod Bay.

From the parking area, follow the trail northeast, where you can spy a few houses off to the right. Soon, you're deeper into the woods and nearer the marsh. The path forks, signaling the beginning of the loop trail. Take the right fork, and you pass through mixed forest until the broad, open salt marsh habitat momentarily comes into view. Enjoy a nice vista here on the fringe of the largest salt marsh on Cape Cod Bay, which extends eastward several miles to Barnstable Harbor.

Because of its short length and loop design, this hike offers a friendly introduction to those unfamiliar with the coastal outdoors. The path is flat.

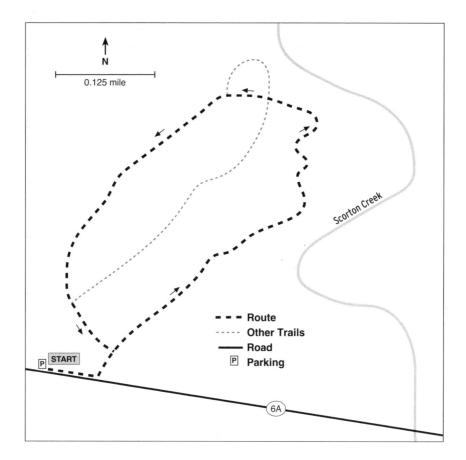

It includes both woodlands and salt marsh, and you can enjoy the entire experience within an hour or less, leaving most of the remaining day to visit the antique shops, gift stores, and restaurants that dot this pretty stretch of Route 6A.

Especially in spring, Murkwood is a popular stop for the millions of birds migrating northward of the Atlantic flyway. Look and listen for a variety of warblers, as well as cardinals, sparrows, wrens, flickers, red-winged blackbirds, and ravenous shorebirds feeding in the marshes after having arrived from South America. Also keep an eye out for poison ivy, which can be found here in abundance.

As you approach the northern section of the hike, you pass through a grove of red cedar, which were some of the first "colonizers" of this piece of land after it began to return to forests, many generations after its trees were cut down by early settlers. Sandwich is the Cape's oldest formally recognized town, dating from 1637.

In fact, Murkwood is a former working agricultural landscape, where pastures and crop fields had long replaced the original forest. (Farmers soon learned that such wholesale clearing of the land was ruinous to the soil and other aspects of the Cape Cod natural environment. Today's Cape farms, including those in Sandwich, tend to be smaller efforts, specializing in sustainable organic practices.)

Stand amid these red cedars and ponder the changes humans and nature have inflicted on this landscape over the past four centuries. Or stop at a trailside bench that offers panoramic views of the marsh and imagine scenes from a century ago: fishers netting herring in the tidal creeks or farmers combing the marsh as they harvest salt hay to feed their livestock and insulate their building.

Leaving the "top" of the loop, the pathway now veers back southward. To your right spreads more of the Scorton Marsh, rolling out toward Ploughed Neck, the main access to a popular bayside beach in East Sandwich. (A short spur trail to the right brings you to a broad clearing.) The views across the this expanse of the estuary are equally impressive, and are even more memorable if you happen to be enjoying your hike at day's end with the setting sun illuminating the cordgrass that traces the creek channels. In autumn, the marsh grass is golden-tipped and is even more striking when backlit by the last rays of the low-angled sun.

Return east along the spur to the main trail, and continue to the right. You pass though a small woodland of oak and maple as you trace the west side of the property where it touches the salt marsh. Those shrub-like trees with pointy leaves and (in season) red berries you pass are holly, which were probably planted, because southeast Massachusetts is the northern edge of their range.

Just a short distance beyond, the trail completes the loop, and you are back at the small entrance point at Route 6A. If you've parked by the fire station, remember to be extremely careful when crossing the often busy road.

TRIP 8
SANDY NECK

$ 🐕 🏊

Rating: Moderate
Distance: 6.0 miles to the tip at the entrance to Barnstable Harbor
Estimated Time: 4 hours
Location: Barnstable

Explore the dunes and shorefront of this barrier beach jutting into Cape Cod Bay and protecting a remarkable salt marsh.

Directions
From Route 6 east, take Exit 3 in Sandwich, and proceed north on Quaker Meeting House Road to Route 6A. Turn right on Route 6A east to Sandy Neck Road on the left at the Sandwich-Barnstable line. The road terminates at a gatehouse. Parking is just beyond it.

Trip Description
Sandy Neck is a classic Massachusetts coastal barrier, similar in structure to Nauset Beach and Great Island in Orleans and Wellfleet, respectively, and Crane Beach in Ipswich on Boston's North Shore. Each protects an inland marsh/estuary system; the collection of tidal creeks and cordgrass that sprawls between the backside of Sandy Neck and the mainland is nourished by Barnstable Harbor, an inlet of Cape Cod Bay and Scorton Creek, which extends from the upper bay. As the weather warms, this fish-rich environment draws migrating osprey, whose nest poles can be easily seen from the Marsh Trail, the main hiking route leading from the Sandy Hook gatehouse.

This reservation, owned and managed by the town of Barnstable, is a popular beach. But hikers and nature lovers drawn to the dunes and small uplands of scrub oak and maple can often explore the back side without encountering the hordes. Indeed, I've hiked along the back side of the spit, encountering northern harriers, great blue herons, and tracks of coyote, fox, raccoon, and myriad other critters without meeting another person.

This is essentially easy hiking on flat terrain; it merits a "moderate" rating only if you and your party are intent on covering the entire distance:

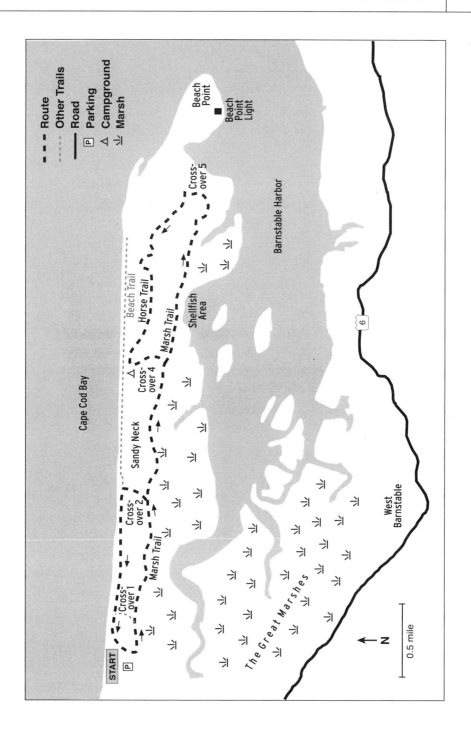

Route
Other Trails
Road
P Parking
△ Campground
⊥ Marsh

Cape Cod Bay

Sandy Neck

Beach Trail

Horse Trail

Marsh Trail

Cross-over 4

Cross-over 2

Marsh Trail

Cross-over 1

START
P

Cross-over 5

Beach Point

Beach Point Light

Barnstable Harbor

Shellfish Area

The Great Marshes

West Barnstable

6

N

0.5 mile

This six-mile stretch of beach on Cape Cod Bay is a beachcomber's paradise.

that's more than a dozen miles, out and back! You can organize your own loop route by following the Marsh Trail and then turning left onto one of four sequential sand routes that lead to the beach, just north. Then follow the beach back westward to your starting point.

From the parking lot, walk south about 0.25 mile and turn left onto Marsh Trail. As you start out, listen for the cry of osprey overhead and off to your right, over the marsh. If they are nesting, you might see a parent circling overhead, a fish in its talons, before dropping onto the nest pole, where a hungry young bird often awaits. The rugged thickets shelter warblers and other songbirds during spring migrations; you can spot red-winged blackbirds, swallows, and blue jays, as well. You also find island hummocks supporting small maritime forests and vernal pools are a part of this magical landscape.

If you're planning a family hike, you might want to consider following the Marsh Trail to the first sand path leading left, which is about 0.5 mile from the trailhead. Turn here and make your way through a small series of dunes before emerging onto the beach. Take another left and follow the shore back to the beach parking lot. The entire trip is less than 1.5 miles, but offers a taste of what this coastscape offers.

If you're up to a longer trip, continue east on the Marsh Trail for another 1.5 miles to beach outlet number 2. If it's an especially warm day, the bay waters glistening and rippling at the shoreline might seem especially inviting. (But be prepared for plenty of company; Sandy Neck, remember, is one of the most popular beaches on the Cape.) By the time you've completed the loop, you have hiked almost 5.0 miles.

Those who choose to wander farther out the Neck should be equipped to spend a good part of the day. In summer, be sure you wear a hat and pack plenty of sun block and water. You will find copses of trees and small groves of maritime forest to explore, but little or no shade to protect you from the high, strong sun.

Along your route, you pass the remains of ruined structures (the U.S. military trained World War II troops for fighting in the Sahara here), vernal pools, and other wet areas where wild cranberries and other moisture-dependent plants can grow. And don't be surprised if you see the occasional horse and rider, especially farther down the Neck where there are fewer people and vehicles.

Past entry path 4, the beach-side trail moves landward into a semi-remote stretch of dunes and small forest that are similar to what you experience in the Province Lands at the very tip of the Cape. This spit was once more heavily forested, but colonial woodcutters made quick work of that bounty. Cultivation of salt hay on the marsh and extensive cranberry bogs also took their toll. This section of trail, accessed from beach entry path 4, meanders through the interior of the Neck for more than 1.0 mile before intersecting at beach entry path 5.

To turn around, follow beach path 5 south to where it meets the Marsh Trail. You can enjoy fine views of several islands, including Green Thatch and Little Thatch, rising out of Barnstable Harbor to the southwest. Look across the embayment to the village of Barnstable and then turn right and begin the 5.0-mile hike back to your starting point. I recommend the Marsh Trail on this longer exploration for three reasons: fewer people (and no off-road vehicles); easier footing than on the thicker, softer sand at the beach front; and memorable views of this spectacular marsh.

Cape Geology

When English colonists stepped off the Mayflower in what is now Provincetown Harbor in November, 1620, American Indians had already been on the Cape for many centuries, of course. Yet the land was among the youngest on the North American continent. It's little more than a 60-mile spit of sand, after all.

The vast ice sheets that covered much of the earth during the Ice Age didn't descend from Canada through New England until about 20,000 years ago. As it advanced, the ice was sufficiently heavy and powerful enough to scrape and tear at the rock it covered. The largest bulldozer in the history of the world, the glacier pushed massive amounts of material ahead of it, until it reached a warmer climate and came to a stop. By about 12,000 years ago the last ice sheet was in retreat.

The rock material and other deposits left in the glacier's retreating wake formed the foundation for the coastscape you explore today. As the climate warmed and glacial ice melt flowed off the coasts, the seas began to rise. About 6,000 years ago, the resurgent ocean reached the disorganized land deposits of the Cape and began to shape them into beaches, dunes, and cliffs. The first barrier beaches (such as Nauset and Sandy Neck) also formed.

Along the Cape Cod Bay perimeter of this amazing hook are uplands formed by moraines, the debris pushed ahead of glaciers into folded hills. One such moraine extends eastward from Sandwich into Barnstable, south of the sprawling salt marsh behind Sandy Neck Beach. Another one runs lengthwise along the Cape side of Buzzards Bay. All are supported by bedrock more than 150 million years old, upper edges of the earth's crust that were nonetheless impacted by the advance and retreat of the glacier.

Much of this rock was gouged out by the ice sheets and transported far from where it originated. When the glacier retreated, the broken rock was sometimes left in the form of huge boulders, called glacial erratics. One of the largest in southeastern Massachusetts is Doane Rock in Eastham, located just east of the Cape Cod National Seashore Visitor Center. The boulder is 15 feet high, 40 feet long, and 25 feet wide, with much of it hidden underground.

The Cape Cod National Seashore, a shining example of political and environmental foresight that features a 30-mile stretch of ocean-side beach from

Glacial boulders such as this one were left behind by retreating glaciers.

Eastham to Provincetown, includes many of these geologic features. A massive wall of clay-backed cliffs climbs to more than 100 feet in places in Wellfleet and Truro (interrupted only by swimming beach parking lots) despite the constant pounding they take from storms, especially winter nor'easters. Natural forces are still molding the Cape; it's just that the eons-old volcanic upheavals and the glacial action of 12,000 years ago have been replaced by water, wind, and weather.

The long swath of sand that runs parallel to the base of the National Seashore cliffs was called the "Great Beach" by Henry David Thoreau, who knew it well. And if you've ever hiked a couple of miles in soft sand, you understand that "great" can mean something other than wonderful or terrific. It can also mean challenging and imposing, as the environmental visionary learned for himself— Thoreau walked it three times between 1849 and 1855.

TRIP 9
LONG POND CONSERVATION AREA

Rating: Easy to Moderate
Distance: 5.0 miles
Estimated Time: 3 hours
Location: Falmouth

**Wander through almost a thousand acres of Falmouth water-
shed land and explore woodlands and wetlands bracketed by
Long Pond and Grews Pond (you can enjoy a picnic or take a
swim at the latter).**

Directions

From Route 28 in Falmouth, exit at Brick Kiln Road, turn left, and proceed
southeast approximately 2.0 miles to Gifford Street. Turn right on Gifford
Street and proceed about 1.0 mile to the Goodwill Park entrance on the right.
Proceed 0.25 mile to parking near Grews Pond.

Trip Description

Almost all this land was pasture when it was donated to the town by Joseph
Fay and his descendants, about a decade before the Civil War. The cultivated
landscapes were typical of this period on Cape Cod, when very little forest
remained anywhere along the 60-mile spit, from Sandwich to Provincetown.
From any high point, a traveler could literally see from town to town, church
steeple to church steeple. But Fay was determined to plant trees, and some
of the hardwoods you pass on the cart paths and dirt roads passing through
this landscape are remnants of his legacy.

These watershed lands straddle a glacial moraine that forms an "L"-
shaped frame for the Upper Cape, connecting the uplands of Cape Cod Bay
and Buzzards Bay. This hilly, rocky habitat on the north and west is marked
by more substantial woodlands and soils whereas the southern side features
flatter, wetter, and sandier habitats, part of the glacial outwash that defines
much more of the Cape.

In the vicinity of the pond you find fields of boulders, more reminders
of the pronounced glacial action that created the Cape; as the last ice sheets

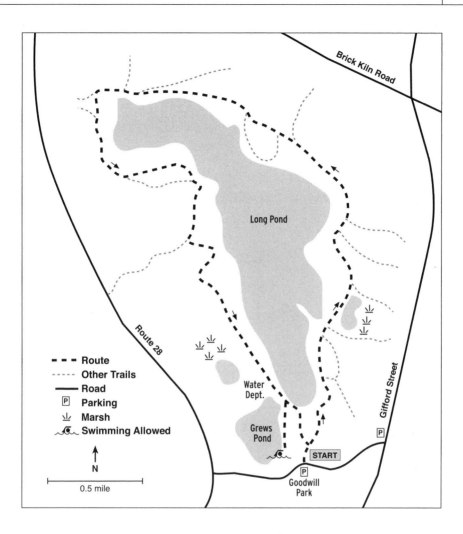

Long Pond

Brick Kiln Road

Route 28

Gifford Street

- - - Route
- - - - Other Trails
——— Road
P Parking
⸽ Marsh
⟅⟆ Swimming Allowed

↑
N

0.5 mile

Water
Dept.

Grews
Pond

START

Goodwill
Park

retreated some 12,000 years ago, these massive rocks were transported, crushed, and then "dropped" by powerful natural forces. Of much more recent vintage are the uniform stands of white pine that are now part of the landscape, planted by the Civilian Conservation Corps in the 1930s.

The Long Pond Trail begins beyond an orange vehicle gate. Walk north to a dirt road that bears left and then soon splits. Head right (north) toward Long Pond on a wide, easy-to-follow carriage road. Continue another 1.0 mile, bearing left as the road traces the north shore of Long Pond. In less than 0.5 mile, you meet a narrow path leading right, which takes you to Brick Kiln Road. This 0.5-mile spur takes you through a thicker habitat, including

Feel free to go swimming in Grews Pond.

cat briar and other thorny flora, more welcoming to rabbits and songbirds than humans.

This northern edge of the pond features steep slopes and is part of higher ridges running north that sit within the moraine that anchors this part of the Cape.

Returning to the main dirt road circling Long Pond, you pass between the northwest arm of the pond and a substantial wetland on your right. This swamp, home to numerous red maples, blazes into color each fall. Keep an eye out for turtles, frogs, and the scarlet epaulets of male red-winged black-birds. In addition to the sandpapery whistle of the red-winged blackbirds and the more pleasing songs of other birds, you might also hear traffic on Route 28; as you continue to hike westerly and then south, you approach to within 0.25 mile of the busy artery.

Proceeding directly south, you trace the pond's relatively short (0.25 mile) northwest shore. Continuing around a section of the pond that resembles an elephant's trunk, you continue south and then begin to head left (east) where the track bows to maintain its proximity to the shore.

The road jogs more abruptly left and then turns right briefly (south) before the main track straightens out for 0.75 mile in a southeasterly direction, with the pond shore still on your left. A narrow causeway between Long Pond and Grews Pond appears ahead, as well as a cluster of Town of Falmouth buildings.

As part of the town drinking supply, Long Pond cannot accommodate swimmers, but Grews Pond features the Town of Falmouth beach on its south shore, complete with lifeguards and snack shop. Here is where Joseph Fay was perhaps at his most benevolent. He donated Goodwill Park in 1894 and made sure his penchant for tree planting was celebrated in this lovely public recreation area.

Look for American holly, hickory and hornbeam, and beech and birch in the areas adjacent to the pond. Rhododendrons were also planted, and these flowering bushes add their own pink and white color displays when in bloom. Indeed, Grews Pond is definitely worth considering, whether you're solo, part of a couple, or with a family.

To return to your car, follow the track for another 0.25 mile, and you are back on the trail leading from the parking lot.

TRIP 10
BEEBE WOODS AND PETERSON FARM

Rating: Moderate
Distance: 4.0 miles
Estimated Time: 3 hours
Location: Falmouth

Explore a former sprawling estate and former working farm, now 400 acres of protected uplands and deep woods, ponds, pastures, and wetlands—all situated within 5 minutes of busy downtown Falmouth.

Directions
Take Route 25 east on the Bourne Bridge and bear right at the rotary onto Route 28. Continue south through Bourne into Falmouth, where Route 28 becomes Palmer Avenue. Just before Route 28 jogs left to become Main Street, take a right onto Depot Avenue. Cross the track (now part of the Shining Sea Bikeway) and continue west on what is now Highfield Drive to a parking lot between the Cape Cod Conservatory and Highfield Theater. Enter the woods on a path just right of the conservatory.

Trip Description
The former Beebe Woods estate and 88-acre Peterson Farm, which forms the south portion of this admirable open space, present one of the loveliest walking and nature-watching experiences on the Upper Cape. The trails and cart paths are either flat or gently undulating, which makes this preserved space welcoming to families.

Depending on where you choose to walk, you pass restored woodlands of oak, maple and black locust; crystal clear ponds and imposing boulders (both natural features fashioned by glacial action); and stone walls and pastures. With development threats continuing, the Lilly family donated the majority of the property to the town in 1966. Two decades later, the town purchased the adjacent farm, which dates from the 1600s and is one of the oldest on the Cape.

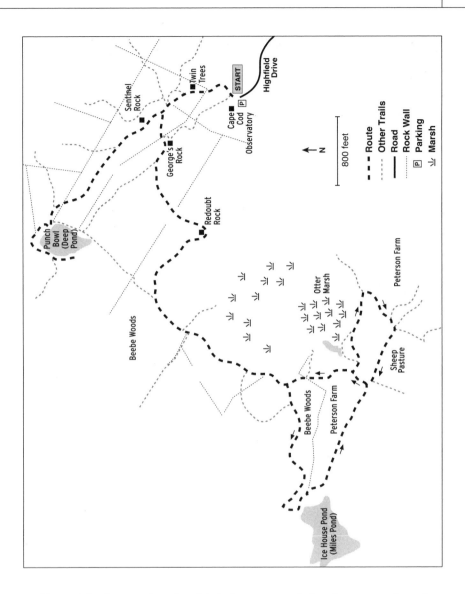

You might have enjoyed a drink from a punch bowl at some time, but you probably haven't ever hiked around one. Now you have that singular opportunity. From the Highfield Theater parking lot, you take a loop route on a northwesterly walk to the Punch Bowl, a pretty little pond named for its steep sides and circular shape. It's less than 0.75 mile out to the pond, easily doable if you're bringing young ones along.

The iconic Bourne Bridge is only minutes from Beebe Woods.

Like most of the other ponds on the Cape, this body of water is a classic example of a retreating glacier having left behind a massive "ice cube" that melted over thousands of years. Look for moisture-tolerant trees including red maple and tupelo. And during the warm-weather months, look and listen for that signature summertime activity: swimming. The Punch Bowl is a popular destination for those seeking a delightful dip.

After exploring the pond, and perhaps taking a swim, retrace your steps, take your first right toward George's Rock, and from there continue to Redoubt Rock, where you will turn right. Follow the trail until you reach Ice House Pond (Miles Pond). There is no trail around the pond, so take the trail that leads east from the pond to the remaining structures of Peterson Farm.

Wander amid barns, outbuildings, and the livestock that still live here. You can enjoy any number of short loops amid the fields and pastures, but my wife and I chose to head north, across the property to a marshy wetland and pond, where we saw (and heard) red-winged blackbirds and watched a hawk—couldn't tell what kind—soaring serenely overhead. The going got a little soggy as we made a loop that explored a small feeder stream and dam that helped form the pond.

You can add a loop of about 1.0 mile by turning left at your first chance and wandering into the western reaches of this property. Just keep bearing right and you eventually return to the main stem.

Before reaching the Highfield Theater trailhead, you find yourself only a short walk away from a wetland that hosts a small colony of rare Atlantic white cedar trees. Take the last left before reaching Highfield, and the swamp is only about 0.25 mile ahead. The cedars still exist because they were not cost-effective to cut; much of Beebe Woods has been transformed several times by humans—burned, cleared, and plowed for pasturage and crop fields, or timbered for wood fuel and building materials.

Look for stone walls just about everywhere. They were built partially to support carriage roads, but more generally as property boundaries and to control the movement of livestock. Most of the rocks came out of the ground courtesy of farmers' muscles, but some were pulled from the fields of boulders that are part of this upland moraine—all part of the grinding and gouging of glacial advance and retreat many thousands of years ago.

I strongly recommend a visit to this engaging and varied property. Whether you are a fan of glacial ponds, stone walls, large boulders, meandering woodland trails, or a flock of sheep, you and your family are probably going to find it here. Best of all, the property is situated within easy driving (and even walking) distance of Falmouth center, which features dining spots, gift shops, galleries and ice cream parlors, and plenty of other attractions to please families, couples, and every other outdoors enthusiast.

TRIP 11
OLD YARMOUTH NATURE TRAILS

Rating: Easy
Distance: 1.5 miles
Estimated Time: 1 hour
Location: Yarmouth Port

Just a few steps away from Route 6A you find a 50-acre refuge through which hikers and nature lovers can enter Yarmouth's colonial past.

Directions
From Route 6, Exit 7, take Willow Street north 1.0 mile to Route 6A. Turn right on Route 6A and follow for 1.0 mile to signs for the U.S. Post Office and the Historical Society on right (Thacher Street meets Route 6A on the left). Park at the end of the lane beyond the restored cobbler shop on the right.

Trip Description
An attractive blend of uplands and restored forest, complemented by a lovely pond environment, this property was given to the community by the Thacher family, whose forebears were early settlers of this part of the Cape. The trail system comprises a pair of interlocking loops. The larger one is about 1.0 mile around; a smaller loop circles Miller Pond.

This walking habitat is another good choice for families or novice hikers—you follow trail markers that guide you through varied natural habitats along a mostly flat trail system. And the network is short enough to get you and your party back to the parking lot with the rest of the day to explore Yarmouth Port, the mid-Cape town's most scenic and historic section. (Be sure to drive down Mill Lane to where a tidal inlet enters from Cape Cod Bay and then down Center Street to the 900-foot boardwalk at Gray's Beach.)

Managed by the Historical Society of Old Yarmouth, the trails invite you to pass through the type of pine and hardwood forest that today is common on many parts of the Cape that were stripped of trees by settlers and farms through the sixteenth and seventeenth centuries. In the late 1880s, the land became the first golf links on Cape Cod. It was a private, 9-hole course that existed until World War II.

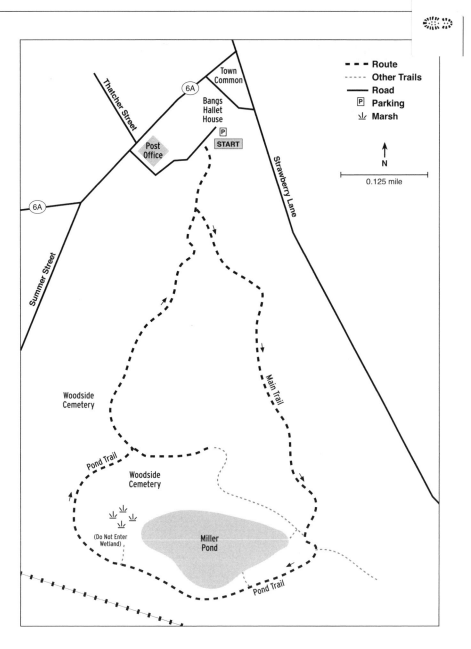

Please note that while the trail network features several benches, picnicking is not allowed on this property. Biking and all forms of motorized transportation are also forbidden.

Follow white blazes as you ascend the main trail on a short rise. You cross into a former pasture that is again returning to forest, including red cedar,

The gentle Old Yarmouth Nature Trails are perfect for a peaceful stroll.

chokecherry, and sumac, all trees that are among the first to take root in fields and other clearings. You also find the hardy pitch pine here, a signature tree across much of Cape Cod. (Henry David Thoreau traveled to the Cape in 1840 along the Old King's Highway, today's Route 6A, five years before he built his cabin on Walden Pond. Making his way through Yarmouth Port, he commented on the robustness of the pitch pine.)

Continuing south into the woodlands you soon come to the first of several benches, perfect for resting or contemplation. Farther on, shade-tolerant oak are beginning to supplant the pitch pine. You also pass taller, straighter white pine and thick rhododendron, the latter blooming beautifully in late spring. Amble through more grown-over pasture, where livestock once grazed. As you pass another bench, the surrounding woodlands become hillier; glacial deposits from 15,000 years ago were more pronounced along the mid- and upper Cape. The trees with roundish-lobed leaves are white oak; those with pointier leaves are black oak, both of which do well in these sandy soils.

You now reach a point where the main trail jogs right while the pond loop, marked by yellow blazes, continues straight ahead. Miller Pond is a typical kettle hole, formed by melting ice left behind as the last glacier retreated. You see trees that thrive in wetter soils here, including maples. Proceed onto the pond loop, moving clockwise and leaving the water on your right. Several access paths off this trail lead to the shore, where you might spy turtles basking in the sun or kingfishers zipping from one shore to the other.

Meanwhile, not too far off to your left, the rail bed of the former Old Colony-Penn Central line runs parallel. (Beginning one town east in Dennis, the rail bed has been converted into a bike trail and recreation path that extends more than 20 miles to South Wellfleet.)

Continue along the south side of the pond to where this footpath curves around to the right and rejoins the main trail. If you turn right on the trail, you shortly reach a bench nestled among rhododendron and holly that is a nice resting spot above the pond. Retrace your steps to continue west on the trail, away from Miller Pond, and you reach an opening where oaks are moving in, "succeeding" the previous habitat of shrubs and bushes, including blueberry and ground-hugging bearberry.

Another example of this property's history as a working landscape is a former clay pit, which you soon come upon, with a cemetery situated just beyond the property's border. The trail arcs north here and begins to angle back toward your starting point. The open area you now pass through was part of a former golf course developed in the late nineteenth century for the Thacher family; today's plethora of courses on Cape Cod has long roots as recreational diversion. The trail continues for a short distance through more "successional" woodlands before reaching the parking area.

On your left you can note a restored house of worship dating to the 1870s, the Kelley Chapel, today made available for weddings and other celebrations. The landscape you enjoyed here is more wooded than it has been in three centuries. Farming, logging, construction of settlements and towns, the charcoal and whale oil industries—all required a large amount of wood and took their toll on the forests the first European settlers found. Less than 200 years after the Mayflower landed in November of 1620 (in Provincetown, four months before reaching Plymouth), the Cape was essentially denuded of trees. Over the intervening two centuries, the landscape has slowly been restoring the balance, with forest returning in some quantity, if not in the variety of species the Pilgrims found.

Before you leave, you might want to visit the Captain Bangs Hallet House, just up the hill, a repository of Yarmouth history and lore. Hallet was a local sea captain active in the nineteenth-century China trade. The museum is open to the public seasonally. The first building you passed on your way in, the Benjamin T. Gorham Cobbler Shop, serves as the historical society's headquarters and research center. It is also open to the public.

TRIP 12
INDIAN LANDS CONSERVATION AREA

Rating: Easy
Distance: 2.5 miles
Estimated Time: 1 hour
Location: Dennis

Follow icons of modern civilization—a power line and former railroad—before arriving at a serene landscape along the tidal Bass River that once was the site of a centuries-old American Indian gathering place.

Directions

From Route 6 east, Exit 9, take Route 134 for 0.75 mile south and take a right on Upper County Road. Take the first right onto Main Street and proceed 0.25 mile to the Dennis municipal complex on the left. Park in the lot at the right of the buildings.

Trip Description

The Bass River comes pretty close to cutting the Cape in half. From Nantucket Sound it winds its way north for 6.0 miles into ponds and creeks that reach within 0.5 mile of tidal waters emptying into Cape Cod Bay. The aptly named waterway (striped bass chase baitfish along the river, spring through fall) is also the largest environment of its kind in the region, supporting an array of plants, trees, fish, birds, and mammals. This fact goes a long way toward explaining why the Nobscussett spent time here, especially during the colder months, when they sought dependable shelter from the more extreme winter weather buffeting the exposed shore lands.

On the other side of a cemetery, situated just north of the Dennis Town Hall, a power line follows the former Old Colony rail bed running east-west. Follow a dirt road west that runs parallel to the power line for less than 0.5 mile, where you see trail signs on the left indicating the Indian Lands. The trail soon splits. Take the path heading left, and soon you reach a scenic panorama that, right to left, includes broad marsh lands, and flowing southward, the blue ribbon of the Bass River. Continue on this path to where you can turn right to begin a short, 0.5-mile loop.

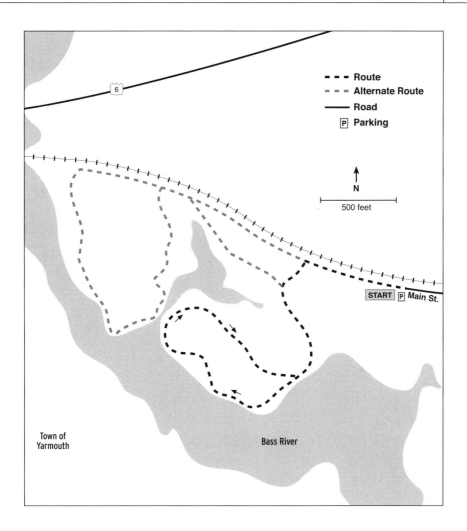

In spring, look for pink lady's slipper orchids growing in the damp, shaded areas near the marsh. Here you might also find ducks and wading birds taking advantage of the bounty of the soggy habitat, from nutritious marsh plants to frogs and small fish. This serene wetland is worth a few quiet minutes; your stillness and silence are often rewarded with a little natural theater, from dragonflies flitting above the marsh surface to turtles sunning themselves on logs or blue herons slowly taking flight on 3-foot wings. Chattering kingfishers also make themselves known throughout the warm-weather months. Look for highbush blueberry near the shore. This habitat attracts red-tailed hawks, northern harriers, and owls. During the fall migration period, look for a greater variety of raptors passing south on

A woodland trail leads hikers to the serene banks of the Bass River.

the Atlantic flyway. Also in fall, the maples show plenty of red, orange, and purple. This property is also friendly to poison ivy, so be aware.

The meandering waterway is especially enticing here; you are permitted a bit of envy as you regard waterside homes on the Yarmouth bank, their small docks and piers serving as nautical driveways. The Bass River attracts plenty of small powerboaters, including many anglers either returning from trying their luck in Nantucket Sound or heading farther inshore. But over the past decade I've seen an increasing number of paddlers, especially kayakers, plying these waters; boat liveries and other rental outfits located near where Route 28 links Dennis and Yarmouth are taking full advantage of this interest in muscle-powered river exploration.

This is municipal open space, so the town and its various agencies are responsible for its care. Cape Cod towns show an impressive commitment to protecting their recreation areas against vandalism, graffiti, and litter. Indian Lands seem even more pristine than most, perhaps because of the time and effort required to reach the riverside trail network or maybe because would-be defacers simply find this environment too lovely to scar.

White pines have been planted, perhaps as partial reparation for forests the first European settlers found (and cut) here four centuries ago. The thin, sandy soil that was the end result of the denuding of the Cape through the 1700s is present here as well, meaning you pass through a familiar woodland of pitch pine and oak, with other hardwoods mixed in. Throughout, you can enjoy one delightful view after another.

For a long hike that, while less scenic, also delivers you to the banks of the Bass River, retrace your steps to the original fork where you turned left starting out on the loop. At the fork on your return trip, bear left and continue for a couple hundred yards, passing the edge of the marsh on your left, to where the dirt road paralleling the rail line merges from the right. Follow this route left less than 0.5 mile. You ascend a short rise and there the road ends at the river, with a bridge carrying the rail line into Yarmouth. This location is a popular fishing spot as well as a swimming hole in summer.

For another view of the marsh that you passed on the loop route, take a foot path south along the river. Descend the small hill, take a quick right, and follow an intimate route that passes through thick vegetation and a forest of pitch pine, with the river on your right. In about 0.25 mile, the north side of the marsh appears before you. Directly across this rich, tidal wetland extends the loop trail that introduced you and your party to this pretty habitat at the beginning of your excursion.

There is no passage across the water, so you must retrace your steps to the dirt road that runs along the power line and rail bed. Follow the dirt road back for about 1.0 mile to the town offices' parking lot and your vehicle.

Bartholomew Gosnold

In the spring of 1602, Captain Bartholomew Gosnold, a son of Otley in Suffolk, England, commanded a small vessel called the Concord that had been commissioned to gauge mining opportunities in the New World. Gosnold first reached the waters off the coast of what is now Maine. The Concord sailed down the New England coast, passed inside Race Point and Provincetown, and continued into the broad bay embraced by the arm of the Cape.

Gosnold might have been seeking Nantucket Sound, which had been described earlier by Italian explorer Giovanni da Verrazzano and was known to other explorers. Gosnold hoped to somehow pass through the long upland rising before him. He made landfall near what is now Rock Harbor, on the Orleans-Eastham line, but found no water passage. The Concord then sailed west, along the shores of Brewster, Dennis, and Yarmouthport, the ship's crew and captain growing increasingly frustrated—until they spied a large opening in the coast.

Unfortunately for Gosnold and company, they had reached the broad entrance to Barnstable Harbor and soon bumped up against shoal water and sand bars—not to mention the extensive salt marsh fed by Scorton Creek. In his frustration, Gosnold gathered several of the crew together and went looking for a hilltop from where they might get their bearings (and locate Nantucket Sound), which they did after bushwhacking from the harbor to what might have been Shoot Flying Hill, located just south of Route 6 Exit 6 in Hyannis. From the summit, Gosnold could see Wequaquet Lake just below, Hyannis Harbor, and just beyond, the broad spread of Nantucket Sound, so near and yet so far.

Upon returning to his ship, the irritable skipper found the decks practically awash in a tasty, ground-feeding whitefish, taken by bored crew members. The sailors "had pestered our ship so with Cod fish, that we threw numbers of them over-boord againe," later reported John Brereton, who had gone to shore with his captain. It was during this encounter with all these fish that Gosnold supposedly named the peninsula Cape Cod.

He still had to get his ship to the south side of the Cape. American Indians were utilizing tidal creeks and portages as a shortcut to reach Buzzards Bay from what is now Sandwich (and the site of the Cape Cod Canal), but no passage existed large enough for a ship. Gosnold was forced to retrace his route out of Cape Cod Bay, make the long passage around Race Point and down what is now the backside of the National Seashore, negotiate the dangerous shoals and currents at Chatham and Monomoy, and enter Nantucket Sound from the east.

On this same voyage he would also name the larger of the two offshore islands in the Sound Martha's Vineyard and would anoint the string of smaller islands at the entrance to Buzzards Bay. These islands comprise one of the quietest, most remote, and ruggedly beautiful corners of coastal New England. Its lone incorporated town, located on Naushon Island, is called Gosnold.

Five years later, after captaining a ship that brought the first English settlers to the ill-fated Jamestown colony in what is now Virginia, Bartholomew Gosnold would perish there of disease.

TRIP 13
NICKERSON STATE PARK

Rating: Moderate
Distance: 5.0 miles
Estimated Time: 3 hours
Location: Brewster

Explore woodlands, marshes, and scenic ponds along miles of trails and footpaths that wander through one of the largest state parks in Massachusetts.

Directions
From Route 6, Exit 12 in Orleans, turn left off the ramp onto Route 6A west. Follow for 2.0 miles to the park entrance on the left.

Trip Description
At more than 1,900 acres, Nickerson State Park is the interior Cape's largest area of open space committed to public recreation. Campers, swimmers, hikers, anglers, cyclists, and nature watchers all enjoy the natural attractions of this Department of Conservation and Recreation-managed park that dominates the eastern part of Brewster.

Old cart paths and farm roads that were constructed when the park was a Nickerson family estate more than a century ago have been augmented by other roads and trails. Nickerson also shelters a cluster of kettle hole ponds, spring-fed bodies of water that emerged from the retreating glacier 12,000 years ago. Hiking trails encircle the four largest, Cliff, Little Cliff, Higgins, and Flax, and bike routes pass by several others.

My favorite time of year for exploring Nickerson by foot is in autumn. Summer is high season for campers, and the scene is simply too hectic. Spring can be wet and buggy (certainly by May). If you choose to visit in the winter, I recommend using snowshoes and cross-country skis when the white stuff flies.

Inside the park, you reach Flax Pond first. But Flax Pond is smallish, less than 1.0 mile around. I prefer to follow Flax Pond Road to where it passes between Cliff Pond (at almost 200 acres, the largest in the park) and, on your

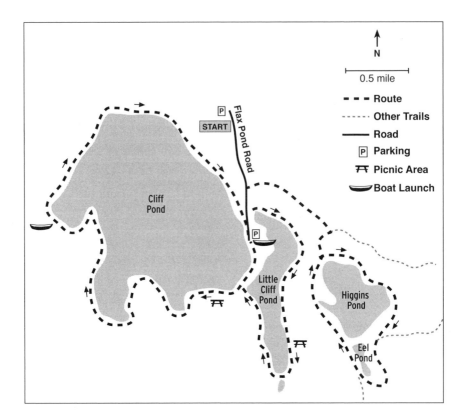

left, Little Cliff Pond. From a parking area-boat launch site, you have easy access to the 3.0-mile trail that loops Cliff Pond.

Amble along the narrow strip between the ponds until the trail bears southwest along the Cliff Pond shore and a white sand beach. Campsites and other facilities appear on your left. At the southern-most edge of the pond you reach a marshy area that once was a pond, now in transition as it fills with vegetation. Cross this neck and follow the trail as it ascends from pond-side into a mix of white pine and maple. (Tall, straight white pines are plentiful within Nickerson; a Depression-era tree-planting program by the Civilian Conservation Corps was apparently very successful.)

As you move through this upland and leave the woods, look for blueberry bushes amid the low-lying shrubs, goldenrod, and wildflowers. The trail juts northward into a small peninsula before reaching another boat launch, called Fisherman's Landing. Anglers have always enjoyed the freshwater fishing in Nickerson, more so since the state began seasonally stocking ponds with trout to add to the naturally breeding bass, perch, and sunfish.

Nickerson State Park's crystal-clear ponds are popular with visitors and residents.

The trail angles northeast along a rocky shore before entering a pine grove, with sandy beaches lining the shore. You again pass campsites on your left and then a picnic area near the northern shore. The trail continues to follow the pond until it returns to the town landing at Flax Pond Road.

From your starting point here, you can also explore Little Cliff Pond and Higgins Pond, to the east. To hike around Little Cliff Pond, a long, crooked finger of a pond, leave the north end of the Flax Pond Road parking area and follow the path that traces its north shore. This is another loop trail, about 1.0 mile a length, and is a favorite birding spot: Swans, ducks, and geese patrol the surface of the pond, while songbirds and kingfishers dip down from the ledges.

Returning to the north shore of Little Cliff Pond, continue east on a bridle trail to Higgins Pond. Follow a dirt road that extends easterly beyond Higgins Pond. The road turns south, then westwards. Eel Pond, one of the smallest in the park, appears on your right. The dirt road angles north past Eel Pond back to Higgins Pond, where you find several footpaths leading down to the shore. Continue until you reach an intersection and turn left and hike back to Flax Pond Road.

TRIP 14
PUNKHORN PARKLANDS

Rating: Moderate
Distance: 5.0 miles
Estimated Time: 3 hours
Location: Brewster

Wander through a semi-remote area of resurgent forest, herring brooks, wetlands, and former cranberry bogs, bracketed by ancient kettle hole ponds and cart paths dating back two centuries.

Directions
From Route 6 east, take Exit 9B in Dennis. Go north on Route 134 for 1.7 miles and then take a right on Satucket Road and travel for 3 miles just past Stony Brook Road. Take a right onto Old Run Hill Road and follow it 1.5 miles to where it turns into the parking area.

Trip Description
Within two minutes of entering this lightly visited, under-appreciated recreation area, my wife and I met two women on horses. One of the horses was wearing what appeared to be mosquito netting over its mouth, but it was just a food muzzle, the horse's rider informed me. The animal likes to stop and nibble anything and everything, "and he can be very headstrong." Then again, the Punkhorn Parklands can accommodate every mood, from feisty to serene. Located in the extreme southwest corner of Brewster on the border with Harwich, and bounded by Route 124 on the east and Slough Road and Satucket Road on the southwest and northwest, Punkhorn comprises an intriguing environment indeed. The forest of oak, pine, and other mixed hardwoods has reclaimed land that once was farmed, drained for cranberry bogs, or provided fuel and water for nineteenth-century Cape industry, including timber harvesting, granite quarrying seaside jetties, and tar production.

However, much of the land had been cleared by the eighteenth century for croplands and pasturage. The name "Punkhorn" is perhaps a derivative of an American Indian name for "place of spongy wood," although establish-

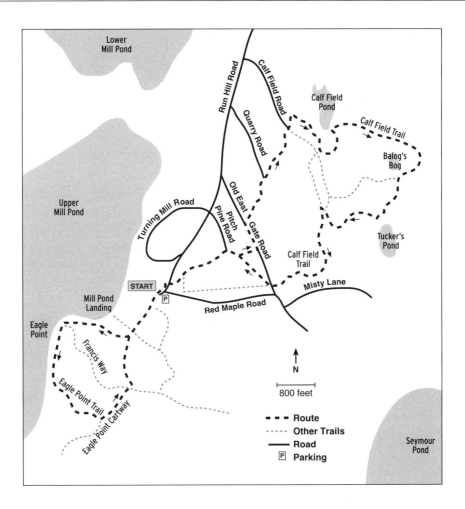

Lower Mill Pond

Run Hill Road

Calf Field Road

Calf Field Pond

Calf Field Trail

Balog's Bog

Quarry Road

Old East Gate Road

Upper Mill Pond

Turning Mill Road

Pitch Pine Road

Tucker's Pond

Calf Field Trail

START

Misty Lane

Mill Pond Landing

Red Maple Road

Eagle Point

Francis Way

Eagle Point Trail

Eagle Point Cartway

N

800 feet

Seymour Pond

- ▪ ▪ Route
- - - Other Trails
—— Road
P Parking

ing more definitive origins has proved difficult. Today, more than 800 acres have been preserved by the Town of Brewster, for hiking, freshwater fishing, mountain biking, and passive recreational enjoyment.

We should all be thankful the Punkhorn environment is located far enough inland (just north of Route 6) that early settlers determined it was too far from where most of the colonial action was: along the coasts of Cape Cod Bay and Nantucket Sound.

The parklands are laced by dirt roads and cart paths, with colorful names including Deep Punkhorn Path, Black Duck Cartway, and Eagle Point Cartway. Color-coded trails—blue, red, green, yellow—meander away from and then return across the larger routes. (For updated trail maps of this area, be

Families enjoy walking the carriage roads of Punkhorn Parklands.

sure to visit the information center at the rear of the Brewster town offices on Route 6A.)

Begin at Calf Field, which offers a series of loop options that total several miles. You also have the chance to visit two glacial ponds and a bog if you make the effort. Start at the first Punkhorn parking lot you encounter along Run Hill Road. From the parking area, walk back on Run Hill 200 feet to where you pass Red Maple Road on the right. Just beyond Red Maple Road, look for a pathway (with sign) entering the woods, also on the right. The trail leads east to Old East Gate Road, which originally traced a farm landscape. Take a left on Old East Gate Road and then follow the trail northeast into the woods. You pass Quarry Road and Calf Field Road before you see the southern tip of Calf Field Pond.

This route loops back to Calf Field Road. From here you have a couple of choices: continue south on Calf Field Road and follow the path as it slowly veers southwestward back to your starting point or take the footpath east and farther into the woods on a larger loop. You leave Calf Field Pond on your left and proceed about another 0.25 mile to Balog's Bog, a former kettle hole becoming a wetland. Continue in a clockwise direction around the bog and then bear left onto another trail section leading to Tucker's Pond. This side path leads back to the main stem as you hike west; take a left and follow Calf Field Pond Trail back to your starting point.

A short walk farther south on Run Hill Road, you reach the main parking lot at Eagle Point Cartway and the Eagle Point Trail loop, ideal for families. The path proceeds along the east shore of Upper Mill Pond, climbs a small rise to Eagle Point (yes, bald eagles have been sighted), and continues in a counterclockwise loop to where it returns to the Eagle Point Cartway and leads you back (north) to where you started. This walk is less than 0.5 mile long, but offers plenty to families with young hikers.

TRIP 15
MONOMOY NATIONAL WILDLIFE REFUGE, MORRIS ISLAND

Rating: Moderate
Distance: 2.0 miles
Estimated Time: 2 hours
Location: Chatham

Amble along the shoreline and through the dunes of Morris Island, gateway to the Monomoy National Wildlife Refuge at the elbow of Cape Cod.

Directions

From Route 6 east, take Exit 11. At the bottom of the ramp turn left onto Route 137 south and follow to the terminus at Route 28. Take Route 28 east to the rotary in the center of Chatham. Proceed through the rotary onto Main Street and past the shopping district. Where Main Street ends at T-intersection, turn right onto Shore Road and proceed past Chatham Lighthouse and the Coast Guard Station. Bear left after the lighthouse onto Morris Island Road and then take the first right. Follow Morris Island Road over the causeway and up a slight rise to signs for the refuge on the left.

Trip Description

Morris Island is linked to mainland Chatham by a causeway and, therefore, has not been cut off by the tide for many years. Indeed, the 40-acre island is the only part of the 2,750-acre Monomoy National Wildlife Refuge not primarily accessible by boat. But when planning your hike here, it would be wise to bring a local tide chart along, or know in advance the hour of high tide because it regularly covers the beginning section of trail just south of park headquarters, rendering it generally impassable—at least for a short period, until the tide begins to ebb.

You have a few ways to approach this memorable walk at the southeast corner of the Cape: Follow the shore 0.25 mile to the first trail sign, which leads you into the dunes on a counterclockwise self-guided interpretive tour,

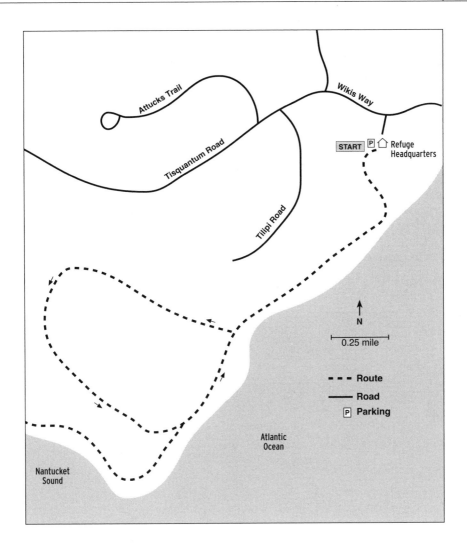

or continue straight along the shore a few hundred yards farther, watch for another sign on the right, and follow the trail clockwise on the same dune-and-upland tour. Either one of these choices offers a 0.75-mile loop that is both fun and educational (bring a trail guide from headquarters) and is manageable for children.

A third option is to continue along the shore, gently arcing southwest-ward to the entrance to Stage Harbor on Nantucket Sound. From here you can enjoy panoramic views of the Chatham flats and North and South Monomoy Islands (which comprise the majority of the refuge) and wonder at the ever-changing coastscape, carved by wind, current, and storm.

But first, let's explore the loop trail. From the refuge parking lot, follow signs that take you right, leaving the restroom complex on your left and entering a small dune-top wooded area. Almost immediately you reach a lookout area on your left. Stop here and marvel at the harbor channel, criss-crossed by boats of saltwater anglers and by shuttles taking people to South Beach and the islands. Farther east, beyond these ever-changing sand barriers spreads the broad Atlantic. Descend a long flight of wooden stairs to the beach and turn right.

You quickly observe the effects of coastal erosion here, on the sand and dunes, but also on the substantial shore-side homes that dominate most of the island. The remains of wooden piers and pilings stick out of the sand (be careful where you step), and the beach constantly uncovers burlap and other material people have packed against the dune to support its integrity. The most aggressive constructions, however, are the high walls of "riprap," vertical fields of large rocks and boulders homeowners have built into the dune. Just beyond these anti-erosion defenses the uplands end, and the dunes take over.

Here's where the loop trail begins. Take a right at a U.S. Fish and Wildlife sign (USFW oversees the national refuge system), and climb onto a pathway that snakes through this remarkable natural environment. Pass among thick beach grass and keep an eye out for coast-loving poison ivy, (mostly green in summer, the three-leaved scourge turns a dark, red-wine color as the weather cools). Shorebirds find shelter in these dune grasses when they're not scurrying along the surf line. Proceeding farther inland, you see more varied and larger plant life (including maples and oaks), and perhaps the droppings of rabbits and those of the coyote that prey on them. Deer also lurk in the thicker growth.

The harsh coastal conditions are tolerated mostly by trees that are especially hardy and adaptable: pitch pine and scrub oak. You also come across ground-hugging bayberry and lowbush blueberry, although the birds that nest and feed at this corner of the Cape generally get to the berries before you can. Overhead, raptors including northern harrier (marsh hawks), red-tailed hawks, and owls (active from dusk to dawn; almost never seen at day) watch and listen for potential meals of small mammals, birds, and snakes.

From a bluff overlooking the Atlantic Ocean, the views are spectacular.

While on the subject of birds, I should note that Cape Cod sits below the Atlantic flyway, one of the world's busiest north-south migration routes. And the Monomoy National Wildlife Refuge is apparently a major "highway services" resource for avian resting and refueling. Millions of birds spend time here each spring and fall, gathering together in great flocks and rafts, feeding on finfish, shellfish, and small beach organisms before continuing thousands of miles north (in spring) or south (fall). Whether you're an avid birder or not, you are sure to find a trip to this part of the Cape during migration season memorable. You can share the beach with thousands of living creatures; they just wouldn't be people.

As you continue looping counterclockwise and begin heading back to the beachfront, a salt marsh begins to appear on your right. This marsh is nurtured by a small tidal creek that enters from the Nantucket Sound side of the beach. When I was here in the early summer of 2008, the sand had cut off the stream, and the cord grass and other marsh vegetation looked less healthy. But with the way the ocean widens, splits, and regularly molds the shore, who knows what another season is going to bring? Look for the blue-purple buds of sea lavender (but please don't pick; all plant life here helps support the fragile soil). With the salt marsh still on your right, continue back to the beach, reaching it 200 yards south of where you started. You can turn left and return to refuge headquarters along the beach trail—or turn right and explore more of the island.

Along the shore, look for shells, large and small, living and dead. I've seen everything from sand dollars and small crabs to periwinkles and horseshoe crabs. The Monomoy Islands also support a substantial rookery of gray seals, and I've spotted them here, their elongated faces (hence the nickname "horse head") and black eyes staring back from just offshore. The beach ends where the Stage Harbor channel meets Nantucket Sound; across the channel rises Stage Harbor Light, no longer staffed but still one of the loveliest on Cape Cod.

Spend a few moments here, a serene spot even on the busiest summer weekend. Then set off along the beach again and enjoy the hike back to the parking lot, packing out a few more memories than you had when you started.

Erosion

Cape Cod remains a place of great and regular physical change. Beaches grow, shrink, and are cut in two. Tidal streams and ponds are breached, their water content going from salt to fresh and back again; the flora of their shores and shallows thriving, dying, and reviving with every dramatic alteration.

The effects of erosion on this remarkable—and remarkably resilient—60-mile hook are significant. A definition of erosion that is appropriate (especially for the Cape) is *the wearing away of land or soil by the action of wind, water, or ice.* Don't forget the latter, even though ice enjoyed its heyday here thousands of years ago. Glacial action created the Cape, and as the last ice sheet retreated, sea waters began to rise, pound the shore, and carve out beaches. It's a process that continues to this day.

Any part of the Cape that is exposed to wind and wave energy is susceptible to erosion and its opposite, accretion (that is, *the increase of land by the action of natural forces*). Such changes are taking place all along the shores of Cape Cod from Buzzards Bay to Nantucket Sound and Cape Cod Bay.

But the most demonstrable and dramatic changes have taken place along the east-facing shoreline, from the majestic Truro dune cliffs south to the Monomoy Islands in Chatham. This side of the Cape confronts the unrestrained Atlantic Ocean, a powerful force in any season. But the Atlantic is at its meanest in winter, when "nor'easters" blow in off the ocean. With their winds roaring in from the northeast, the storms bludgeon and tear at the exposed shore of the Cape. And because the Cape's surface is mostly sand and thin soils, it can suffer great damage.

The blizzard of 1978 swept away the remains of the Eastham cabin in which acclaimed naturalist Henry Beston wrote *The Outermost House*, a chronicle of a year spent on a Cape Cod beach, in the 1920s. Other storms have sent the ocean ripping across the great sand barrier of Nauset Beach, chief natural protector of Orleans' and Chatham's eastern flank. In the late 1980s, several Chatham homes were lost to the sea, the victims of a break in North Beach.

In recent years, a springtime breach on Nauset Beach split a summer colony in two; as the new break widened, cottages had to be demolished and removed before they would fall into the sea. Beyond the human heartbreak, these natural forces continue to alter the Cape's shoreline. *Elastic, dynamic, movement, creep—* all these words are used by scientists when they seek to describe the Cape's ever-changing geology.

It will be interesting to see what emerging climate-change data, and rising sea levels, might mean for the Cape. Some research suggests the sea level rose about 6.5 feet in the last 2,000 years—but about 1 foot over the last 100 years. It might be worth considering if the rate of erosion will increase, as well.

Still, don't worry about next year's vacation; you can expect a few thousand more years before the entire cape is a beach, submerged at high tide. In fact, all the sand that's being eroded has to go somewhere—and a lot of it is going to other parts of the Cape.

The very tip of the Cape in Provincetown, Long Point, continues to grow through a process called longshore drift: Sand is carried by waves striking a barrier beach at a diagonal and the grains wind up deposited at its terminus. Long Point continues to curl, much like the Cape itself, and now points northeastward.

TRIP 16
NAUSET BEACH

$ 🐕 🏊

Rating: Moderate
Distance: 14.0 miles
Estimated Time: 6 hours
Location: Orleans and Chatham

Venture beyond one of the Cape's most popular swimming destinations onto a 7-mile barrier of sand, dune, and upland that sustains horseshoe crabs, shorebirds, and even coyotes.

Directions
Take Route 6 east to Exit 12 and take a right off the exit onto Route 6A, heading toward Orleans center. At the first traffic light, turn right onto Eldredge Parkway. Follow approximately 1.0 mile, through the traffic-light intersection with Route 28 to the stop-sign intersection with Main Street. Turn right and proceed on Main Street to a fork; bear left onto Beach Road, which terminates at the Nauset Beach parking lot.

Trip Description
One of New England's most popular summertime destinations, Nauset Beach each year attracts thousands of saltwater-loving vacationers, swimmers, sunbathers, and surfers to its 7.0 miles of sand and dune, upland and salt marsh. Nauset is a barrier beach, running parallel to the mainland coasts of Orleans and Chatham and protecting them from the Atlantic Ocean. (Though part of the Cape Cod National Seashore, the beach is co-managed by two towns.) Pleasant Bay spreads between the beach and the mainland, gradually narrowing into Little Pleasant Bay, and farther north, the marshes of Pochet (pronounced "PO-chee") and snaking tidal creeks.

The sand and surf belong to the beach crowd, whereas the paddlers call the upper bay and creeks their own. Nauset's broad middle ground, marked by dune lands, coastal scrub, and a few wooded uplands and split by a sand route extending the length of the barrier, draws the hikers and nature observers. This delightful environment hugging Massachusetts' most easterly edge is young, created by the last retreating glacier a mere 15,000 years

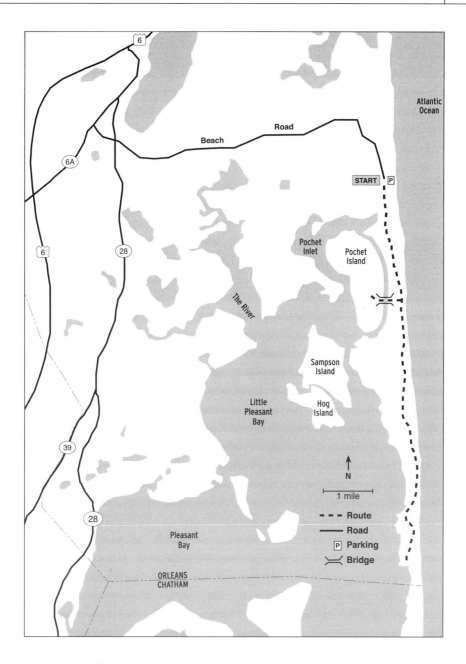

ago. In fact, Nauset continues to endure growing pains; over the centuries storms have broken through and removed billions of tons of sand, only to deposit it elsewhere. The beach has broadened and lengthened, narrowed and shortened, as nor'easters and other storms have caused breaches and changed patterns of current and tide.

The most recent dramatic event took place in April of 2007, when a surprise spring storm sent the sea crashing through a cottage colony at the Chatham end of the barrier, cutting off the southside summer shacks, which now sit upon an island. It has been the north cottages, those still part of the main beach structure, that have fallen prey to erosion, either into the demanding sea or to the wrecker's ball. On the other side of the new channel, the island upon which those vulnerable "south" cottages sit is seeing an accretion of sand piling up. The sea, in effect, is building new land.

Park at the far (south) end of the parking lot, beyond the public beach facilities that include showers, restrooms, and a snack bar. At the southwest corner of the lot, a short paved road leads to an open area where off-road vehicle drivers can deflate/inflate their tires and where all vehicles check in at a guard shack. (Pedestrians need not check in but I recommend it; beach personnel can often provide tips for an enjoyable hike and updates on the barrier.)

Beyond the guard shack, the sand road begins. For the first 0.5 mile, the road is fairly wide, and you find plenty of room for walkers and drivers. But always stay to the right and be mindful of traffic, coming and going. Farther onto the spit, the track turns to soft sand and narrows; be even more mindful as you hike that a vehicle can approach at any time. The boardwalk and small bridge you pass on your right about 0.5 mile along leads west to a mainland neighborhood and are private. Go 0.25 mile farther, and Pochet Island appears on your right; continue on the sand road a short distance to where a trail/jeep track on the right leads along the edge of Little Pochet Island. Follow the trail to where it meets a road on the right that crosses a bridge onto Pochet Island. The bridge crosses a tidal creek where you can spy small fish and shellfish going with the flow. This vantage point also offers nice views of the surrounding marsh and uplands, and of the long spread of dunes to the east. (Because this area is located within the wash of the tide, note that a trip at low tide is best; you might be sloshing across to Pochet Island when the water is in. Also, high tide on this inside edge of the barrier can be 90 minutes later than it is on the ocean side.)

The path becomes a grassy track that meanders through thickets and woods, interrupted by a few houses and outbuildings. Stop to take in addi-

Visitors to Nauset Beach enjoy a pleasant walk along the Atlantic Ocean.

tional views of the marsh and, looking west, of Barley Neck at the uppermost shore of Little Pleasant Bay.

Continue south along the main trail for more panoramic views of the bay and Sampson and Hog Islands, which form the western side of the Broad Creek channel. Follow the trail to where it spurs back to the bridge, and from there east to the sand road. Turn south and continue your hike past Little Pocket Island, and soon the first of a series of dune shacks appear. The generations-old structures, built by families and friends, are idiosyncratic, following their owners' architectural whims. But each seems to include an outhouse and rain-collecting apparatus. Again, they are private, best to be admired from afar.

Along the route 3.0 miles, my wife and I spied white-tailed deer, marsh hawks, and osprey. As you continue, the occasional beach-entry point appears on the left; these spurs to the ocean are for both vehicles and hikers. *Do not* cross the dunes at any other point, as this environment is especially fragile and home to nesting shorebirds.

To the west, a salt marsh spreads to the edge of Little Pleasant Bay, with the mainland of Orleans, Harwich, and Chatham in the distance. Take one of several jeep tracks that lead to the marsh, but again, mind the tide and, in mid-summer, be on the lookout for greenhead flies, which breed (and bite) throughout the estuary. Continue to wander south, eventually reaching the cottage colony, now riven by the 2007 breach. Stand in awe of what nature has wrought—an energetic new passage between ocean and bay, still evolving—then make your long way back north to the mainland, along the way pondering your place in the greater scheme.

TRIP 17
NAUSET MARSH TO COAST GUARD BEACH

Rating: Moderate

Distance: 6.0 miles

Estimated Time: 4.0 hours (including time for exploring, optional
swims)

Location: Eastham

**Explore two distinct but interconnected environments: the
upper reaches of the sprawling Nauset Marsh and the barrier
of sand and dune that helps protect and support the estuary.**

Directions
From Route 6 east in Eastham, watch for signs to Salt Pond Visitor Center
on the right. Turn right, and take another immediate right into the visitor
center.

Trip Description
This hike is a good introduction to a pair of natural habitats that define
Cape Cod: tidal marshlands and the beaches that stand between them and
the open ocean. Most people think of ocean swims and suntans on the beach
when they conjure up a vacation on the Cape, but as this trip shows, you can
find a lot more to enjoy and experience—and still have plenty of time to hit
the surf.

The Salt Pond Visitor Center provides plenty of information for all ages,
including films and videos, discussions, lectures, and presentations, but we
recommend saving indoors for the end of your trip. Right now, head out behind the main building to the outdoor amphitheater that sits just above the
upper reaches of Nauset Marsh. Stay to the right of the amphitheater stage
and look for signs to the marsh trail.

The small, circular pond in front of you is Salt Pond, which comprises the
northwest corner the marsh. Bear left, and follow the pond shore southeast. You're walking between the water and the wooded upland on your left.
Follow the trail as it traces the northern contour of the salt marsh. Watch
for great blue herons rising gracefully above the tidal waterways or standing

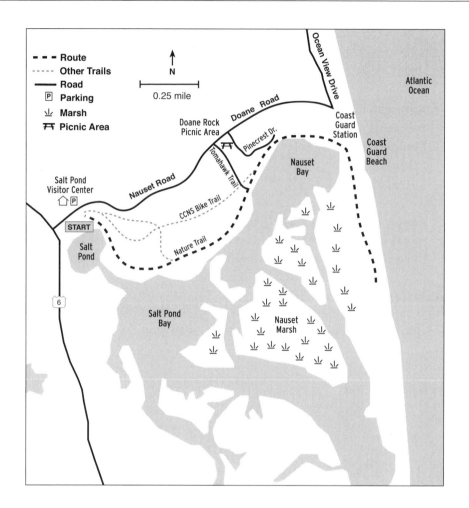

stock-still in the shallows, on the alert for small fish or crabs. As the tide recedes, you also see the tiny "caves" of fiddler crabs, which scurry across the sand and through habitats of intertidal flora, looking to feed before the tide returns.

On the trail, you see signs directing you straight ahead to Coast Guard Beach, but they are hardly necessary—the long spit of the sand barrier is hard to miss. You're also hiking parallel to the bike trail/recreation path that connects the visitor center and the old U.S. Coast Guard station (now a National Seashore facility) overlooking the beach. The recreation path is quite popular through the warm-weather months, meaning you probably hear

The parking lot of the former Coast Guard station offers fine views of a salt marsh.

activity before spotting the paved route on your left. Your passage is soon interrupted by a tidal creek, so hop on the bike trail and cross the bridge that leads to the small hill upon which sits the parking lot for Coast Guard Beach.

When you emerge at the parking lot, head to its south side and stop at a terrific vantage point for viewing the breadth of Nauset Marsh and the long strip of sand that terminates at the mouth of the marsh. It was on this stretch of beach in 1927 that naturalist Henry Beston spent a year in a small cottage, inspiring his classic book, *The Outermost House*. What remained of the two-room cabin was swept away during the Blizzard of '78, but pilgrims continue to visit the site where Beston settled in among gulls, beach grass, and the voices that he would sometimes describe emanating from a storm surf.

From the former U.S. Coast Guard station, head straight out to the beach, one of the most scenic on the Cape, and turn right. (You soon walk on sand that once supported an asphalt parking lot that would fill with cars on summer weekends; the Blizzard of '78 also reclaimed this trifling example of human's intrusion on the shore.)

You can follow the narrowing sand spit for 0.5 mile as the sprawling salt marsh just inland slowly encroaches from the right. You can stay out on the shore or follow a sand route closer to the marsh side (stay away from roped-off areas). I recommend walking out along the open beach, especially in the off-season. You can see a variety of shorebirds at spring and fall migration periods, including plovers and sanderlings, and, out at the tip, perhaps a seal sunning itself on the sand.

(Never approach seals; these marine mammals are cute and a delight to watch, but they have sharp teeth and might use them if they feel threatened. Also, avoid the roped-off dune areas, where piping plovers and Least terns, both federally protected endangered species, mate and raise their young.)

On your return, follow the barrier beach back on the marsh side. You can enjoy remarkable views of one of the Cape's largest estuaries. Depending on the status of the tide, you can cross a wide expanse of sand or hug the shore and watch the water flow around grassy "hummocks" and through a network of tidal creeks. Make your way back along the inside of the barrier toward the former U.S. Coast Guard building and then bear left to where you can see the wooden bridge carrying the bike trail across the creek, the same bridge you crossed coming out.

If you prefer a more direct route back to the visitor center, take the bike trail—and first take a break on the bridge. We've observed lots of avian specials here, from osprey and kingfishers to yellow legs and smaller plovers. In the winter, the coves and protected small embayments of the salt marsh draw sea ducks such as eider, scoter, and bufflehead, seeking protection from the winds and waves that roar in from the ocean. On the bike/recreation path, remember to watch for oncoming traffic, especially cyclists, but also in-line skaters and skateboarders (we've encountered both).

Watch for signs to Doane Rock on your right. The large boulder sits near the north end of a parking lot and picnic area, just off Nauset Road, the main vehicle route to Coast Guard Beach. Doane Rock shows plenty of granite above the surface, but hides even more of its mass underground. It might be the largest glacial erratic in southeast New England, and it's worth a look.

Return to the recreation path, and follow its undulations back to the visitor center. Head inside and immerse yourselves in the ecological, historical, and cultural attributes of this remarkable environmental jewel.

TRIP 18
ATWOOD-HIGGINS HOUSE/
BOUND BROOK ISLAND/RYDER BEACH

Rating: Moderate
Distance: 4.0 miles
Estimated Time: 2 hours
Location: Wellfleet and Truro

Visit one of the oldest houses on the outer Cape and then explore a wooded upland bordered by thick wetlands and Cape Cod Bay.

Directions

From Route 6 east in Wellfleet, turn left onto Pamet Point Road (the last road before entering Truro). Drive for 1.5 miles to the intersection with Old County Road. Bear left and look for a brown National Park Service (NPS) sign on the right that reads "Atwood-Higgins House." Turn right onto Bound Brook Island Road. Parking and the entrance to the property are less than 0.25 mile ahead on the left.

Trip Description

Named for two of the oldest families in this part of Cape Cod, the Atwood-Higgins House is now in the National Register of Historic Places. The restored site includes fields and outbuildings, as well as the main house. Originally a half-Cape Cod-style house built in 1730, it was expanded several times over the next two centuries.

You approach the home from the rear: The front door is oriented to the south, toward the warming sun and the Herring River. The river is much overgrown today and is hard to see even from the high bank at the edge of the Atwood-Higgins property. But 200 years ago the tidal waterway was much more a central element in this community, providing food and transportation. A small shipbuilding enterprise was also based nearby.

Walk west on the dirt road. In about 0.25 mile, the road forks to the right. Bear left and continue into the woodlands until you reach another fork. Stay to the right and continue toward Cape Cod Bay.

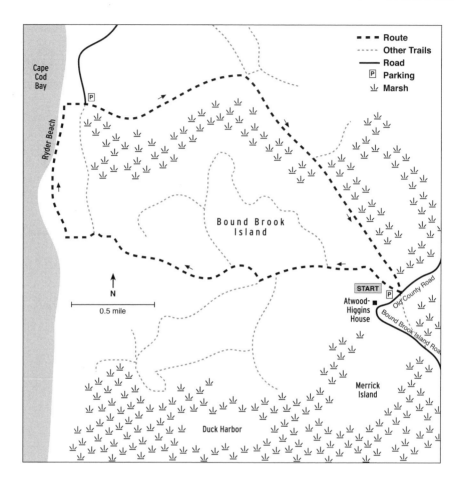

Look for ground-hugging bearberry; small, wild cranberry bogs; blueberry; and beach plums. The dune habitat here is relatively young. The bay had openings here and at Duck Harbor (which really was an inlet from the bay when settlers named it) to the south well into the 1800s; that regular tidal action nourished the coastal landscape in a much different way than you see today. As the beach dunes grew, the openings gradually closed up. Without its daily dose of salt water, this cluster of salt marsh habitats began to dry up. The water eventually transformed from salt to fresh; most of the cordgrass that flourished along the banks of the then-tide creeks disappeared with the waterways, replaced by thick shrubs and trees that thrive in freshwater wetlands.

Fences prevent people from walking on the fragile habitat.

In less than 0.25 mile, you reach a dune overlooking Cape Cod Bay at the northwest corner of Wellfleet, one of the prettiest stretches of beach on the bay side of the Cape. (Sunsets here are especially memorable.) Descend to the shore and kick off your shoes. Even on a weekend day at the height of summer, you often have this paradise on the Massachusetts coast all to yourselves. The swimming and beachcombing—and the fishing for stripers and bluefish—are unparalleled, and the views northwest to Provincetown are especially memorable.

Walk north along the beach a few hundred yards to the parking lot for Ryder Beach, just over the town line in Truro. A pathway runs parallel on the inside of the dune, but it can be a very wet walk along the marsh, so I recommend hiking the beach—not a bad alternative!

From the south side of the parking lot, a sand road leads right. Follow this road until you reach what looks like a dirt road but is, in fact, the rail bed of the former Old Colony-Penn Central line that once ran all the way to Provincetown.

Turn right on the rail bed (the straightest part of this hike and a stretch you might be sharing with mountain bikers) and follow it for about 0.75 mile to Old County Road, near where you drove in from Pamet Point Road. From this point, you again turn right and take Bound Brook Island Road back to the parking lot at the Atwood-Higgins House.

TRIP 19
GREAT ISLAND

Rating: Moderate
Distance: 8.0 miles
Estimated Time: 4 hours
Location: Wellfleet

**Explore a remarkable barrier beach on Cape Cod Bay that pro-
tects Wellfleet Harbor and once sheltered a rowdy colonial-
era tavern.**

Directions
From Route 6 in Wellfleet, turn left at the sign for Wellfleet center (traffic
light). Bear left onto East Commercial Street and follow it past a marina and
a large parking lot to where it jogs right and becomes Kendrick Avenue. With
the harbor on the left, continue as road joins Chequessett Neck Road. Cross
the bridge where the harbor becomes Herring River, ascend a rise, and follow
the road to the entrance and parking on the left.

Trip Description
Great Island is not an island at all but rather a long coastscape of shore, sand
dunes, and upland. It is a classic barrier beach, much like Long Point in Provincetown, Nauset Beach in Orleans, and Sandy Hook in Barnstable. Each
parallels the mainland and protects interior bays, harbors, and marshes. In
the past, Great Island was a "stand-alone" environment. It was a true island
into the early 1800s and is now the chief upland of this land mass, rising 0.5
mile south of the parking lot. (Another natural feature of this hike, Great
Beach Hill, located farther down the barrier, was also surrounded by water
at one time.)

Today, the entire peninsula runs south for 5.0 miles, thanks to a steady
accretion of sand, in which hardy grasses, plants, and even trees have taken
root and serve to anchor the thin, unstable soil. The action of tide and current continues to manifest itself most directly at the Great Island's southerly
tip, Jeremy Point, which can be reached only at low tide.

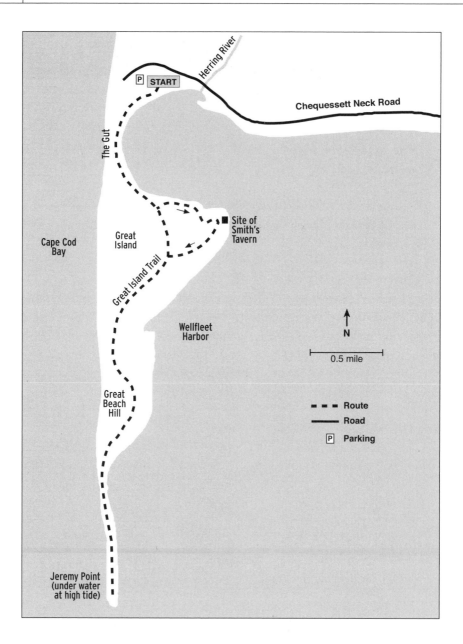

Wind, wave, and sand have combined to create—and erode—this coastal environment in varied ways over many centuries. Early colonists set up a fishing camp on a 60-acre site just south of Jeremy Point and called it

Billingsgate Island, in honor of a London fish market. Billingsgate Island thrived, at one point boasting 30 homes and its own lighthouse. But a storm in the mid-nineteenth century that bisected the island spelled its doom; erosion continued to wear away at Billingsgate Island until homes were floated over to the mainland and the last lighthouse was torn down in the early twentieth century. By World War II, the island had been essentially reduced to a large sandbar. Today, Billingsgate Shoal is popular with anglers, seals, and boaters, the latter arriving to picnic when low tide exposes the sandy hump in the bay.

Begin your Great Point hike from a trail extending from a National Park Service kiosk in the parking lot down to the edge of the marsh on the uppermost reaches of Wellfleet Harbor. The path jogs right, along the edge of the marsh, reaches a line of dunes fronting on the bay, and bears left on the approach to Great Island, which looms ahead.

The narrow strip of land you're crossing to reach Great Island is called The Gut. Follow the trail as it bears east, away from the dune. Almost immediately, the route splits, one path hewing to the marsh side, the other heading inland. Follow the marsh-side trail, passing thick lawns of bearberry and beach plum out to a point that overlooks the inner harbor. Enjoy the view up and down the harbor and across to Wellfleet town.

Nearby, you also come across the site of Smith's Tavern, marked by a sign and a boulder. It was a notorious colonial-era meeting place for fishermen, smugglers, and, reportedly, pirates. From here, the route loops back around to the interior of this upland, and you soon intersect a trail that runs parallel to the barrier beach. Take a left and continue south on this trail, passing through a hardy forest of pine and hardwoods.

Follow the trail farther south to where Great Island proper meets another salt marsh. Turn right and trace the north side of this marsh out to the dunes. The trail again jogs south along another spit (similar to The Gut), which connects Great Beach Hill, itself another former island.

Head up the hill and check out the views across the outer harbor to Lieutenant Island, a lovely spit in South Wellfleet reached by a causeway. Continue through woodlands that descend to the southern base of Great Beach Hill and to the beginning of a broad tidal wetland leading to Jeremy Point. This long sand spit is submerged at high tide, so if you want to walk to the true terminus of the Great Island barrier beach, you must align your hike so

Great Island is a popular destination for many visitors to the Cape Cod National Seashore.

that you arrive here during low tide. Be sure to ask a park ranger about the timing of the tides.

You've covered about 3.0 miles to this point; many hikers turn back here. But exploring Jeremy Point is a worthwhile option. Sand flats extend for more than 2.0 miles and you will see spectacular views of the bay and harbor. Also, you never know what you might find in an environment that is under water for hours at a time; my wife and I literally stumbled upon a large whale vertebra in the sand.

Returning from Jeremy Point, head back up Great Beach Hill and retrace your steps. Along the way, enjoy panoramic vistas of the bay and the coastline as it arcs northwest toward Provincetown.

Upon reaching The Gut, look for a boardwalk on the right that crosses the dunes and meets the sand road that leads back to the parking lot.

TRIP 20
CAPE COD NATIONAL SEASHORE HEADQUARTERS
—ATLANTIC WHITE CEDAR SWAMP TRAIL

Rating: Easy to Moderate
Distance: 1.3 miles
Estimated Time: 2 hours
Location: Wellfleet

Follow a boardwalk that meanders through a coastal swamp-land where one of the last colonies of Atlantic white cedars still exists. Then explore trails passing through woodlands and across heath leading to the seashore.

Directions
From Route 6 in South Wellfleet, turn at the traffic light leading to the Marconi Area and Cape Cod National Seashore headquarters. Follow signs to the swamp trail (bearing left), approximately 1.0 mile. You find an ample parking lot here.

Trip Description
This habitat of rare (in this region) Atlantic white cedars sits amid a swamp at the western border of the Cape Cod National Seashore headquarters. The trail leads from the parking lot in almost a straight line to this former kettle hole pond, now a peat environment many feet deep. The reddish-brown cedars grow ramrod straight from raised hummocks in the tannin-hued waters of the swamp spreading under the loop boardwalk trail. Visitors should appreciate these declining trees, which are inexorably giving way to swamp maples and other more dominant species. Other remnant pockets of Atlantic white cedar exist, but this fine example is the most accessible to the public—and the boardwalk helps immensely, both in terms of providing access and protecting the trees.

Follow the dirt path for about 0.5 mile through a typical coastal Cape forest of pitch pine and scrub oak, which have adapted to the harsh winds and weather of this exposed environment. As this is a self-guided hike, small

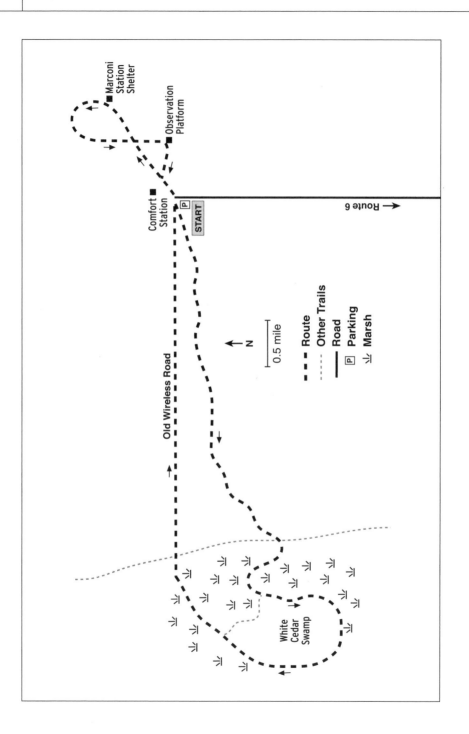

Marconi Station Shelter

Observation Platform

Comfort Station

START

Route 6

Old Wireless Road

N

0.5 mile

Route
Other Trails
Road
P Parking
Marsh

White Cedar Swamp

A portion of the Atlantic White Cedar Swamp Trail is on a boardwalk.

signs describe the habitat and the plants that make their homes here, including blueberry, crowberry, and other hardy, sandy soil-tolerant species. Within the more protective environment of the wetland, and away from the exposed heath, you pass stands of taller hardwoods, including maple and black and white oak.

You cross another dirt track, dating to the time when radio pioneer Guglielmo Marconi made his historic transmission across the Atlantic Ocean to Cornwall at the beginning of the twentieth century. Bear to the right, and soon you are in the swamp proper and on the boardwalk. This loop offers visitors, especially those interested in the ecology of the Cape, a truly memorable experience.

The water beneath the elevated hiking platform is dark and foreboding, suggesting a southern swamp full of gators and dangerous snakes, but this environment is hardly threatening. Instead, the swamp and its peat underpinnings are what allow the Atlantic white cedar to survive, even thrive, at this northernmost frontier of its range. This hike is more mystical than haunted, with the thick-canopied cedars providing a misty cast to the understory.

The boardwalk forks; bear left here and continue in a clockwise direction. Examine the root systems, bark, and upper branches of these remarkable evergreens. Sit on one of the benches that have been placed along the boardwalk for closer observation of the swamp or for simple contemplation. Be aware that this area is extremely buggy in the summer. Continue north, then northeast, until you reach the dirt track that was part of another roadway dating to Marconi's time. The Old Wireless Road leads eastward to where his station stood. Follow this route back to the parking lot.

Walk east through the parking lot toward an observation tower erected amid the open heath. From here, take in panoramic views of the Outer Cape, from Cape Cod Bay to the west to the broad Atlantic just a short distance to the east. Both the bay and ocean can be visible because you are standing at the narrowest part of the 60-mile hook, which is only about 1.0 mile wide in this part of South Wellfleet.

A few yards farther out on the cliff is a pavilion that commemorates the achievement of Guglielmo Marconi in the early 20th century. In 1901, he built telegraph towers at this site, and two years later, Marconi successfully transmitted a Morse code message from President Theodore Roosevelt to King Edward VII of the United Kingdom, changing communications forever.

The combination of the historic Marconi station, park headquarters, and the public beach draws many thousands of visitors a year, but it is amazing that you can hike these trails on a mid-summer weekend and meet very few other people. This location is definitely worth a visit, especially because the restaurants and ice cream parlors lining busy Route 6 are just a few minutes away, ready to assuage your hunger, thirst, and sweet tooth.

TRIP 21
PILGRIM HEIGHTS

Rating: Moderate
Distance: 4.0 miles
Estimated Time: 3 hours
Location: Truro

Explore a small, upland forest, enjoy panoramic vistas of a long, thin marshland, and then enjoy a "dunescape" leading to the Atlantic Ocean.

Directions

From Route 6 east, look for the brown and white National Park Service sign to Pilgrim Heights. Follow the driveway to the first parking lot.

Trip Description

This modest National Park Service recreation area on Route 6 is popular—especially with history buffs—because it was the supposed place where a party from the Mayflower, just-arrived in Provincetown Harbor and desperate for fresh water, found a spring that saved them. The "site," located near a present-day spring where the Pilgrim Spring Trail descends to meet the Head of the Meadow Bike Path, is marked by a plaque, but its historical veracity is in doubt, and the story is now considered apocryphal.

But both the Pilgrim Spring Trail and the Small's Swamp Trail, each less than 1.0 mile long, offer easy and enjoyable hiking loops, ideal for families. The trails begin near a gazebo/information kiosk at the north end of the parking lot. (First, take time at the gazebo to learn about Pilgrim Lake on the Truro-Provincetown border, which has been re-christened with the name given it by the Pilgrims, East Harbor, when it was still open to Cape Cod Bay.)

Beyond the Gazebo, head onto Small's Swamp Trail (named for the man who farmed this area in the nineteenth century, Thomas Small), which my wife and I found more interesting, for both the natural elements and the views. Proceed beyond the gazebo and bear left onto the trail. The path soon

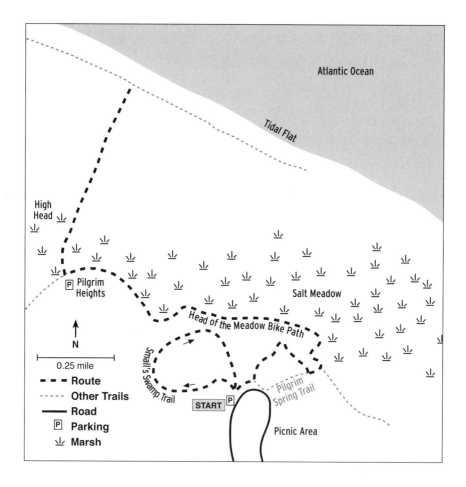

splits; take the left fork and slowly descend into a small valley, remnants of a glacial kettle hole. The wetland is dense with highbush blueberry, black cherry, and swamp azalea, and other moisture-dependent flora.

Where the boardwalk reverts to a dirt path, you begin to ascend back to your starting point. In quick succession, you come to a pair of viewing spots (attracting birders during spring and fall migration seasons) that present even more dramatic views. The dune lands command the distance, but the foreground belongs to a former salt marsh in transition (now the meadow of "Head of the Meadow" fame). It's an impregnable valley full of hardy shrubs, bushes, and poison ivy. Deer and coyote are at home here, and so are hunters, in season. Continue on the trail, which gently ascends to the gazebo and parking lot.

Look for the Pilgrim Spring Trail, which bears left and meanders through the recreation area, passing through scrub oak-pitch pine woodlands before descending to the Pilgrim Spring. Along the way, stop to enjoy a southeasterly view of a salt meadow and dunes. Just beyond the spring, you reach the Head of the Meadow Bike Path.

Turn left on the paved bike route, and follow it for less than a mile to its terminus at the High Head parking lot. A 0.25-mile sand road leads right to the beach, passing through a spectacular dunescape, presenting hikers with the most memorable section of this trip. The beach front is striking; a long line of dunes stretches north to Provincetown and south to Eastham. Here, at the very edge of what Henry David Thoreau called the "Great Beach," you can revel in the sort of peace and solitude unexpected in one of the nation's most popular vacation regions.

Depending on the season, sandpipers and plovers trace the surf line, while black-back and herring gulls harass one and all with their raucous cries. A quarter-mile offshore, gannets plunge into the sea for fish, air sacs in their chest cavities inflating like vehicle air bags just before impact. Each violent immersion sends up a small plume of spray. And don't ignore larger plumes you might spy—these could be the exhalations of whales that also populate Cape waters for parts of the year. When you're ready to return, retrace your steps down the sand road to the bike trail, and from there back to the spring and the parking lot.

Whales

When people think of whaling and its illustrious history, *Moby Dick* and the far-away South Seas may come to mind, as well as the renowned ports of Nantucket and New Bedford, from which American whaling sprung. The first whale hunters hailed from outer Cape Cod villages, especially Truro. The men (and boys) of the Cape developed the whaling trade in the colonies mostly because these largest of marine mammals came to them. Seventeenth- and eighteenth-century fishermen discovered pods of whales inside Cape Cod Bay, in the Atlantic off the Cape's long eastern shore, and, most famously, feeding in the rich, relatively shallow waters of what today is known as Stellwagen Bank.

Located less than 10 miles off Race Point, Provincetown's northern tip, the Bank is a shallow underwater plateau. In fact, for millennia it was dry land, where huge mammals including wooly mammoths once lived. It was created by glacial action and rising sea levels. Today's Stellwagen Bank was named in 1855 for Henry Stellwagen, a U.S. Navy surveyor who mapped it. It is a rough rectangle, 26 miles long and about half as wide, narrowing to several miles wide at its northern edge. The top of the bank rises more than 150 feet above the surrounding sea floor, and some parts sit only about 65 feet below the ocean surface.

This shallower, and thus warmer, underwater upland draws a tremendous variety of fish and other marine life. And all this bounty draws whales, primarily during the warm-weather months, when they travel north, often with young, from the Caribbean and other southern waters. They feed on krill, copepods, other tiny organisms, and small fish. Stellwagen Bank attracts several species, including humpback, finback, minke, and the endangered North Atlantic right whale.

The Cape whaling legacy lives on in a more benign, marine mammal-friendly way through whale watches. Whale watch boats that have been specially outfitted for large numbers of passengers and that carry whale videos, onboard guides, and other educational elements depart daily in season from Provincetown's MacMillan Wharf. Provincetown is the epicenter of the whale-watching industry in New England. These trips are exceedingly popular; making a reservation is a smart move.

On a whale watch, you need to take some simple precautions to help insure a comfortable and enjoyable trip. Although you spend much of your excursion

A group of whale watchers observes a humpback whale.

in sight of land, the ocean and bay can turn choppy, making for a sometimes bumpy ride; seasickness pills might be a good option. Also, although most whale watch boats are equipped with snack bars, always bring along plenty of fresh water.

Also, be sure to eat before you leave shore. Those worried about having a full belly should know that an empty stomach produces acids which, in turn, can actually make you sick. Toast, cereal, bagels, and even pancakes are okay. But forget fried foods. Eating dry snacks also help to block acid buildup.

Finally, be prepared for both sun and cold temperatures. Even on an overcast day, the sun's rays shine through—onto you. Make a billed or brimmed hat and sunblock part of your carry-on supplies. Also, don't forget sunglasses, preferably with a cord that goes around your neck.

And yes, you can get a chill on a 90-degree day because of the cool breezes that blow off the ocean. Be sure to bring along a windbreaker and a middle layer. It's much easier to strip down to a T-shirt or tank top than it is to have to hunker down below decks in the cabin while whales are frolicking just outside. Also, there's no need to race to a side of a boat where a whale has been spotted; they usually surface for a reasonable period, and you can almost always get a good look without hurrying. Stay where you are; you might get a private performance!

TRIP 22
BALLSTON BEACH

Rating: Easy
Distance: 2.0 miles
Estimated Time: 1.5 hours
Location: Truro

**Explore the oak-and-pine forest behind the dunes of pictur-
esque Ballston Beach and visit the site of a former cranberry
bog.**

Directions
Driving north on Route 6 in Truro, take the Pamet Roads exit and turn left
at the end of the ramp onto North Pamet Road. Follow North Pamet Road
as it bears right toward the seashore. At 1.75 miles, just before an old Coast
Guard Station (now an education center during the school year, and a hostel
during the summer months) on your right, look for a series of parking spaces
parallel to the road.

Trip Description
Cross the road and enter the woods at the trail sign and cement steps. Follow the gently ascending path through an upland of pitch pine and oak, away
from North Pamet Road. As you approach a clearing, a mass of ground-hugging bearberry begins to dominate. You soon arrive at a path leading right-
ward, which takes you to the crest of Bearberry Hill, about 0.5 mile from
North Pamet Road.

From this spectacular overlook, which features a delightful sitting platform, you can take in the broad expanse of the Atlantic Ocean beyond Ballston Beach. Given its proximity to the open ocean, the hilltop can be quite
breezy, so a windbreaker might come in handy.

Not only can you enjoy memorable views of a spectacular Cape Cod National Seashore beachfront and the open ocean extending to the horizon,
but the panorama also includes the spring-fed source of the Pamet River and
its surrounding marshlands. Gaze out beyond the high dune supporting two
large homes at Ballston Beach to the east. The headwaters of the Pamet also

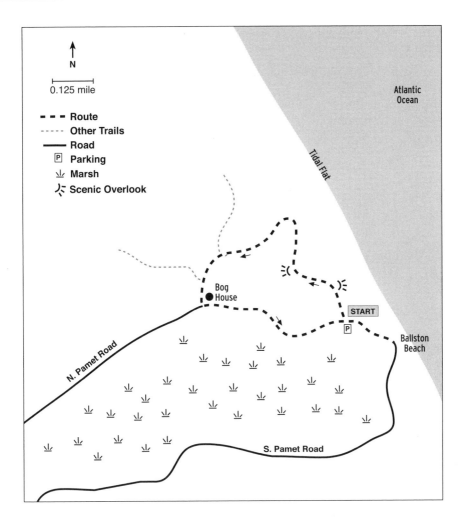

catch your eye. Note how the sand from the beach has crept right up to the marsh, which features a fair amount of dead vegetation. This is a result of a storm that slammed the coast in the fall of 1991, which forced salt water to flood the upper reaches of the Pamet River, killing fresh water-dependent vegetation.

The ocean's incursion into the river is a reminder of the Cape's fragility and vulnerability to the power of water and wind. At your feet you will see bearberry, the small green-leaved, red-berried groundcover that covers most of the hilltop. But look also for blueberry and poison ivy. This ubiquitous plant is a scourge for all seasons and as a border plant loves to establish itself along the sides of cart paths, walking trails, and the edges of open spaces. Turn around, and you will see a former cranberry bog.

Descend to the main trail, turn right and you soon come to another overlook, this one specifically of the bog house. Continue on the meandering trail north and east, gradually descending a series of log stairs. The trail bears right and soon intersects with a sandy fire road. Turn left and follow the road just a short distance to where the trail to the bog house jogs left.

Before returning to the woods, take time to savor this remarkable habitat. Look for coyote tracks, which I have seen frequently on these dune paths. I have also watched northern harriers silently wafting over the dune grass and deer loping across the open terrain.

Now resume your hike toward the former cranberry bog through the understory, which offers occasional glimpses of the surrounding dunes and open landscapes that back the ocean cliff (you can hear the sea roar when conditions are right). Continue to signs that lead to the bog house. Here you'll find an interpretive panel describing the history and restoration of cranberries, the packing house, and how the former cranberry pond had been an important agricultural and community resource for centuries.

From this site, follow a dirt road that leads between the house and bog toward North Pamet Road. Take a left on the road and follow it past your vehicle (on the right) to the road's terminus in sand at the marshy source of the Pamet River.

For generations, North Pamet Road connected here with South Pamet Road; one could drive a horseshoe route around the length of the river east of Route 6. Today, you walk the hundred yards between the river marsh and the modest series of dunes on your right. From the parking lot on the South Pamet side, turn left onto a short sand path that leads out to Ballston Beach. Ballston, which once featured a lively summer colony (including a bowling alley!), remains a popular swimming/sunbathing destination in summer. But, as is the case at most Cape beaches, walk a few minutes north or south along the shoreline and you can feel as if you're on a deserted island.

Depending on the season, you might see shorebirds skittering along the surf line, or rafts of sea ducks. Let your gaze drift just beyond the surf and you may be rewarded with the treat of a gray seal raising its whiskery head above the surface to give you a curious look. With that delightful image stored in your mind, make you way back off the beach on the designated path and then back to North Pamet Road, where your vehicle waits.

The Piping Plover

When the Atlantic Ocean washes over Cape Cod beaches from Chatham to Provincetown, the strong surf and big winds can wipe out nesting habitat for *Charadrius elodus*, the piping plover. The loss of habitat, effects of predation, and other natural forces perhaps less understood have combined to reduce the bird's numbers. Federally recognized as an endangered species since 1986, the stalwart little plover has achieved semi-iconic status among birders, conservationists, and others who realize the value of biodiversity.

Named for its whistling "peep-lo" call and other "piping" notes, the 7-inch shorebird arrives each spring on Cape beaches to mate and raise young. The female lays a clutch of four eggs in late spring, one every other day. The female and male share watching the nest, and if incubation is successful, the eggs hatch 28 days later. The young birds can fly by mid-July. But some piping plover hatches have been averaging less than two per nesting. The cause of this breeding challenge continues to confound ornithologists, field biologists, and other experts.

Plovers breed from the Canadian Maritimes to as far south as the outer banks of North Carolina. However, because Massachusetts can account for a third of the Atlantic seaboard population, the Bay State is a crucial breeding area.

The piping plover is just one of numerous species that are annually drawn to the Cape. Shorebirds feed on tiny marine organisms and plants at the water's edge. They are prodigious seasonal commuters, flying from the Northern to the Southern Hemisphere and back (sometimes in a wider loop that can include Europe and Africa) before making their way back to the Cape, often to the same beach and even the same stretch of sand.

Semipalmated plovers are the same size as piping plovers, but are dark brown on top with whitish bellies and dark neck bands. Black-bellied plovers can be a foot long, with black-and-white speckled wings and backs. Plovers tend to run in starts and stops.

Sandpipers are similar in their habits but tend to be a bit longer and sleeker. One of the most common is the yellowlegs, with brown-black, speckled backs, long beaks, and, of course, yellow legs. The willet, another sandpiper with a thicker bill and lighter-colored body, grows to 15 inches. Sanderlings are smaller, more the size of piping plovers, but much more common. You can see them in

A piping plover is the size of a sparrow.

groups racing along the edge of the surf line, somehow never getting their feet wet.

Piping plovers are perhaps the best camouflaged of the shorebirds, the color of light sand, with orange-yellow legs and feet. Against a beach backdrop, they are almost invisible when still. They don't make nests but rather lay eggs in small indentations in the sand. They don't avoid places frequented by people, and countless numbers of eggs and offspring have been killed as a result of such proximity.

However, since the piping plover was designated endangered, aggressive efforts to nurture them (including beach closures, fencing off nesting areas, and placing anti-predator cages around nests) have resulted in an increase to upwards of 500 breeding pairs on the Cape.

So, the good news is that there have been overall gains in breeding pairs. But pressures on the plovers, ranging from beach overwash and erosion to animal predators and human presence, continue to affect the numbers of birds able to fly from the nest. Visitors can do their part by volunteering with piping plover restoration groups, or by just giving these vulnerable little birds plenty of space.

TRIP 23
RACE POINT LIGHTHOUSE

Rating: Moderate
Distance: 4.0 miles
Estimated Time: 3 hours
Location: Provincetown

Follow a fire road through a pitch pine forest and cross the top of a dike spanning a salt marsh, past Hatches Harbor to Race Point Lighthouse and the Atlantic Ocean.

Directions

Near the terminus of Route 6 east in Provincetown, take a right onto Province Lands Road at signs for Herring Cove Beach. Follow the road for about 1.5 miles to a small parking lot on the left.

Trip Description

For decades, this National Seashore fire road just west of the Provincetown airport sat under the radar, so to speak, drawing only locals, seasonal hunters, and National Seashore employees on patrol or with specific maintenance assignments. But in recent years, the route has become a favorite with birders, dog walkers, and those seeking to reach the lighthouse on firmer footing than the leg-challenging beach route from the Race Point parking lot.

Park your vehicle and pass through a typical fire road gate. Note the signs for ticks and poison ivy. (This route—at least the initial section bounded by wetland and woods—is especially mosquito-friendly, so don't forget the bug repellent.) The fire road is nestled within an area that floods occasionally, and the puddles that sometimes form can remain for days. That occasional commotion coming from the left is the sound of cyclists on the bike trail; although it is just a few yards away, in summer thick brush renders the paved route almost invisible.

The bike path soon veers off west, and the terrain to your left is replaced by a freshwater wetland, marked by moisture-tolerant vegetation including swamp maple and wild cranberry. I have spied deer in this habitat, as well. A seemingly endless patchwork of dune, sandy ground, and pitch pine/oak forest is on your right. It wasn't always so; when the Pilgrims first trod their new wilderness, the soil of what is now the stark Province Lands was thicker and richer, supporting a healthy mixed forest of hardwoods and evergreens. But centuries of unrestrained cutting took the trees, and the wind did the rest, blowing away whatever topsoil remained and replacing it with sand.

Amble northwest along the fire road, watching for chickadees in the pines, blue jays, and (especially during spring migration) musically inclined warblers. Off to the right, you can observe plenty of tracks in the sand, including those of domesticated dogs (paws all over the place); their wild cousins (coyote leave neat and efficient tracks, one foot following the other); and rabbits (ending at impenetrable thickets).

As you approach the dike, the scrub forest falls away. To your left, Hatches Harbor and its snaking tidal creek extensions extend to a break in the ocean beach just northwest of Herring Cove. To your right, you can observe a marsh habitat in transition; a 1930s-era dike shut off this habitat from steady salt-water flow, an interruption in the natural order that has been partially restored by removing tide gates and undersized culverts and replacing them with a large, open box culvert big enough to restore tidal flow. (The dike also allowed construction of the airport.) Today, much of the vegetation that emerged during 70 years of freshwater/brackish environment is dying off and being replaced by the once-dominant salt marsh cordgrass and hay.

Cross the dike, and if you're accompanied by a dog, keep it on a leash, as required by the Cape Cod National Seashore; the combination of tidal water, artificially constructed portals, and pets seeking a swim can spell disaster. You might see shorebirds patrolling sand ribbons along the creeks, as well as great blue herons and egrets stalking the shallows. Overhead, look for gulls, northern harriers, and increasingly, the V-winged profile of turkey vultures.

The route continues and soon devolves into a network of dunes. I recommend descending the dike to the left and following the northwest shore of Hatches Harbor out to the lighthouse, which is becoming increasingly visible with each step. Depending on the time of tide, you might find yourself crossing a dry habitat of gravel and sand, small dune hummocks, and the harbor bed, which features salt hay, cordgrass, saltwort, and sprays of sea lavender. Or, with an oncoming tide, you can watch small pockets and corners fill to become enticing wading pools.

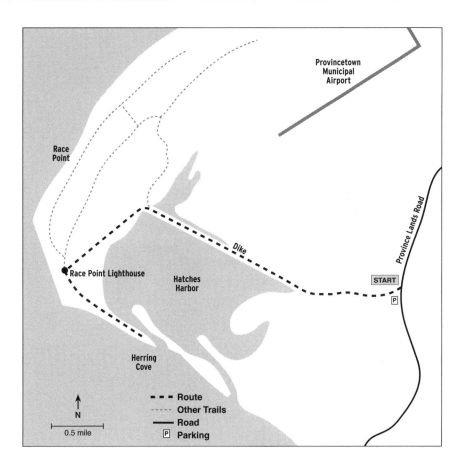

Proceed across the sand flats directly toward the lighthouse, where a trail leads to a jeep track and to the complex. Take care as you approach; you may find a fair amount of glass, metal, and other detritus in the immediate vicinity. First built in 1816, the original Race Point Lighthouse was just a 20-foot stone tower, the first of Provincetown's three, the other two built at Wood End and Long Point. These warning beacons for mariners became increasingly important as nineteenth-century coastwise shipping increased, along with a growing number of wrecks along the treacherous outermost shores of the Cape. In 1852, the lighthouse's warning system was improved by the addition of a fog bell, and three years later a stronger Fresnel lens beamed for miles out to sea. In the year of the nation's centennial, 1876, the structure was replaced by the 40-foot-high iron tower that stands today.

The keeper's house (to the left of Race Point Lighthouse) is powered by renewable energy.

Formerly, two keeper's houses occupied the site. One was torn down in 1961, the year the National Seashore was created. In 1978, the light was automated, and in 1995, the stalwart American Lighthouse Foundation leased the house and light. Both were in need of much repair. The restoration resulted in the keeper's house being transformed into a rough overnight accommodation, today available for rentals. Tours of the keeper's house and lighthouse are given from June through September on the first and third Saturday of the month.

Continue out to the beach through a short dune field. Follow the sand trail and avoid walking on the dune grass. Dune grass is fragile and protects the sand dunes from wind erosion. Turn left and walk southeast along the sand strip, Cape Cod Bay on your right and Hatches Harbor on your left. Continue to walk southeast, to where the inlet reaches open water. Across the channel is Herring Cove Beach, popular especially with vacationers and surfcasters. On the other hand, you stand a good chance of having this stretch of seashore to yourself. Then turn back and, keeping Hatches Harbor on your right, follow the embayment shore inland until you reach the dike road.

TRIP 24
HERRING COVE/WOOD END

Rating: Moderate
Distance: 5.0 miles
Estimated Time: 2 hours
Location: Cape Cod National Seashore, Provincetown

Trek from one of the Outer Cape's most popular beaches to one of its quietest corners, where a long finger of sand and dune comprises the very tip of Cape Cod.

Directions
Driving north on Route 6 in Provincetown, turn right onto Province Lands Road at signs to Herring Cove Beach (and traffic light). Take the first left into Herring Cove parking lot, then left again to far south side of lot.

Trip Description
This hike along the outermost reaches of the National Seashore allows you to partially trace by land what the exhausted and frustrated Pilgrims saw from the wet, cold deck of the Mayflower as they rounded the tip of the Cape before finding refuge in Provincetown Harbor.

You can reach Wood End and its lighthouse either by walking the outer beach or on a sand road that passes through a lovely dune habitat before emerging at the inner shore, at the edge of the upper harbor and salt marsh. I suggest heading out on the ocean side and returning on the inside, taking advantage of distinct but connected coastal habitats each way.

Exit your vehicle at the southwest corner of the parking lot and follow a sand path out to the beach. To your right, you can spot the crumbling remains of an asphalt strip that formerly anchored part of the beach (bad idea). To your left, you see nothing but sea and sky, sand and dune. Start walking.

As you wander toward the beginning of Long Point, the outermost sand barrier of the Cape that protects Provincetown Harbor, you pass a series of barrier beach microcosms: small bars and pools constantly being created

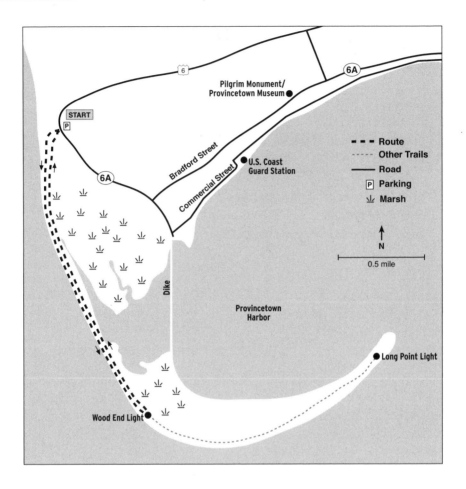

and destroyed by the movement of sand and water. This stretch of shoreline draws a lot of beachcombers and collectors; you might pass a makeshift shelter or two, constructed from flotsam and jetsam gathered along this shore where the ocean meets the bay and thus heavy with washed-up fishing gear, traps, line, and wooden beams.

On your left, the long low wall of dunes hides an expansive salt marsh that marks the upper harbor. At spring and fall migration periods, this stretch of beach southeast of Herring Cove can be a fine destination for birding. Sandpipers zip along the surf line, bulking up on tiny organisms, while crowds of sea ducks gather in large "rafts" just offshore. Above the horizon, those white birds repeatedly diving into the sea for fish are gannets, which inflate

The Wood End Lighthouse has been guiding mariners since the nineteenth century.

specialized upper-body pockets, much like vehicle air bags, just before making impact with the water to soften the landing and protect their bodies.

On a clear and calm day here, you might experience a special treat: The sighting of a whale's spout, that steamy exhalation through its blow hole that first drew whalers and today attracts whale watchers. So always bring binoculars! The Provincetown whale-watch fleet is the largest in the Northeast and has become a major tourist engine for this town particularly and the Cape in general. Each spring, several whale species arrive from the warm waters of the Caribbean and southern Atlantic to feed in the rich waters of the bay and at Stellwagen Bank, just north of the Cape's tip. Sometimes, when the ocean surface is calm, they can be spotted from these shores.

Continue walking southeast along the beach and as the shoreline curves, the bone-white Wood End Lighthouse begins to appear ahead on your left. The light, situated at Provincetown's southernmost point, was built in 1872, a half-century after its older cousin, Long Point Lighthouse. The 38-foot tower was originally painted brown. The lens flashed red, as it does to this day (Long Point flashes green). A keeper's house for the new lighthouse was also built. In 1961, Wood End Light was automated, and all support structures other than the small oil house were destroyed. The lighthouse went solar in 1981. It is not open to the public.

The Long Point sand barrier extends from the "fist" of mainland Provincetown and crooks like a finger more than 180 degrees, from southwest to northeast. At its rough-washed gravelly tip, the sand extension points back across the harbor to East Harbor (formerly Pilgrim Lake), over the dunes, and to the Atlantic Ocean. This narrowing spit continues to pile up with sand deposits; where other parts of the Cape shore suffer from breaks and loss of coastline, Long Point keeps getting longer.

During the summer, the spit is popular with boaters and kayakers, but you can still find stretches of deserted beach. If you were hiking here in the first half of the nineteenth century, however, you would have seen upwards of 200 people, making up a small village on Long Point. By the time of the Civil War, the settlement had failed, and the houses were floated on barges across the harbor to be relocated in the West End, where many still stand today.

The hike to the end of Long Point adds another 2.0 miles—and lots of time—to your trip, cutting into whatever you might have planned for the rest of your day (hint: experiencing Provincetown's singular sights). To begin your return from the Wood End lighthouse, follow a path that leads down to the harbor shore; you might want to time your trip to the low or receding tide so that you can venture across the marsh along the sand flats.

To the right you can see the impressive stone dike that connects Wood End to the rotary and viewing area at the western terminus of Commercial Street. You might find it tempting to return to the mainland on this popular route, but that course means walking along busy roads with fast-moving traffic, mostly without benefit of a pedestrian path, to reach the Herring Cove parking area. Stick to the shore. The views of the marsh are terrific, as are those of the town rising beyond. Make your way northwest, with the marsh on your right and the dunes now on your left. You reach a network of paths and the main sand road that leads across a small upland of pine and oak before reaching the parking lot. Use the prominent path instead of the small paths that cross the dunes. These paths have increased significantly over time, leading to a weakened dune system and erosion.

2

Biking Cape Cod

YOU CAN FIND FEW MORE ENJOYABLE REGIONS to take a bike ride in than the Cape. The scenery is unparalleled, and you can find bike rental/repair shops from one end to the other. The Shining Sea Bikeway and Cape Cod Rail Trail are two of the loveliest routes on the East Coast, and the bike paths of the Cape Cod National Seashore are just as memorable.

The routes described in this section are of modest length, ranging from a couple of miles to a dozen or so. The chief exception is the Cape Cod Rail Trail, which covers 22 miles—one way. The Cape is also home to plenty of off-road options, especially on the cart paths that lace the National Seashore. And while this coastal landscape is mostly flat, in some stretches, particularly on the outer Cape, you might feel like you're in the Green Mountains. Can't make it too easy for you!

One last note of caution: Although you might observe cyclists riding along scenic Route 6A, one of the prettiest roads in New England, I cannot recommend biking there. No bike path exists along Route 6A, which carries a lot of traffic, and the sidewalks are inappropriate. Instead, I suggest pedaling side roads that run parallel to this main artery, which can be just as enjoyable.

Trip Times

The times listed for the bike rides in this chapter are fairly conservative and based on what I feel it might take a rider in average physical condition to complete the trip. Infrequent bikers might need more time. Those who ride consistently from week to week are probably going to need less time. You should add extra time when trails are wet or when rain is expected.

Trip Ratings

As with the hikes, ratings for the bicycle trips are based on my own experience, mostly aboard an aging hybrid bike. These trips are geared to novices and families with riders of varying experience levels, and those who might enjoy a half-day in the saddle. Few of the trips are especially strenuous, although you do have to endure some elevation gain and loss on the rides through Wellfleet and Truro and the off-road portion in North Truro. Trips that are mostly flat are listed as *easy*, though longer mileage trips on gently rolling terrain might be listed as *moderate*. Moderate rides usually feature more ups and downs and are of longer distance. The Cape Cod Rail Trail has been broken into a few trips, although the 22-mile pedal from Dennis to South Wellfleet can be completed in an active morning.

Etiquette

- Pedal defensively: That means always keep an eye out for others, either oncoming or passing from behind. On rail trails and recreation paths where you can also expect to encounter walkers, joggers, and skaters, slow down and keep to the right. Stop at intersections, even if you see no stop sign or traffic light (including on rail trails). Remember, pedestrians *always* have the right of way, and motor vehicles are not worth messing with! And always set a good example for young riders; they mimic your bike behavior, for good or ill.
- Leave no trace. Be sensitive to the pavement/dirt beneath you, and the surrounding environment. Don't litter.
- Control your bicycle. Inattention for even a second can cause problems. Obey all bicycle speed regulations and recommendations.
- Yield to others. Do your utmost to let your fellow trail users know you're coming—a friendly greeting or a ring of a bell is a good method. In general, riders need to strive to make each pass a safe and courteous one.
- Plan ahead. Know your equipment, your ability, and the area in which you are riding—and prepare accordingly. Be self-sufficient at all times, keep your equipment in good repair, and carry the necessary supplies for changes in weather or other conditions. Always wear a helmet and appro-

priate safety gear. As mentioned previously, the Cape is home to plenty of bike shops (some are located right on the Cape Cod Rail Trail), but don't plan to rely on them.

Safety and Comfort

Many biking accidents on the Cape occur on paved recreation trails, where a rider's confidence overtakes experience and the ability to react. Speed is often a factor, but so is a slick riding surface. For a safe and comfortable biking experience, keep your bike under control at all times and consider the following tips:

- Helmets on every head!
- Select a trip that is appropriate for everyone in the group. Match the ride to the abilities of the least capable person in the group.
- Plan to complete your trip at or about the time suggested in this guide. Determine a turnaround time and stick to it even if you have not reached your goal for the day.
- Check the weather forecast. Avoid riding during or immediately after heavy rains. Give yourself more time to stop in the rain, because wet brakes do not work as well as dry ones.
- Bring a pack or pannier with the following items:
  - ✓ Water: Bring two or more quarts per person depending on the weather and length of the trip.
  - ✓ Food: Even for a short, one-hour trip, bring some high-energy snacks like nuts, dried fruit, or snack bars. Bring a lunch for longer trips.
  - ✓ Map and compass
  - ✓ Extra clothing—at least a windbreaker
  - ✓ Flashlight
  - ✓ Sunscreen
  - ✓ First-aid kit
  - ✓ Pocketknife
  - ✓ Basic bike-maintenance tools and a spare inner tube and/or tire repair kit
- Wear appropriate footwear and clothing: sturdy sneakers or cross-trainers, and clothes that can stand up to weather. Avoid wearing cotton clothing, which absorbs sweat and rain, making for cold, damp riding. Polypropylene and fleece are good materials for keeping moisture away from your body and keeping you warm in wet or cold conditions.

Maps

Town halls and municipal information kiosks usually have maps available that can guide cyclists. Maps of the National Seashore bike paths can be obtained at the Salt Pond Visitor Center in Eastham, National Seashore headquarters in Wellfleet, and at the Province Lands Visitor Center in Provincetown. Or visit www.nps.gov/caco. Towns along the Cape Cod Rail Trail provide maps of the bikeway. For Rail Trail maps, you can also visit www.mass.gov/dcr/parks/southeast/ccrt.htm.

These trips range from leisurely, family friendly rides along the Falmouth shore via the flat-as-a-sand-dollar Shining Sea Bikeway to hilly road journeys from Wellfleet to Truro. You can also blend a Rail Trail cruise with a bumpy ride on a backcountry jeep track. That's what biking on Cape Cod is all about. Short and sweet. Mix and match. Take your time or just take a brisk pedal before meeting with everybody at the beach. You are going to enjoy a great view no matter where your wheels take you.

TRIP 25
CAPE COD CANAL BIKE PATH (CAPE SIDE)

Rating: Moderate
Distance: 10.5 miles
Estimated Time: 4 hours
Location: Bourne and Sandwich

Pedal along the banks of a marvel of New England maritime engineering. Watch ships from 20 to 200 feet long ply the canal's waters and then stop to take in fine views of this threshold to the Cape.

Directions
Follow Route 25 over the Bourne Bridge. Take the first right on the Cape-side rotary and follow to a T-intersection. Turn right, pass under a bridge, and look for the parking area immediately on the left.

Trip Description
The service roads on both the north and south banks of the Cape Cod Canal were built as access routes for vehicles and equipment of the Army Corps of Engineers, which has managed the canal since 1928. But the paved pathways—similar in design and length: 7.0 miles north side, 6.5 miles south—have developed a much broader appeal to the recreation-loving public. In addition to bicyclists, you pass in-line skaters, skateboarders, walkers, joggers, and anglers. (Remember to always wear a helmet, be constantly aware of oncoming and passing traffic, and carry plenty of water to sustain you through the trip.)

Today's outdoors enthusiasts are following an ancient tradition of travel along this corridor. For centuries, American Indians followed the Manamet River and other tidal waterways that laced the narrow isthmus connecting what is now mainland Massachusetts and Cape Cod.

This family-friendly trip on nicely flat terrain follows the recreation path on the canal's south side from the Bourne Bridge east beyond the Sagamore Bridge to East Basin and Sandcatcher Recreation Area, where the canal meets Cape Cod Bay in Sandwich.

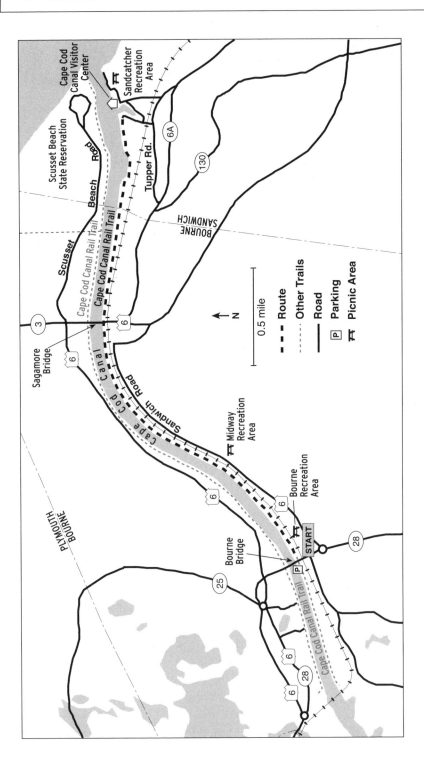

Sandcatcher
Recreation
Area

Cape Cod
Canal Visitor
Center

Scusset Beach
State Reservation

Tupper Rd.

6A

130

BOURNE
SANDWICH

Beach Road

Scusset

Cape Cod Canal Rail Trail

Cape Cod Canal Rail Trail

3

6

6

Sagamore
Bridge

Cape Cod Canal

Sandwich Road

Midway
Recreation
Area

0.5 mile

N

Route
Other Trails
Road
Parking
Picnic Area

6

Bourne
Recreation
Area

6

PLYMOUTH
BOURNE

Bourne
Bridge

START

P

28

25

6

28

6

Cape Cod Canal Rail Trail

You can enjoy terrific views, easy pedaling, and a mix of attractions, from overlooks and picnic areas to a busy marina and visitor center. Plus, you have the chance to see plenty of commercial and recreational boat traffic And maybe more: In the fall of 2008, a 45-foot right whale stopped traffic, literally, as it lazily made its way through the canal on its way to Buzzards Bay and the open ocean.

The Bourne Recreation Area, located just adjacent to the parking lot, features picnic facilities (where you can fuel up at either the beginning or end of your ride) and an information booth to obtain up-to-date information. As you pedal along, look for park benches that have been placed to present the best views of the canal. The distance between the Bourne Bridge and Sagamore Bridge is 3.25 miles, but you can spy the top of the Sagamore Bridge arch long before you arrive.

After pedaling about another 1.5 miles, look for the aptly named Midway Recreation Area on your right, where you find picnic tables and restrooms. Go 1.0 mile farther, and you reach another fine lookout, on your left; across the canal, look for a series of fish ladders rising into the uplands. You've spotted the Bourne herring run, a popular tourist attraction, where for eons herring have been ascending the waterway to spawn in fresh water. Each spring, thousands of tourists enjoy watching the herring "parade."

Continue east along the recreation path and under the massive, concrete-and-steel span of the Sagamore Bridge, which carries mainland traffic from Route 3 onto the Cape and Route 6. Like its similar-looking sister farther west along the canal, the Sagamore Bridge was built between 1933 and 1935, in the midst of the Great Depression, and building it put hundreds of men to work. From the roadbeds of both bridges, it's more than 140 feet to the water. However, the total length of the Bourne Bridge is 2,384 feet, almost 1,000 feet longer than the Sagamore Bridge.

Make your way beyond the shadow (and traffic noise) of the bridge into the quiet and lovely Bourne village of Sagamore, with the canal on your left and the railroad tracks on your right. As you pass from Sagamore into the town of Sandwich, the tracks bear off right on their way to Hyannis at Mid-Cape, whereas the bike route continues straight, into East Basin, home of the Sandwich Marina and Sandcatcher Recreation Area, located just beyond.

Here you pass through a busy, boat-centric mix of docks, moorings and berths, marine-support businesses, and picnic amenities and broad lawns. The marina is also home to a large fishing fleet, and ships passing through the canal often wait out bad weather and fog here. (You find boat shuttles

The Cape Cod Canal is a popular recreational destination, as well as an inland shipping route.

and canal tours available here, too.) However, the chief attraction at Sand-catcher Recreation Area is the Cape Cod Canal Visitor Center, located between Ed Moffit Drive and the water.

The visitor center (open May to October) tells the story of the canal's construction and is a welcoming, interactive repository of the history and culture of this Upper Cape region through which the waterway was cut. Highlights include a 41-foot Corps of Engineers patrol boat (inside!), a theater where videos explain canal history and ecology, and even radar images that reveal real-time canal and boat traffic profiles. For those cyclists just looking to rest their legs, the center boasts rocking chairs on a deck that offers great views of the canal as it reaches Cape Cod Bay. You can also come away with plenty of informative brochures, postcards, and souvenirs.

Return to your bike, and take time to appreciate what the canal meant to Cape commerce, and to shipping, trade, and passenger travel. The 7.0-mile waterway effectively became a 135-mile shortcut for ships moving up and down the Northeast coast. Perhaps most important, because ships could pass through the protected bays and canal, thus avoiding the historically treacherous shoals and "ship's graveyards" off the Cape's eastern shore, the canal was an immeasurable advance in maritime safety.

Leisurely make your way back to the parking lot at the Bourne Bridge (again, you see the topmost steel truss work long before you reach the span).

Cape Cod Canal

Several years after establishing the Plymouth Colony, Pilgrims set up a trading station between the Manomet and Scusset Rivers in what is now Bourne. The outpost was strategically placed along a Wampanoag route of inlets, tidal streams, and small uplands that ran between Cape Cod Bay on the northeast and Buzzards Bay on the southwest.

Today the Aptuxet Trading Post and Village is a fascinating museum and interpretive site, popular with visitors who have either just crossed or are traveling along the modern incarnation of that ancient trade route: the Cape Cod Canal. The canal was completed in 1914, but only after three centuries of dreams, plans, and proposals. The earliest suggestion that a canal be built might have been aired by Myles Standish, who was among those Pilgrim leaders who saw the value of a more direct sailing route to Narragansett Bay and Long Island Sound and the Dutch settlements at New Amsterdam (now New York).

In the early twentieth century, an established tycoon and business visionary named August Belmont, Jr., saw a canal as a commercial opportunity. The grandson of Commodore Matthew Perry, who opened trade with Japan, he had mariner's blood in his veins and may have seen how a canal could reduce the terrible toll exacted by the Atlantic Ocean just off the eastern shore of the Cape.

Hundreds of ships had fallen victim to the storms, strong currents, and especially, treacherous shoals that awaited all who dared venture close to the "graveyard" along the back side of what is now the Cape Cod National Seashore. Recorded wrecks of ships start soon after the Pilgrims arrived in 1620. (The Mayflower itself was bound for more southerly shores at New York when it reached Cape Cod instead. The ship's master determined that sailing south along the shoreline in unpredictable conditions was too great a risk and retreated to the safety of Provincetown.) Many other ships continued to be claimed by the seas through the eighteenth and nineteenth centuries.

Also, as the Age of Sail faded by the mid-nineteenth century, sailing vessels were succeeded by steam-powered ships. Some hauled huge barges, which carried more freight than the largest, five-masted schooners could, but barges were even more vulnerable to the Atlantic.

Belmont surely had all of these issues in his mind in 1909 when he and his newly formed enterprise, the Boston, Cape Cod & New York Canal Company, began in earnest to design the Canal. At the Cape Cod Bay entrance, the first step was to put in place rock barriers to impede sand and other sediments that lead to shoaling.

It took five years to build the canal, which was 13 miles long, 100 feet wide, and 15 feet deep; the official opening took place on July 29, 1914. It was a crowning moment for Belmont; the canal was to be a toll road, with ships paying a fee to pass through. However, many private captains and shipping companies found his tolls too high, and thus, many still chose to brave the back side of the Cape.

The canal's constricted width and shallow depth became problematic almost immediately, as larger vessels were developed. More frustrating, the strong tides that rushed twice daily into each end of the canal carried more sediment than could be handled.

Belmont began to lose money. Eventually, the federal government entered into negotiations to purchase the canal and officially took control in 1928, four years after Belomont's death. The U.S. Army Corps of Engineers has managed the canal ever since.

The canal was transformed into a marine-engineering marvel five times as wide and more than twice as deep as Belmont's original, in a massive public works project started in 1935, as the nation was staggering through the Great Depression. It was budgeted at $5 million and employed a total of 1400 men throughout the five-year construction period, providing a huge boon to the local and regional economy. The "new" canal was opened in 1940 and ended up costing $20 million.

Today the Cape Cod Canal is a National Historic Civil Engineering Landmark. The world's widest sea-level canal, it measures more than 500 feet across. The busy waterway is spanned by a railroad bridge at Buzzards Bay and by two highway spans, the Bourne and Sagamore Bridges, which carry vehicles onto the Cape from the mainland along Route 25 and Route 3, respectively. Both the railroad and highway bridges were designed for high clearances, to accommodate large freighters, tankers, and even ocean liners.

TRIP 26
SHAWME-CROWELL STATE FOREST
AND SANDWICH VILLAGE

Rating: Easy to Moderate
Distance: 4.0 miles
Estimated Time: 4 hours
Location: Sandwich

Explore an Upper Cape state forest/campground and then pedal into Sandwich Village, past historic houses, a glass museum, and a colonial-era grist mill.

Directions
From Route 6 east, take Exit 2 and then Route 130 north into Sandwich. Follow signs to the state forest entrance on left.

Trip Description
You can pick up a lot of colonial history and local lore on this trip from a popular state forest and camping area to Sandwich's quaint village and back. Even the name of the park—Shawme-Crowell—represents specific historical eras in this part of Cape Cod. The first European settlers drifted down from the Plymouth Colony shortly after the Pilgrims landed at Plymouth Rock in 1621. They explored this northwest corner of the Cape the local indigenous people called "Shawme"—and renamed it Sandwich, in honor of the town in England. Sandwich, *nee* Shawme, is Cape Cod's oldest town. Crowell was the name of a renowned twentieth-century forester who made his reputation defending and promoting these open spaces.

Park in the campground lot near the welcome center, or go where rangers direct you. This 700-acre property offers about 5.0 miles of paved and dirt roads, where road bikes and hybrids will have no problem. Jog quickly north (right) to where a paved road passes the camp store and then follow this main road into the campground proper.

Continue along the main road and follow the undulating paved path to the intersection with Bayview Road. (The Upper Cape, supported by a massive glacial moraine that parallels part of Cape Cod Bay and then angles

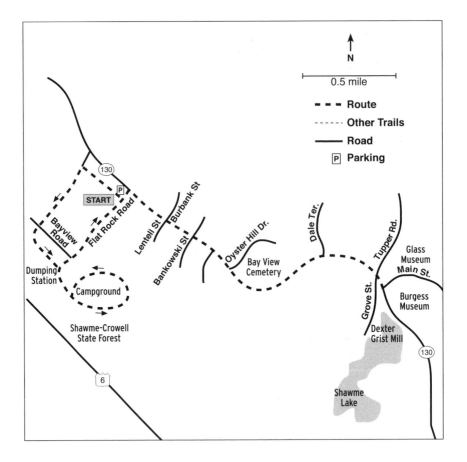

down along the Cape Cod Canal toward Falmouth, is the hilliest section of the 60-mile spit—hence the up-and-down nature of the ride.)

Bayview Road gets its name from the elevation you reach on the way to Mount Perry, at 300 feet the highest point on the Cape. If you were to turn right here, you would reach Mount Perry and get a nice view of Cape Cod Bay, but the road quickly becomes a rough, rutted route best enjoyed on a substantial mountain bike. So, we suggest sticking to the paved and smoother dirt roads of the campground. Pedal through the intersection with Bayview Road and bear off to the left. You're leaving camping Area 1 and entering Area 2, passing a maintenance area on the right.

That noise you hear off to the right is the traffic on Route 6, several hundred yards through the woods. (These woods of pine and oak are relatively new, having succeeded forest that burned in a series of fires that plagued this part of Cape Cod in the early twentieth century.)

Area 2 is a larger complex of tent, yurt, and camper sites. You can follow this main road to its terminus (about 0.5 mile farther) at a rotary on the east border of the property or bear off to the right at your first chance. Follow this paved road on a counterclockwise loop that eventually returns you to the main stem. At this point, bear left and follow the campground road back toward the maintenance area and dumping station, now on your left.

Now look for Flat Rock Road, which leaves right, just across from the dumping station. This route, with usually less motor vehicle traffic, parallels the main campground road as you make your way back to the parking lot.

Head out onto Route 130 and take a right. Sandwich Village begins less than 1.0 mile east. Just past Oyster Hill Drive, look for lovely Bay View Cemetery on your left. Route 130 becomes Main Street, which leads past houses that date to the seventeenth century and past sea captains' homes from the 1800s, when whaling skippers and merchants involved in the China trade made fortunes.

Just beyond the intersection with Water Street, at 129 Main Street you find a museum dedicated to the town's once-world renowned glass industry, the Sandwich Glass Museum. Turn around here and head back to the intersection of Main Street and Water Street. On the far side, picturesque Shawme Pond once powered the centuries-old Dexter Grist Mill, which ground grain for bread, biscuits, and other basic foodstuffs in colonial times. The mill-and-pond complex is worth getting off your bike to experience—just ask the numerous just-wed couples who have their photos taken here.

Depending on your memories, or the reading level of younger pedaling partners, you might want to wander into a nearby museum dedicated to Thornton W. Burgess, author of the Peter Rabbit tales for children. As you begin to pedal back to Shawme-Crowell State Forest, check out Yesteryears Doll Museum at the corner of Maine Street and River Street. If not for the doll-lovers among your party, then for the history-lover in you—the museum is housed in the First Parish Meeting House, the oldest parish on the Cape, established by the Pilgrims in 1638.

Pedal back out of town on Route 130 and in about 10 to 15 minutes you make your final turn back into the state forest. Put the bikes back on your vehicle (unless, of course, you're staying at one of the campsites) and con-

Built in the 1640s, Dexter Grist Mill was used to grind grain during the colonial era.

sider these two other family-friendly ways to cap your trip: Drive back into the village, turn left on Jarves Street, and at the intersection with Route 6A, look for a great ice cream parlor on your left. Or, you can continue through the village on Main Street to where it joins Route 6A a little farther east. Almost immediately on the right you see signs for a state fish hatchery. Fish food dispenses for a quarter from what looks like gumball machines, and the frothy mass of brown and rainbow trout go crazy for the stuff. *Everybody* loves this place.

TRIP 27
SHINING SEA BIKEWAY

Rating: Easy to Moderate
Distance: 8.0 miles
Estimated Time: 3 hours
Location: Falmouth, Woods Hole

This leisurely pedal goes from Falmouth to the quaint village of Woods Hole, following a former rail spur along picturesque Vineyard Sound.

Directions

From Bourne Bridge—At Cape-side rotary, bear right onto Route 28 and follow it through Bourne and North Falmouth into the center of Falmouth. Where Route 28 bears left, continue straight onto Locust Road for 0.5 mile. Parking is on right, just after Pin Oak Way on the left and just before the road crosses the bikeway. From Sagamore Bridge—Take the first Route 6 exit (1) immediately after crossing the bridge onto the Cape. At the bottom of the exit, turn left at the traffic light onto Sandwich Road and follow south to the rotary at Bourne Bridge. Then follow directions above.

Trip Description

Shining Sea is an apt description for this lovely rail-trail linking the center of Falmouth with its southwestern-most village, Woods Hole. The sun indeed glitters on Vineyard Sound and at Woods Hole Harbor, two highlights of your trip. But the bikeway's name is more specifically derived from the phrase "from sea to shining sea," the final words to "America the Beautiful," by Falmouth native Katherine Lee Bates. Visitors from both coasts and many points in between—and beyond—have pedaled this path; we followed a cycling French family on one of our trips.

The bikeway, which opened in 1975, follows a former spur of the New York-New Haven rail line that once ran the length of the Cape. But it's older by three years than the Cape Cod Rail Trail, which today follows the main rail from Dennis on the mid-Cape out to Wellfleet. For most of its history, the Shining Sea Bikeway began at Locust Road and terminated at the parking

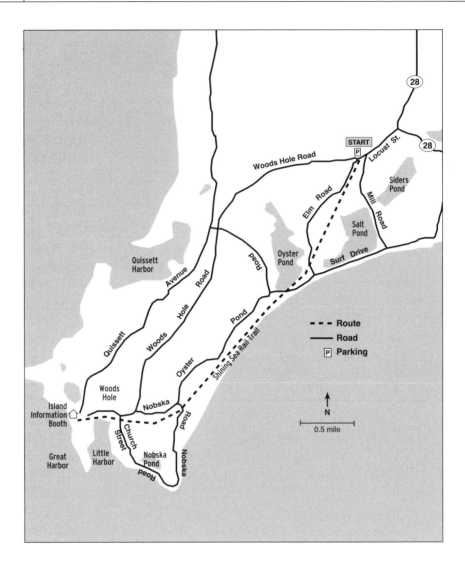

lot for the Woods Hole–Martha's Vineyard Ferry. It was later extended 1.0 mile north, to Carlson Lane, and present plans call for it to run to North Falmouth, near the Bourne line, which will more than triple its length to 11.5 miles.

The more southerly portion is by far the prettiest, however: a lovely, flat excursion passing sandy beaches, salt marsh, and shore-side ponds once open to the ocean. The route eventually emerges at Little Harbor in Woods

This rail trail from Falmouth to Woods Hole is perfect for families.

Hole, offering fine views of boats bobbing at anchor, anglers trying their luck from shore and pier, and the pretty rooftops of the village.

Leaving the Locust Road parking lot, you pedal less than 0.5 mile before Salt Pond appears on your left, the first of four ponds now cut off from Vineyard Sound by a thin sand barrier—the one that you're riding on! It hardly seems time to dismount, but the Salt Pond Bird Sanctuary might be worth a stop, especially if you (and any children in tow) enjoy watching ospreys, either atop their nest poles or stalking fish. You might be joined by someone with binoculars or a scope to provide a close-up view of these raptors and other avian species in the area.

In fact, numerous species are attracted to this coastal plain, from plovers and other shorebirds patrolling the beachfront to the larger wading birds of the marshes, including great blue herons and egrets. Swans, Brant geese, and of course, the ubiquitous gulls are also part of the coastal tableau. Sit down at a bench at the scenic overlook here and take it all in.

The bikeway runs between Salt Pond and Oyster Pond, which soon appears on your left. We once watched several dark-headed, bright-orange-billed American oystercatchers noisily calling and zipping about its shores, hunting for food. (These not-so-common shorebirds must have had a good feeling about a body of water called Oyster Pond; they do indeed feed on these and other mollusks, using their bills as pry bars to open the shells.)

At Trunk River Beach a parking lot also offers access to the bikeway, but a sticker is required, always a complication for visitors. This stretch of the ride is also notable because you are now heading southwest, into the prevailing breeze of the summer season. Riding along the shore of Vineyard Sound, you might find the pedaling a bit more of a struggle, the wind gaining power as it whips across the open water. If you and/or your fellow cyclists are in need of a rest, Trunk Beach offers a nice place to take a swim, allowing all to cool off and rest up. (This portion of the trip is also a pretty good place to go fishing for stripers, bluefish, and other warm-weather species. We've seen plenty of cyclists with fishing rods attached to their bikes; it's an easy ride from the Locust Road parking lot to here and back.)

Beyond Oyster Pond, you pass a pair of smaller salt ponds on your right and Quissett Beach on your left. You also are treated to some nice views of Martha's Vineyard, rising across the Sound. Your last view of this scenic shore before the path moves inland is of iconic Nobska Light, a renowned navigational beacon and a familiar waypoint on the annual Falmouth Road Race. The 7.0-mile race follows the shore from Woods Hole to Falmouth Harbor and attracts an international field.

The bikeway passes through woodlands and more open areas before arcing westward toward the village of Woods Hole. Soon, the red roof of the U.S. Coast Guard Station appears across Little Harbor at the tip of Juniper Point, a sign that you're almost at the Woods Hole terminus of your ride. You emerge at a long parking area (partially created out of the old rail bed). Follow this to where it ends at the ferry station.

Secure your bikes (or stay on them) and explore this pretty seaside community. Woods Hole is home to funky restaurants and bars, gift shops, and the world-renowned Woods Hole Oceanographic Institute, where a lot of brainpower is working to increase our understanding of oceans, weather, and an array of marine-related disciplines. You might want to circumnavigate tidal Eel Pond, which serves as Woods Hole's version of a village green. If you don't have the time or energy for this side-trip, hang around the bridge between the pond and the harbor, where a semi-steady stream of boat traffic has the bridge going up and down all day.

Watching this parade of boats is itself worth the bike trip!

COTUIT CENTER TO CROCKER NECK

Rating: Moderate
Distance: 6.0 miles
Estimated Time: 3 hours
Location: Cotuit

Meander through one of the Cape's prettiest villages down to a scenic peninsula and nature refuge on Popponesset Bay.

Directions

From Route 6 east, take Exit 2 (Route 130) south to Route 28. Turn left on Route 28 and then take the first right onto Main Street, which leads to Cotuit center. Follow Main for about 1.25 mile and to Lowell Park on the left (at Lowell Avenue) and parking.

Trip Description

Cotuit is one of the seven villages that make up the municipality of Barnstable, at 60 square miles the largest town on the Cape. Barnstable's westernmost village on Nantucket Sound, Cotuit is understated, eye-pleasing, and mostly removed from the Route 28 tourist hubbub—a self-contained island without being an island.

From Lowell Park (where Cotuit's Cape Cod Baseball League team plays its home games), pedal south on Main Street to where it intersects with School Street. Turn right onto School Street and continue another 0.5 mile to where you see Lewis Pond looming on your right. To your left, directly across from the pond, Crockers Neck Road leads south. Take this route down the long peninsula that marks the extreme southwest corner of the community.

This pretty peninsula is bracketed by several bays: Cotuit Bay on the east, Shoestring Bay on the west, and the largest, broad and sparkling Popponesset Bay, on the south and southwest. The breezes racing over Nantucket Sound waft across these smaller embayments and offer cool relief on the hottest days of summer.

After 0.5 mile, Crockers Neck Road enters Santuit Road. Continue on Santuit Road until it becomes Cotuit Cove Road. You soon reach a gate to the

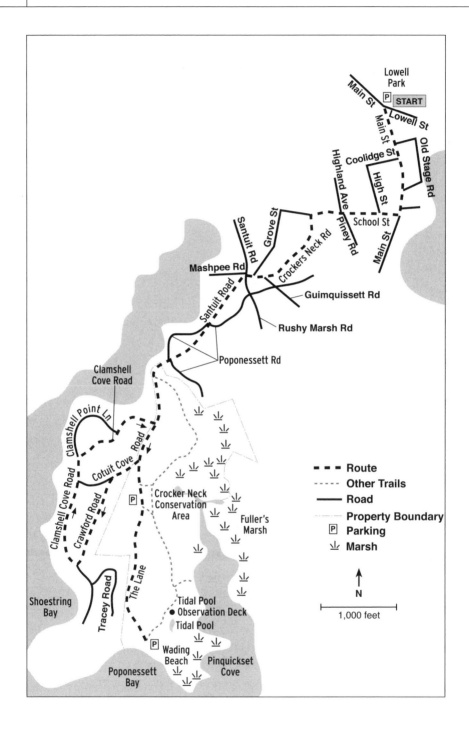

Lowell Park
P START
Main St
Lowell St
Main St
Old Stage Rd
Coolidge St
Highland Ave
High St
Grove St
Santuit Rd
Crockers Neck Rd
Piney Rd
School St
Main St
Mashpee Rd
Guimquissett Rd
Santuit Road
Rushy Marsh Rd
Poponessett Rd
Clamshell Cove Road
Clamshell Point Ln
Cotuit Cove Road
P
Crocker Neck Conservation Area
Fuller's Marsh
Clamshell Cove Road
Crawford Road
The Lane
Shoestring Bay
Tracey Road
Tidal Pool
Observation Deck
Tidal Pool
P Wading Beach
Pinquickset Cove
Poponessett Bay

- - - Route
····· Other Trails
─── Road
─·─· Property Boundary
P Parking
☽ Marsh

N
1,000 feet

Crocker Neck Conservation Area on your left. You enter a coastal environment of almost 100 acres defined by multiple habitats including saltwater and brackish marshes, wooded uplands, and shoreline, from the deep blue waters of Popponesset Bay east to Pinquickset Cove, which feeds an expansive salt marsh.

The dirt road you pedal onto at the conservation area is called The Lane, and it continues southward for more than 0.5 mile to an overlook and beach on the shore of Popponesset Bay, one of the loveliest coastal bodies of water on the Cape. Crocker Neck Conservation Area, in fact, is part of the larger coastal formation stretching southwest from Osterville to East Falmouth. (This environment of sand barrier and bay, upland woodlands and marsh includes Popponesset Bay, South Beach, Waquoit Bay, and Washburn Island, much of which is situated within the Waquoit Bay National Estuarine Research Reserve, described elsewhere in this guide book.)

The views and overall experience one enjoys here (especially if you are on vacation and not a local) are somewhat uncommon, if only because of Crocker Neck Conservation Area's location and its status as public open space. First, the Cape's south-facing shore on Nantucket Sound is notable for the amount of private property along the beachfront, reducing public access. Second, Route 28, as a major east-west artery, carries people *beyond* these worthy areas, either farther down the Cape or into Falmouth, into Woods Hole, and to the ferry boats to Martha's Vineyard.

All of which is to say, visitors to Crocker Neck Conservation Area often have much of the place to themselves, which can make the experience all the more memorable. And fewer human visitors can often mean more sightings of birds and mammals, primarily the former. To be sure, you can spot squirrels and the occasional chipmunk (and perhaps even the elusive gray fox, which seems to prefer coastal habitats), but the plovers, yellowlegs, sanderlings, and other shorebirds, and the egrets, herons, and raptors are more common.

Continue to pedal along The Lane to its terminus on a small beach on Popponesset Bay. Dismount and wander out on the sand strip (which expands into flats on a receding tide). Look for the long spit across the water that forms the southwest arm of the bay. This spit shelters and nurtures terns and other shorebirds.

Before returning to your bike, consider walking a couple hundred feet up a trail to your left, where you can reach an observation deck overlooking

Fuller's Marsh and serene little Pinquickset Cove. Watch for osprey overhead and, in the shallows, bone-white egrets or great blue herons standing in wait for an unsuspecting fish or crab.

Pedal back north along The Lane. You pass through a forest of Cape-toughened pitch pine and scrub oak, species hardy enough to survive in this feisty habitat of sandy, shallow soil, harsh winds, and leaf-killing salt spray. Also, be aware of equally resilient (and seemingly ubiquitous) poison ivy; it especially loves the edges of trails and dirt roads.

Upon leaving Crocker Neck Conservation Area, turn left onto Cotuit Cove Road for a short loop that overlooks Shoestring Bay, between Cotuit and the next-door town of Mashpee. Pedal about 100 yards and bear left onto Crawford Road. Crawford intersects Clamshell Cove Road in about 0.25 mile. Turn right here, and pedal north on Clamshell Cove Road (with bay on your left) to where it enters Santuit Road. Take a left on Santuit Road, which puts you back on the road that you traveled to reach the conservation area.

Stop at the narrow strip of land passing between Shoestring Bay on your left and the uppermost reaches of Fuller's Marsh on your right. You see a boat landing area on your left and broad marshlands on your right. In this rich estuarine environment, the osprey is right at home, and you might spot the determined "fish hawk" hovering or even diving for a meal.

Continue on Santuit Road to where it again meets School Street. Turn right on School Street, continue back into the village, and follow Main Street north (left) back to Lowell Park.

Rating: Moderate
Distance: 5.0 miles
Estimated Time: 3 hours
Location: Centerville and Hyannis

Escape busy downtown Hyannis and pedal past Craigville's tidal creeks and half-moon beach over to Squaw Island, home of the Kennedy compound.

Directions

From Route 6 east, take a right off Exit 6 (Route 132) toward Hyannis for 1.2 miles. Turn right on Phinney's Lane and follow 2.0 miles to Route 28. Cross Route 28 to Main Street. Take a right on Main Street (which becomes Craigville Beach Road) to the beach parking lot.

Trip Description

At the height of summer, Hyannis can be a daunting destination; thousands of vehicles and even more people swarm to the largest, busiest, liveliest spot on Cape Cod. But this most "vacation-y" of Cape towns can also be a place for a memorable bike trip, especially if you head west and hug the coast. Craigville Beach can be mighty busy, but is one of the loveliest of the south-facing beaches on Nantucket Sound. And just east is Hyannis Port and Squaw Island, home of the Kennedy compound, which contains the homes of Joseph Kennedy and his sons, John and Robert.

In between you can explore a quiet, modest neighborhood that evokes "old Cape Cod" and offers nice pedaling, especially for young families.

Hyannis, Hyannis Port, and Centerville are all villages within the greater town of Barnstable, and each is located right on the spectacular Sound. The main artery is busy, touristy Route 28, but a goal of this trip is to get off that road and stay off. I recommend arriving at the Craigville Beach parking lot early (you pay a fee in season). The lot has room for more than 400 vehicles, but why take chances on being shut out?

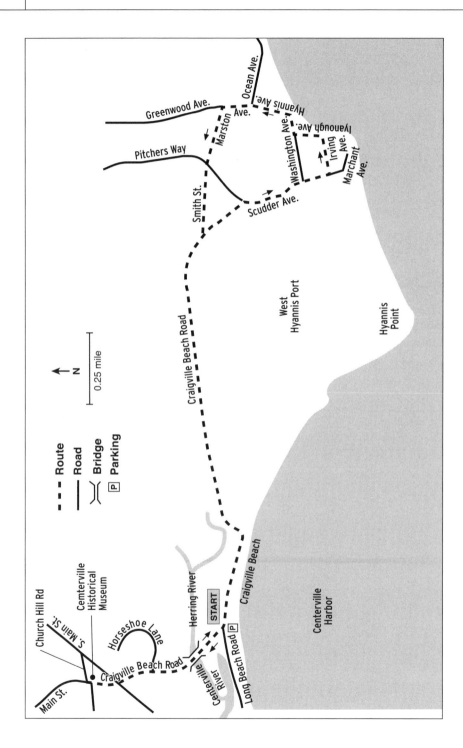

Pedal left out of the lot, retracing your route along Craigville Beach Road. Your trip truly begins a half mile up the road, just south of Route 28. Turn around at the Centerville Historical Museum, and pedal back toward the shore. One of the many Herring Rivers on the Cape passes under a pretty bridge, and you are going to find it worth a stop to take in your scenic surroundings.

This tidal waterway empties into a couple of small ponds just to the east, part of a once much-larger salt marsh habitat. This area is definitely osprey country. And you might spot a great blue heron in the wetlands, as well. To the right of the bridge, the stream widens as it becomes the Centerville River and eventually empties into East Bay and Nantucket Sound in Osterville, one town to the west. Continue pedaling south and east, and you're soon back at Craigville Beach.

It might be too soon for a swim (or maybe not!), but the beach features a changing room/shower complex, open in season, and a snack bar. Pedaling east on Craigville Beach Road, you pass Craigville Beach before the route moves inland, away from the water. You enter West Hyannis Port, an intimate neighborhood of classic Cape and smaller cottages, with newer, larger homes also taking their place.

If you would like to send a postcard, this quiet little neighborhood does have its own post office—a small, handsome structure right on Craigville Beach Road. Farther down the road toward Hyannis 0.5 mile, bear right onto a short connector that flows into Scudder Avenue, the main route to Squaw Island. The Kennedy mystique is wrapped up in elegance, glamour, and yes, wealth, but this legendary neighborhood of Hyannis Port, where the family has summered for decades, can be a bit underwhelming, which is meant as a compliment.

Many large homes line the Sound, reflecting the moneyed class that gravitated here in the early half of the twentieth century, but you also find plenty of "just plain folks" houses. In fact, the most noticeable clue that you're closing in on the Kennedy compound is the series of "All Busses" signs that dot surrounding streets.

Follow Scudder Avenue almost to its terminus at the water. Marchant Avenue is the last left off Scudder. Irving Avenue is the second-last.

President John F. Kennedy's father, Joseph P. Kennedy, rented a small house on Marchant Avenue in 1926, purchasing it two years later and expanding the structure for his growing family. The Kennedy children, including

John, Robert, Ted, and their sisters, spent summers playing on the broad lawns, sailing and fishing, and swimming in the warm Sound. (As a Harvard student, John would become a collegiate sailing champion, having honed his skills in these local waters.)

Three decades later, then-Senator John F. Kennedy bought a home on Irving Avenue, and Robert also purchased a house to add to the family compound of white, clapboard summer houses. The compound is still owned by the Kennedy family and is Ted's residence. No public access to the properties is permitted; if you've come seeking the "Summer Camelot," you are as close as you are going to get.

From here you can pedal back along Scudder Avenue to Craigville Beach Road. Or you can continue a bit farther east, pass a beach and breakwater adorned with a lighthouse, and look across Hyannis Harbor to the long peninsula terminating at Point Gammon in Yarmouth. Take time to enjoy this special harbor panorama: powerboats, handsome sailing vessels, and ferry boats leaving and entering the sparking blue harbor, with the lighthouse serving as a beacon of safety.

Continue on Hyannis Avenue to Marston Avenue and turn left. Marston Avenue becomes Smith Street and then merges into Craigville Beach Road. Follow Craigville Beach Road back to the beach parking lot, a distance of less than 2.0 miles. You might want to reward yourself for your combination recreational/historical ride by stopping at the Craigville Beach Grille, located just across from the parking lot, or by going for a swim.

TRIP 30
CAPE COD RAIL TRAIL—DENNIS AND HARWICH

Rating: Easy to Moderate
Distance: 10.0 miles
Estimated Time: 4 hours
Location: Dennis and Harwich

Explore the upper portion of Cape Cod's most popular cycling path, passing woodlands, cranberry bogs, and lovely ponds.

Directions
Take Route 6 east to Exit 9A. Take Route 134 south for 0.5 mile, past a shopping center and convenience store, to a parking lot on your left and signs for the Cape Cod Rail Trail.

Trip Description
The paved pathway follows the former Old Colony rail bed for almost 25 miles, from South Dennis through Harwich, Brewster, Orleans, and Eastham, terminating in South Wellfleet. The Old Colony line eventually became part of the New York and New Haven railroad, which once carried passengers and freight through much of the Northeast. By 1848, the line had reached Sandwich and six years later had extended mid-Cape, to Hyannis. The line had extended as far as Orleans by 1861, but its progress was delayed by the onslaught of the Civil War. After the war, the railroad quickly reached Wellfleet (1870) and its terminus in Provincetown (1872).

The line remained active well into the twentieth century, until the growing popularity of automobiles and the development of the federal highway system spelled its doom. By 1959, all passenger service to the Cape was ended, followed by the suspension of freight service.

This trip focuses on the first two communities the rail trail passes through, Dennis and Harwich, which were part of the first section of the trail to open in 1978. The ride starts inauspiciously, as you pass through "industrial" Dennis: construction yards, building materials suppliers, boat storage facilities, etc. (Remember: Commercial enterprises needed to be near the railroad, which furnished supplies and transported goods off the Cape.)

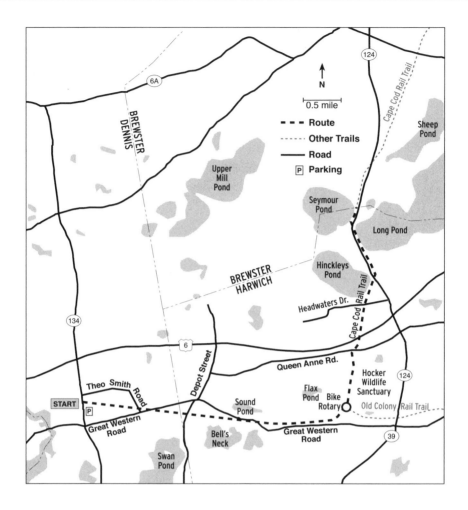

Within 1.0 mile, however, you're pedaling past woodlands of oak, beech, and pine, and when you cross into Harwich, you see your first cranberry bogs, the primary agricultural landscapes of the mid-Cape. You see swaths of cranberry production on both sides of the route as the rail trail continues east before gently bearing northeast, toward Route 6. At the North Harwich Cemetery, the bike trail jogs right and runs through the most common woodland type on the Cape: sandy soil-loving scrub oak and pitch pine.

The trail meanders through town conservation lands and crosses the herring run leading into West Reservoir with an attractive view of the watershed feeding the marshes of the Herring River, which empties into Nantucket Sound. At a rotary (a nice resting spot, complete with benches) the Cape

Cod Rail Trail bears left, while a more-recent rail trail through Harwich to Chatham (following a spur of the Old Colony line) continues straight. Follow the Cape Cod Rail Trail (CCRT) signs, and you soon pass the Hacker Wildlife Sanctuary on your right, part of the Harwich conservation lands system.

Just beyond this lovely refuge, the trail crosses Route 6 on a bridge specially constructed for just this purpose. For most of the rail trail's history and before the bike rotary was constructed, cyclists had to continue east into the village of Harwich at Route 124 and then negotiate the challenging exits at Route 6 before returning to the safety of the bike path. The bike bridge over the highway has made all the difference; the Route 124 traffic challenge is totally avoided.

After you are over the bridge—from which you can watch often sluggish highway traffic with satisfaction—you cross Headwaters Drive, so named because it passes ponds north of Route 6 that eventually feed the Herring River, which empties into Nantucket Sound. Today, you encounter a rail trail parking lot at Headwaters Road, where you often find other cyclists to talk about the route ahead and share experiences. Cross the road, and soon you approach the first of several beautiful kettle hole ponds, so named for the glacial action that carved them into deep bowls.

Welcome to Hinckleys Pond, also known as Pleasant Lake. Over the next 1.0 mile, you pass two more scenic ponds, both shared with the town of Brewster, before reaching the Brewster line about a mile father along the rail trail.

Here you can turn around, leaving plenty of cycling to be enjoyed ahead on another day. After you are back at Hinckleys Pond, stop at the Pleasant Lake General Store, which sits where the rail trail crosses Route 124. The store offers all kinds of comfort food, including great sandwiches and ice cream, of course. And because a town beach is right across the way, you might want to take a dip, before or after.

On the return trip, slow down to notice the smaller flora that decorates your surroundings, including goldenrod, asters, cornflowers, ferns, and highbush blueberry. These modest splashes of color (okay, the goldenrod is pretty eye-catching) nicely interrupt the steady visual diet of pine and oak.

Overhead, red-tailed hawks soar, while sharp-shinned hawks pursue small birds through the understory. You might even see a box turtle making its sluggish way from one side of the bike path to the other, but these delightful creatures are becoming increasingly rare. You might also encounter

A group of bikers riding through a rotary on the Cape Cod Rail Trail.

snapping turtles where the bike trail passes bogs or marshy areas; your best move is to keep on pedaling, because snappers are most aggressive when they are out of their water habitat and thus feeling more vulnerable.

As you continue on your return trip, you pass Depot Street in North Harwich. You might consider leaving the rail trail and taking this road south for 0.5 mile, where it crosses into Dennis. Almost immediately, Swan Pond, one of the prettiest ponds in the mid-Cape region, looms on your right. It's surrounded by private property, but the Swan Pond Cemetery is a serene place to stop and enjoy the view of the pond.

To return to your car, head back to the rail trail and turn left.

TRIP 31
OLD COLONY RAIL TRAIL

Rating: Easy to Moderate
Distance: 15.0 miles
Estimated Time: 6 hours
Location: Harwich and Chatham

Follow a former spur of the Old Colony rail line from the scenic center of Harwich through aging woodlands and new residential development into the heart of Chatham.

Directions

From Route 6 Exit 10, take Route 124 south for 1.5 miles to the Harwich Town Hall parking lot on right (if you cross the bike path, go back 100 feet).

Trip Description

This former rail line reached Chatham in the 1880s, primarily to promote tourism; by the 1930s, the last trains were running to the elbow of the Cape, victims of the automobile (and tourist-filled busses). The Harwich section was revived as a rail trail 60 years later. Today you can pedal an undulating route that parallels Queen Anne Road into the center of Chatham. Park and explore the town—choose from an array of shops, galleries, and restaurants; then enjoy a leisurely return to Harwich.

The Harwich-Chatham route actually begins about 1.0 mile west of Harwich Center, at a specially designed bike rotary where this spur branches east of what is now the Cape Cod Rail Trail. Pedaling on a modest ascent toward Harwich Center, where Route 124 and Route 39 (Main Street) meet, you pass quiet Island Pond on your left, followed by equally serene Island Pond Cemetery, elegantly designed with tree-lined alleys and pathways. You quickly reach the historic center of this community, with its town hall, white-steepled church, gas station, post office, and rail trail-friendly café.

Continue east past verdant Brooks Park. Here, the bike route is shared by cyclists, in-line skaters, and pedestrians in goodly numbers; I passed a number of older residents clutching grocery bags.

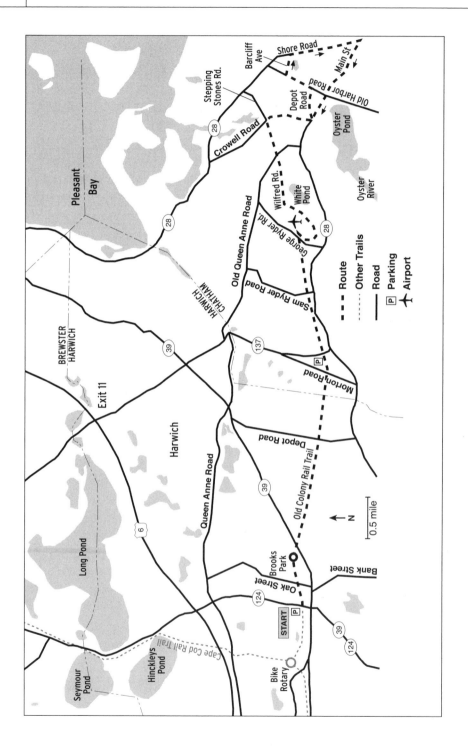

You soon pass a rest area with picnic tables—a bike route enhancement project courtesy of Boy Scout Troop 67. Pedal through the Thompson's Field Conservation Area, adjacent to the Harwich watershed property. Another rotary looms as you approach Route 39, a major secondary Cape artery. Attention families with young riders: The bike rotary allows cyclists to turn around without having to cross this busy traffic route. East of Route 39, the trail passes through pine/oak woodlands on both sides and makes a modest, twisting descent before crossing Depot Road. This crossing is your last intersection with vehicular traffic before reaching the Chatham line about 0.5 mile farther along.

The Harwich section of the rail trail was completed in the late 1990s, but the Chatham section was not constructed until 2003–2005. The delay was due in part to the issue of how to design the rail trail around the Chatham airport—the field covers a large portion of the original rail spur, and other sections of the track had disappeared decades ago, buried before encroaching residential and commercial development.

Pedal through part of the Chatham Town Forest and across Morton Road, the first traffic intersection you meet in this town. Go 0.25 mile farther, and you reach Route 137 and a parking area/information kiosk for the trail (an enterprising homeowner has set up a snack shop in their back yard just east of the parking lot). Busy Route 28 can be seen a couple hundred feet to the right. On your left, you pass the wide-open spaces of the town landfill (not as unattractive as it sounds). About 0.75 mile farther, you cross Sam Ryder Road, and a town park appears on your left. In less than 1.0 mile you reach the airport at George Ryder Road. The bike route jogs right onto George Ryder Road; you leave the airport to your left.

The bike path picks up (left) after you pass the Veterans of Foreign Wars (VFW) Hall, and now you pedal along the south side of the airport. The trail reenters a more natural landscape here, passing alongside a cluster of freshwater ponds. (At White Pond, the largest, you might want to take advantage of the town swimming beach and restrooms.) Here, you again leave the formal bike route and pedal onto Wilfred Road for about 0.5 mile before crossing Old Queen Anne Road onto Stepping Stones Road. The bike path picks up again and takes you to the intersection of Crowell Road and a Department of Public Works (DPW) yard.

Take a right on Crowell to Route 28 (Main Street) for an easy pedal into downtown (watch for traffic). After you reach Route 28, take a quick left

This Cape Cod Rail Trail is a mostly flat route that is great for adults with children.

onto Depot Road, which takes you to the old train station, now a museum and visitor center. Inside, you can find out more about this rail spur and what it meant to Chatham so many years ago.

Depot Road intersects with Old Harbor Road; turn left and follow Old Harbor Road about 0.25 mile to Barcliff Avenue. Take a right on Barcliff Avenue to Shore Road and enjoy memorable views of the Atlantic and the famed Chatham "bars," sand shoals just offshore that have bedeviled mariners for centuries.

Just ahead of you sits the bustling Chatham Fish Pier, where commercial boats offload their catches and take on supplies. It's definitely worth a watch. You can also take a boat from the fish pier to more remote Chatham beaches and the North and South Monomoy Islands, which represent the majority of the Monomoy National Wildlife Refuge.

Turn right on Shore Road. Large, handsome homes line your route on the right, and little wonder: They all enjoy spectacular views of the Cape coastline, Nauset Beach, and the broad Atlantic, spreading away to the horizon on your right. Continue south on Shore Road until you reach Main Street. Turn right and head downtown. Explore this quaint tourist Mecca with its gift shops and galleries, ice cream parlors, and restaurants. Fuel up, rest up, and then pedal west on Main Street to where it again becomes Route 28 and Crowell Road enters from the right. Turn right on Crowell Road and follow back to the bike trail and the trip back to Harwich.

Rating: Moderate

Distance: To Orleans center: 12.0 miles, round-trip; to Nauset
   Beach: 20.0 miles, round-trip

Estimated Time: 6 hours

Location: Brewster and Orleans

Explore the Cape Cod Rail Trail as it curves northeastward past cranberry bogs and sprawling Nickerson State Park to Orleans center. Then leave the trail for an out-and-back excursion to Nauset Beach.

Directions

From Route 6 east, take Exit 11. At the bottom of the ramp turn right onto Route 137 north and proceed about 2.5 miles into Brewster to Underpass Road on the right. Take Underpass Road about 0.5 mile to the intersection with the rail trail and a parking lot.

Trip Description

This trip includes a bit of everything. You pedal through classic mid-Cape terrain of woods and wetlands. You pass a pond and then enter Nickerson State Park; at almost 2,000 acres it is one of the largest open spaces on the Cape. (It's even more impressive when you realize the state park is a former family estate!) Beyond Nickerson State Park, the rail trail soon enters Orleans, which features a fairly large "downtown," where Routes 6A and 28 converge. By contrast, Orleans is also home to Nauset Beach, a spectacular, 7.0-mile sand barrier (the southern tip is part of Chatham) that is both a popular sun and fun destination and a semi-wild refuge drawing hikers, birders, and other nature lovers.

From the Underpass Road parking lot, take the rail trail northeast toward Orleans. Pedal through oak-and-pine woods and past open fields and wet areas. After about 1.0 mile of mostly flat riding, Blueberry Pond appears on the right, another of the renowned Brewster kettle holes, crystal-clear,

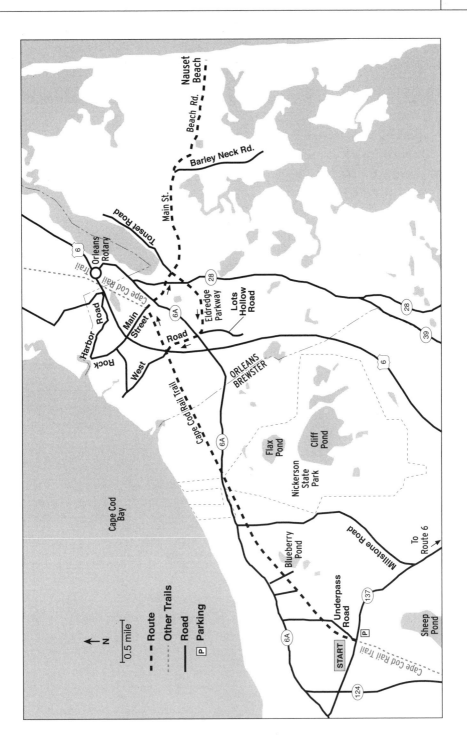

spring-fed pools left by retreating glaciers. Cross Millstone Road and reach the state park at about 2.0 miles. Nickerson State Park, which dominates the northeast side of Brewster, boasts its own network of biking trails; pick up a map at the entrance kiosk. (Flax Pond, just a short pedal into the park, is a popular swimming area—you might want to take advantage.)

To this point, the rail trail has been running parallel to busy Route 6A, which you've been able to hear, and then see, to your left. Here, the bike path runs under the road and emerges into a habitat of cranberry bog and more woods. After about 4.0 miles, you cross the marshy headlands of Namskaket Creek, a tidal waterway that enters Cape Cod Bay.

After you are on the other side of Namskaket, you are in Orleans. Pass through more salt marsh and 1.0 mile farther on you approach the center of town, just north of Route 6A where Main Street crosses. Judging by the lumber business and other long, low-slung commercial buildings, it's easy to tell this was a bustling rail center a century ago. (In fact, the rail trail formerly avoided the center of town and followed a more circuitous route along public roads to Rock Harbor before picking up the rail bed again in Eastham.)

This vacationer-friendly town is worth a visit. You find ice cream parlors, bakeries, restaurants, convenience stores, and shops just mere steps off the bike path. So if you want anything from a cool treat to bottled water to sunglasses to shell earrings, you've come to the right place. Main Street heading north (away from town) leads to the above-mentioned Rock Harbor, an especially scenic inlet on Cape Cod Bay that is also a popular place to watch the sunset.

But if you want a big-time saltwater experience, Nauset Beach, about 4.0 miles east, is where you want to wind up. Pedal a block on Main Street to where it crosses Route 6A. In tourist season especially, you face a lot of vehicular traffic at this intersection; be particularly aware of drivers turning left and those taking advantage of right-on-red situations. Continue on Main Street to where it cross Route 28 (same cautions apply).

Pedaling east on Main Street, you have by now left the major congestion behind, but because you are on the main route to the beach, you still face a semi-steady stream of traffic, with no bike trail. You pass a cemetery and a seasonal playhouse (Cape Cod's summer stock tradition goes back generations) on your left and town offices and the Veterans of Foreign Wars (VFW) Hall on your right. Just before the road forks, you come upon Orleans Village

Pedaling on this paved surface will take you past cranberry bogs and Orleans center on the way to a spectacular beach.

Market, also on your right. Offering everything from gourmet sandwiches and baked goods to fresh produce, the market is worth considering if you want to stock up before continuing the last 2.0 miles to the beach.

At the fork with Barley Neck Road bearing right, keep to the left; Main Street becomes Beach Road. Pedal past quaint cottages, suburban-style homes, and large farmhouses that recall East Orleans' agricultural past. Just past a pair of motels overlooking the Atlantic, you descend to the Nauset Beach parking lot. Dismount at one of several bike racks and explore. In season, you find rest rooms, changing rooms, and a snack bar and store. Walk between the buildings out to the beachfront and enjoy a terrific view of the Atlantic.

If crowds aren't your thing, proceed to the southeast corner parking lot, where a boardwalk trail leads to a more secluded stretch of beach. Or you can follow the dirt road leading from the southwest corner of the lot to where the off-road vehicle (ORV) sand road extends southward the length of the barrier. The road surface quickly becomes too soft for bikes, but you can enjoy some fine hiking here if you have the energy (remember, it's more than 10.0 miles back to Brewster).

Gauge the surf and waves before taking a swim, but I heartily recommend a plunge, particularly on a hot day. Towel off, gear up, and get back on the bike. Your pedal back to Underpass Road is undoubtedly slower (bet you didn't notice that the last stretch of Beach Road was downhill!) but no less enjoyable.

And consider this alternate route through downtown Orleans: Where Main Street (heading west, now) meets Tonset Road, take a left and cross Route 28, onto Eldredge Parkway. On your right is Eldredge Park, home of the Orleans Cardinals, one of the fine Cape Cod Baseball League teams that have served as the launch pad for many college players in their quest to reach the major leagues. Where Eldredge Parkway meets Lots Hollow Road and Route 6A, bear right across Route 6A onto West Road. Continue for 0.25 mile, pick up the rail trail on your left, and start pedaling in the direction of the Namskaket marshes.

Salt Marshes

Sandy Neck in Barnstable, Waquoit Bay and South Cape Beach in Mashpee, Hatches Harbor in Provincetown, Coast Guard Beach in Eastham—each of these areas along the shores of Cape Cod offers spectacular ocean or bay views. But look landward and you're likely to enjoy broad vistas across coastal habitats that are not only beautiful, but also important and connected to our daily lives: salt marshes.

Salt marshes are tidal wetlands of sand and peat, grassy hummocks and salt-tolerant plants, and they are among the richest natural environments in the world, perhaps on a scale with rain forests. They support great diversity, offer coastal flooding protection, act as natural filters, and serve as nurseries for myriad forms of marine life, from microscopic organisms to shellfish and fin fish.

These creatures are nourished by the twice-daily rise and fall of the tides; meandering creeks carry algae and other nutrients in from the open sea, feeding both flora and fauna. Organic detritus, resulting from the breakdown of marsh plants, sustains the tiniest creatures in the marsh.

The complex network of tidal waterways, sand banks, and plant structures also serves to shelter fish and shellfish from predators; many of the species we pursue with fishing rods, nets, or clam rakes first thrive in these rich waters. Humans have used them for other purposes: Salt marsh hay was used for centuries both as livestock forage and as insulation for buildings.

The Cape's salt marshes come in all shapes and sizes. Many are protected by barrier beaches and other coastal land forms that serve to shelter these crucial habitats from direct ocean energy, thus allowing them to grow and remain healthy.

Sandy Neck is a 6-mile barrier beach that protects Barnstable Harbor and the 4,000-acre salt marsh nurtured by Scorton Creek (the largest on the Cape), which stretches westward into Sandwich. South Cape Beach and the arms of Waquoit Bay on Nantucket Sound serve much the same function, as does Coast Guard Beach on the Atlantic. Wander the beach southward to where it ends at a break; here the ocean fills and empties the sprawling Nauset Marsh behind the beach.

At Provincetown, near the northernmost tip of the Cape, Hatches Harbor is undergoing a restoration. As its name implies, this habitat was once more of an open harbor drawing colonial-era fishermen and whalers; a community even sprang up here for a time. However, the ocean gradually reclaimed the harbor (at least partially), and an inland dike furthered its transformation from bay to salt marsh to brackish/freshwater environment. But the National Seashore removed the dike gates and a stronger tidal flow is now restoring the saltwater habitat to a more naturally healthy model.

Across most of Cape Cod, salt marshes remain among the healthiest of natural systems, and among the most enjoyable for visitors. Tidal creeks at full tide offer terrific wading and swimming. When the water is moving, these snaking watercourses turn into water parks, allowing bathers to float along with the current. Kayakers, especially, are drawn to salt marshes for the same reason: to explore the tidal creeks among the cordgrass-topped hummocks, sand bars, and small islands. At above-mean high tides, marshes can become vast inland lakes; you paddle across the top of cordgrass and other plants as they wave eerily beneath your hull. However, on a receding tide, take care. Being stranded deep in a marsh, stumbling through peat and mud as you haul your boat, swatting at greenhead flies, and wiping sweat from your face is not a pretty picture.

TRIP 33
NAUSET TRAIL, EASTHAM

Rating: Easy to Moderate
Distance: 1.6 miles
Estimated Time: 1 hour
Location: Eastham

Follow an undulating paved pathway between wooded upland and salt marsh that leads from a Cape Cod National Seashore visitor center to a former Coast Guard station overlooking the Atlantic.

Directions

Follow Route 6 to the intersection with Nauset Road, marked by signs for the Cape Cod National Seashore's Salt Pond Visitor Center on the right. Turn right onto Nauset Road and take another immediate right into the visitor center parking lot. For a shorter excursion, pass the visitor center and follow Nauset Road to where it jogs left. Continue straight on Doane Road and then turn right into the Doane Rock picnic area. Bike path access is at the end of the parking lot.

Trip Description

This gently undulating bike trail begins at the visitor center and terminates at Coast Guard Beach, where a former station still stands. (From the visitor center, you also have quick access to the Cape Cod Rail Trail—located just west of Route 6 near Old Orchard Road—which extends to Eastham on its way to its terminus in South Wellfleet.) You find plenty to see and do after you've reached the beach (swim, explore the beach, watch for birds and passing boats, etc.), but don't skimp on the ride out to the ocean.

With the small and scenic Salt Pond on your right spreading out into spectacular Nauset Marsh, this trip is one of the loveliest on the Cape. Here, the 40.0-mile National Seashore beach that begins in Provincetown is broken by the sprawling marsh and inlet, which also forms the border between Eastham and Orleans. Pedal slowly and pay attention; you might see a heron

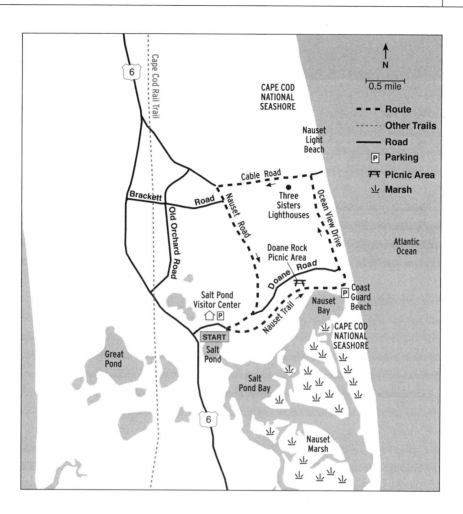

or egret lifting gracefully out of the cordgrass or a long-bodied northern harrier hunting silently just above the waving grasses.

As the path descends to marsh level, you reach a boardwalk deep within Nauset Marsh. Look for osprey here, as well as chattering red-winged blackbirds and yellowlegs skittering across the marsh mud. After you are across the boardwalk, you ascend to the beach parking lot. Pedal up to the former U.S. Coast Guard Station (now a residential education center operated by the Seashore), park your bike at the ample racks and wander over to the far-right (south) end of the parking lot. From this height, your view of the Nauset Marsh is unparalleled; it's much the same view that inspired naturalist

Henry Beston to build a two-room cabin in the dunes between the marsh and ocean in 1927 and spend a year exploring this magnificent place.

Beston's book, *The Outermost House,* became a classic, and the cabin itself hung in against the elements for a half-century, until the Blizzard of 1978 washed away its remnants. On most summer days, however, the beach and ocean are much kinder, and Coast Guard Beach is a great place to swim. Afterward, wash off the salt water at the shower/restrooms and turn your handlebars back toward the bike trail entrance at the west side of the parking lot.

Often because they were in a hurry to reach the beach or are a bit fatigued from all the beach fun, cyclists tend to make a return trip in at a more leisurely pace, which is a good thing, because now is the time to slow down and smell the beach roses. Stop on the boardwalk where a tide creek passes below. Look for horseshoe crabs slowly cruising the shallows or fiddler crabs scurrying into their mud lairs.

Be sure to check out Doane Rock. It is hard to miss: Extending 18 feet skyward, with another 12 feet anchoring it below the ground, the boulder is one of the largest in southern New England. Geologists believe it was left by glacier, whose retreating movement helped carve out the 60-mile curved spit of the Cape 12,000–18,000 years ago. The rock was named for John Doane, one of the first colonists to settle Eastham in the 1600s.

The Doane Rock parking area is situated just off Doane Road, but traveling the road back to the visitor center via bike is not recommended: vehicular traffic can be intense, particularly during the summer months. Return to the bike path and make your way along its meandering route (including a brief uphill stretch).

Cyclists will want to bike northward along the shore for a short distance, passing another emblem of the Cape's maritime history. From the parking lot, leave the bike trail entrance on your left and continue straight through the vehicle egress onto Ocean View Drive toward Nauset Light Beach, about 1.0 mile north. Just before reaching the parking lot to this beach, take a left onto Cable Road. About 0.25 mile down on your right, look for a small sign describing the Three Sisters Lighthouses, often referred to as simply "the Sisters."

They date back to the early 1800s, when it was decided that, given the fact the treacherous waters off the "backside" of the Cape were already con-

The path crosses a bridge over a scenic tidal creek near Coast Guard Beach.

sidered a ship graveyard, another navigational aid should be constructed between the existing lighthouses at North Truro and Chatham. "The Sisters" stood in a row for decades atop the beach in Eastham before coastal erosion and technological advances gradually conspired against them. Restored in 1989 by the National Park Service, the towers stand in their original configuration, about 150 feet apart from each other. Tours are available during the summer months.

After you are back on your bike, continue west along Cable Road about another 0.5 mile to where it meets Nauset Road. Turn left on Nauset Road and follow it south and then west as it arches back to the visitor center, about 1.5 mile away. After you are back where you began, be sure to check out the programs and events the center offers. Some are geared to children, others are appropriate for all ages. You can learn plenty from the maritime and geologic displays, films, and books available inside. Then you can wander outside to the amphitheater, where outdoor talks and demonstrations are held.

TRIP 34
WELLFLEET RIDE

Rating: Moderate
Distance: 12.0 miles
Estimated Time: 4 hours
Location: Wellfleet

Pedal from the Oceanside beaches and past inviting fresh-water ponds, along the byways of the village center, and out to Great Island on Cape Cod Bay.

Directions

From Route 6 east in South Wellfleet, pass the entrance to the Cape Cod National Seashore headquarters and Marconi Beach. Go another mile and take your next right, onto LeCount Hollow Rd., then pull immediately into the parking lot on the right.

Trip Description

You can tell by its name that Wellfleet was a seafaring and fishing village long before it became known as the "art gallery town," and these elements of the community's profile are worth exploring. But so is the Cape Cod National Seashore, with its hollows, its terrific beaches, and crystal clear freshwater ponds. That all of this can be enjoyed by bicycle makes Wellfleet especially attractive for day trippers and vacationers alike. (If you have more than one vehicle available, you might want to leave one in town, at the harbor, or at the parking lot for Great Island; upon reaching this vehicle, you and your party can decide if you want to end the bike portion of your trip or if you want to continue on two wheels.)

Start at the intersection of Route 6 and LeCount Hollow Road in South Wellfleet, where you can park at a small retail cluster (including a bike rental shop). Follow Lecount Hollow Road east for 1.0 mile to Maguire Landing, a town beach on the Atlantic. Enjoy a great panorama of the broad, blue Atlantic before heading north on the aptly named Ocean View Drive. On this scenic route, you have the ocean on your right and the scrub oak-pitch pine forest of the interior seashore on your left.

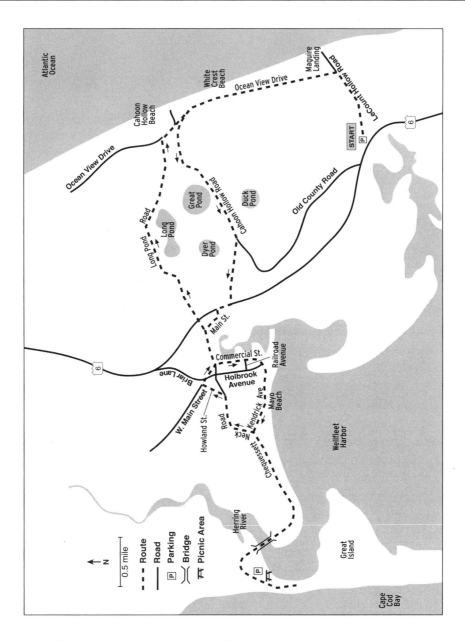

Pedaling Ocean View, you pass White Crest Beach (a surfer favorite) before reaching the entrance on the right to Cahoon Hollow Beach. (A hollow
is a valley or geological depression; some extend to form a natural break in
the seashore's cliff structure, where easy access to the shore prompted the

Built in 1844, Uncle Tim's Bridge was named for Timothy Daniels, an eccentric character who lived in the area.

creation of public beaches.) Cahoon Hollow Beach is one of the most popular beaches on the Cape, made more so by the Beachcomber, a legendary bar/restaurant/party spot.

From here, take Cahoon Hollow Road, which is a left turn from Ocean View Drive. After pedaling about 1.0 mile on undulating Cahoon Hollow Road, Great Pond appears on your right. Slow down and look for a bike rack. This pond always looks mighty inviting at the bottom of a pine-covered hill, and even more so when you're standing there, pond side.

One mile west of Great Pond, Cahoon Hollow Road reaches Route 6; take a right and follow Route 6 a couple hundred yards to a traffic light. Cross Route 6 and you are now on Main Street, leading to the town center. You pass tidal Duck Creek on your left and Duck Creek Pond on the right. From the south side of Main Street near this intersection, Commercial Street enters from the left (south). Follow Commercial Street on a leisurely pedal down to the harbor.

Along the way, you pass quaint Uncle Tim's Bridge, which leads to Hamblen Park; park your bike and cross the bridge over Duck Creek. You might even consider following the short loop around this small harbor-side park.

Back on your bike, you pass galleries, shops, and a funky corner café. As you cross Railroad Avenue, imagine the trestle that once carried Old Colony trains across the upper corner of the harbor and into town.

Go 0.25 mile farther, and the marina and commercial fishing pier loom. Park your bikes and walk around; you find a couple of seafood restaurants along this stretch are worth considering—their ambience alone is worth it. Proceed on Kendrick Avenue along Mayo Beach, where you might see aquaculture farmers tending to their shellfish in the shallows. Kendrick Avenue becomes Chequessett Neck Road, which crosses the broad mouth of the Herring River before climbing left to the parking lot for Great Island. From the marina to this outpost on the town's northwest shore, the distance is about 2.0 miles. The small pine woods and picnic area are the stepping-off point for those hiking Great Island, a 5.0-mile sand barrier that extends southward between Cape Cod Bay and Wellfleet Harbor.

If you're doing the full trip, this spot is a great place to break for lunch, with easy access to the upper harbor and great views of the bay-side coastscape. Pedaling back toward town, follow Chequessett Neck Road left at the fork with Kendrick Road, skipping the harbor and heading for the village center. After about 0.75 mile, turn left onto Howland Street, which intersects with Main Street at the far end of the village. Turn right here and proceed on Main Street past the library, more shops and galleries, a church, ice cream shops, upscale and family restaurants, and even a secondhand store. If you think this list is designed to pique interest, you're right. Get off the bikes and experience what this quaint community offers visitors and tourists.

Then pedal back up Main Street toward Route 6. Because your starting point in South Wellfleet is a straight shot south on this main road, you might be tempted to take it, despite the steady traffic and lack of bike lanes. However, I recommend taking the longer (and much more scenic) way home. But rather than head for Cahoon Hollow Road across Route 6, look for Long Pond Road on your left as you ascend Main from the village center. Take Long Pond Road out of town and cross the bridge that spans Route 6. In about 0.5 mi. Long Pond looms on the right, and a swim might be just the remedy from so much time in the saddle. Back on your bike, continue on Long Pond Road to where it intersects with Ocean View Road; take a right and pedal on Ocean View past Cahoon Hollow Road to where it terminates at LeCount Hollow Road. Follow LeCount Hollow back to the parking lot at Route 6. This route may be longer, but it also gives you multiple chances to hit the ponds and beaches one last time!

TRIP 35
OLD COUNTY ROAD TO CORN HILL

Rating: Moderate
Distance: 18.0 miles
Estimated Time: 4 hours
Location: Truro

Pedal the "back way" from Wellfleet into Truro and meander along country roads and byways, passing the old railroad bed, Truro Harbor, and the Pamet River.

Directions
Follow Route 6 North, past signs for Wellfleet Center and over the Herring River. Take a left on Pamet Point Road, just before entering Truro. Follow Pamet Point Road to a T intersection with Old County Road. Park off the right side of the road. If you are leaving another vehicle at Corn Hill: Follow Route 6 North into Truro, past Old Pamet Road on the left and a plant nursery/garden center. At the top of the hill, look for Castle Road on the left and a sign to Corn Hill (motel and cottages are at the corner). Take a left onto Castle Road and follow down a long hill to a T intersection with Corn Hill Road. Take a right on Corn Hill Road to a parking lot on the left.

Trip Description
This road actually extends from just north of Wellfleet Center where the winding route is West Main Street, before becoming Bound Brook Road and then Old County Road as it approaches Pamet Point Road. Old County Road ends at the Pamet River near Truro Center. But because this trip includes the river, Truro Harbor, Castle Road, and Corn Hill (and its beach) it does not include the Wellfleet section, to make the trip a reasonable length.

Before Route 6 pushed through, this was a main route from Wellfleet to Truro; today, it's the scenic way, although the summer vehicle traffic (lots of tourists) requires that cyclists use extra caution. From Old County Road's juncture with Pamet Point Road, pedal north on a twisty, sometimes hilly road that offers cyclists everything Route 6 cannot: fine scenery, less vehicular traffic, and a close-up experience with a remarkable "old Cape" landscape.

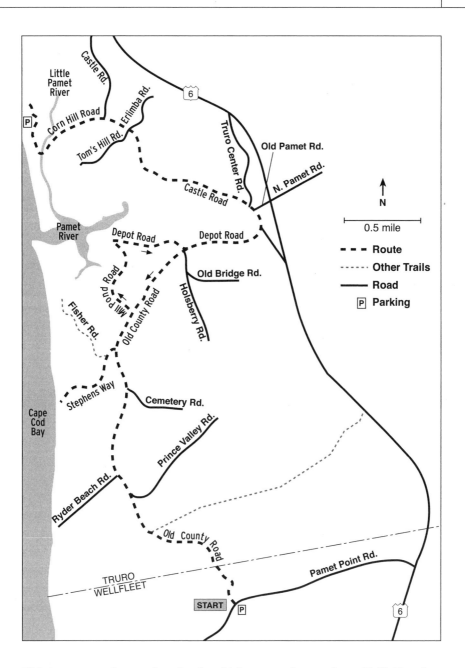

This is an area of coastal wetlands, old farms, and once-cleared hillsides that previously offered vistas of Cape Cod Bay but are now again covered with resurgent forests of scrub oak and pitch pine.

Pedaling north, you see a seemingly impenetrable marsh on your left. Almost immediately, you pass into Truro (note the difference in pavement), climbing short rises and enjoying the dips in the road. Old County Road soon jogs left, while a jeep track leads right. If you are on a mountain bike or hybrid, you can explore this unpaved route through Paradise Valley, a low-lying, semi-mystical hollow bracketed on both sides by resurgent woodlands. You can ride east all the way to Route 6, if you choose, but this off-track adventure is perhaps best saved for another day.

Back on Old County Road, follow its bends and turns until the paved Prince Valley Road enters from the right. Just ahead on your left, Ryder Beach Road leads you about 0.5 mile to a lovely Cape-side beach, Ryder Beach, the most southerly of Truro's public beaches on the bay. You might not yet have earned a wet and cooling respite from the bike, but I prefer Ryder Beach to the much-busier Fisher Beach, farther north. The route continues to undulate with the topography, with houses and newer residential development on your left. At this stretch of Old County Road, the road serves as the western border of Cape Cod National Seashore property; thus, much of the landscape to your right consists of woods and open areas marked by bearberry and other ground-hugging flora.

After about another 1.0 mile, Fisher Road enters from the left. This road not only leads to another terrific bayside beach, but also takes you through "Hopper Country." Painter Edward Hopper (1882–1967) lived and worked here for decades, capturing Cape light and the landscapes it illuminated in singular ways. A short way down Fisher Road, take a left onto Stephens Way. Climb up a rise, and, gazing west toward the bay, enjoy views of both the Cape-style house where Hopper lived and the surrounding dunes and coast that so inspired him.

Back on Fisher Road, either turn left and head out to the beach or return right to continue on Old County Road. Descending a hill on Old County Road, you pass on your left Phats Valley Road, named for a local character of the first half of the twentieth century, Anthony "Phat" Francis. Your next left is Mill Pond Road. Take Mill Pond Road left and follow it past Mill Pond and the inlet from the Pamet River that flows in from the left. For years, Mill Pond had been closed off from any tidal action, but a storm in the early 1990s brought in so much water from the bay that a passage was again opened.

Leaving the wetlands behind, you climb to Depot Road, but farther west. Turn left and you are soon at the harbor/marina area. Take in a remarkable panorama: To your left are the Truro Yacht Club and the main boat launch area. Straight ahead, the Pamet River flows through a channel and past a breakwater into Cape Cod Bay. The southern tip of Corn Hill Beach forms the north side of the channel. To your right is one of the Cape's most delightful views: the old rail bed (which crossed what is now the marina parking lot) picking up on the north side of the river; Tom's Hill; and, spreading for 0.5 mile to your right, the Pamet broad salt marsh.

The marsh that extends northward between the rail bed and the beach was the original harbor until storms and other tidal action altered it in the 1800s. Get back on the bikes and pedal Depot Road to the east. This road is also an undulating, meandering route, so keep an eye out for vehicle traffic. You pass the Mill Pond on your right before moving inland.

After less than 1.0 mile, Old County Road merges in at a stop sign. Continue on Depot Road. It terminates at Truro Center Road (Route 6 is straight ahead). Take a left on Truro Center Road and pedal past "downtown," which consists of a gourmet food shop/general store, post office, and, set back off the road, a small commercial strip. At the three-way intersection just ahead, bear left onto Castle Road. Begin to climb around Castle Hill and then up Tom's Hill, passing nice views of the upper Pamet marsh on your left. After cresting the hill (Tom's Hill Road on your left) proceed carefully down the other side, mindful of the descent and of traffic entering from Corn Hill Road on the right. On the downhill ride, you get a nice view of the Little Pamet River marsh and, in the distance, Corn Hill, topped by a row of former artist cottages.

With the Little Pamet River on your right, continue straight (Castle Road has become Corn Hill Road) 0.25 mile to where the road turns sharply right. Continue right, and the parking lot for Corn Hill Beach is immediately on your left. Corn Hill looms ahead, now pocked by vacation homes. At the northwest end of the parking lot is a plaque recounting how the hill got its name: A party from the Mayflower discovered a cache of corn at the base of the hill. The corn helped sustain them, and their desire to repay the local Payomet resulted in an invitation to share in a feast in November 1621—the first Thanksgiving.

If you didn't leave a car in the Corn Hill parking lot, return to Old County Road by following Corn Hill Road to Castle Road and Depot Road.

Rating: Easy to Moderate
Distance: Head of the Meadow Bike Path: 2.0 miles; Old King's
Highway to Coast Guard Road and Highland Light: 3.0 miles
Estimated Time: 4 hours
Location: North Truro

**Follow a paved bikeway along a former salt meadow, then ex-
plore the upland forest and wetlands that dominate the Cape
Cod National Seashore landscape between highway and ocean.
Finally, enjoy a visit to Highland Light.**

Directions
Take Route 6 through Truro, past Truro Vineyards on your left, and to Head
of the Meadow Road on your right. Follow to its terminus at the beach parking lots. The bike path begins just before you reach the parking lots (at a sign
and kiosk).

Trip Description
This excursion offers a pair of contrasting bike experiences that also allow
riders to share some of the National Seashore's most dramatic environments. You can begin with a flat, family-friendly cruise along the Head of
the Meadow Bike Path, which connects Truro's northernmost public beaches
on the ocean with Pilgrim Spring and High Head.

From the Head of the Meadow parking lot, pedal to its entrance and look
for the bike trail on your right, heading north, one of three paved recreation
paths managed by the National Park Service and the easiest. The Nauset
trail in Eastham is shorter, but with multiple twists and turns and hills. The
Province Lands network in Provincetown is a more ambitious undertaking
in every way.

Head of the Meadow is so named because it begins at the uppermost
edge of a large wetland extending southeastward from East Harbor (for-

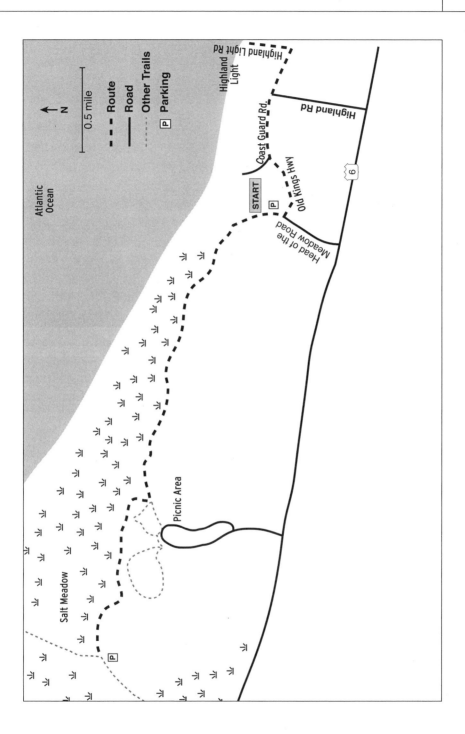

Atlantic
Ocean

N

0.5 mile

- - - Route
—— Road
.... Other Trails
P Parking

Highland Light Rd

Highland
Light

Coast Guard Rd.

Highland Rd

Old Kings Hwy

6

START

P

Head of the
Meadow Road

Picnic Area

Salt Meadow

P

Constructed in 1857, Highland Light is one of the oldest lighthouses in the nation.

merly known as Pilgrim Lake) on the Truro-Provincetown line. This thickly vegetated habitat was formerly a salt marsh nourished by the tidal flow emerging from the outer reaches of Provincetown Harbor into East Harbor. The meadow lost its daily saltwater nourishment when dikes were built at the bay and along the tidal creek at its far end; the habitat's upper portion turned brackish over the decades. As you begin your ride, you notice thick vegetation to your right and extending to the ocean dunes that is the result of human intervention. (In 2002, the dike under Route 6A at Beach Point was re-designed to partially restore tidal flow and today East Bay is welcoming marine life it hasn't hosted in more than a century.)

Take time to enjoy these surroundings: a wall of wetland flora on your right, an upland forest of oak and pine to your left. This mixed environment attracts myriad bird species, especially during spring and fall migration periods. At about 1.3 miles, you see a trail on the left leading to the National Seashore's Pilgrim Heights picnic area. You find no bike access here, but the small park area and trail network is worth a visit. Even if you decide against ascending the trail to the picnic area, you can't miss a small spring just off the bikeway. The plaque reads that this was the site of the first fresh water the Pilgrims discovered during a desperate exploration of their new surroundings in November 1620. Known as "Pilgrim Spring," the historic shrine is today considered suspect to researchers and the story more legend than fact. Pilgrim Heights has great value to birders, who set up their scopes from vantage points on the bluff overlooking the meadow. Many species of raptors, from bald eagles to an uncommon (in these parts) Mississippi kite. More common sightings include red-tailed hawks and northern harriers, the latter cruising low and silently over the marsh and adjacent dunes.

Follow the bike trail to its terminus at the High Head parking lot. A sand road heads right, providing an access route for surf anglers and off-roaders. A gravel road leads from the parking lot to Route 6; cycling it is a challenge. You can carefully cross Route 6 to 6A (Beach Point) here, but your best bet, especially if you are with your family, is returning along the bike path to the Head of the Meadow parking lot. You can end your trip here. Or, if the bikeway was just a warm-up for a more adventurous, off-road experience, continue back down Head of the Meadow Road a short distance to where a dirt road forks in from the left.

Old King's Highway is the name for a former travel route dating to colonial times, tracing the spine of the Cape. Today, it survives as a haven for cyclists (on mountain bikes and hybrids), locals who live and work in the area, and vacationers seeking to give their SUVs a bit of a workout. (Be sure to carry a topographical map in these areas, because the dirt tracks and fire roads—none with names—can be confusing to newcomers.) Pedal the "highway," hilly in places, through an expansive woodland of scotch pine and black and white oak, about 0.5 mile to where it bears left and emerges at another paved route, Coast Guard Road.

Take a right and proceed south to where signs on your left indicate the entrance road to the Highland House, a former tourist hotel and now the museum of the Truro Historical Society. Here you can find a repository of Outer Cape history and culture both quaint and sophisticated in its scope—definitely worth a visit. Next door sprawl the fairways and greens of the Highland Links golf course, a classic seaside layout where you battle wind and salt spray as much as sand traps.

At the end of the road rises the lighthouse known as Highland Light, formally known as Cape Cod Light, the first such navigational beacon built on this 60-mile sand hook and noted by Thoreau and other writers. Erosion on the dune cliff supporting the lighthouse prompted National Seashore authorities to move it inland in 1996; given the wild and unpredictable natural forces of this environment, the light's long-term future is uncertain. Tours are conducted regularly.

To return to your car, pedal along Coast Guard Road to where Old King's Highway enters on your left and continue to Head of the Meadow Road.

TRIP 37
PROVINCE LANDS BIKE TRAIL

Rating: Moderate
Distance: 9.0 miles
Estimated Time: 3 hours
Location: Cape Cod National Seashore, Provincetown

Pedal through one of the wildest—and most starkly beautiful—natural environments on the East Coast.

Directions

At the Race Point Road/Conwell Street Exit on Route 6 in Provincetown (watch for Race Point signs), turn right onto Race Point Road. Follow for about 1.5 miles and turn right up the driveway to Province Lands Visitor Center, just prior to the Province Lands Road intersection. Province Lands Road enters a couple hundred yards after the entrance to the visitor center.

Trip Description

The visitor center sits at the crest of a hill, and from the parking lot the views of the surrounding Province Lands are impressive: miles of undulating sand dune covered with small forests of pitch pine and scrub oak, bayberry and wild cranberry, poison ivy and beach grass. This harsh landscape is nature's response to the gradual depletion of the original hardwood forest for settlers' housing, fuel, and industry; by 1800 most of the original forest of the Outer Cape was gone. When the deeper-rooted trees went, so did the topsoil, ultimately replaced by sand and sandy soil and the tough flora that could thrive in this dry and exposed environment.

For an even better overview, climb to the center's observation deck for a 360-degree panorama that takes in Provincetown, the Atlantic Ocean, and Cape Cod Bay; Herring Cove and Race Point at the western tip of the Cape; the Atlantic Ocean to the north; and looking eastward and southeastward, the dune shacks that have drawn artists, dreamers, and nature lovers for generations. Between your vantage point and these distance markers spread the Province Lands, and snaking among them, the bike trail that leads you into their very heart.

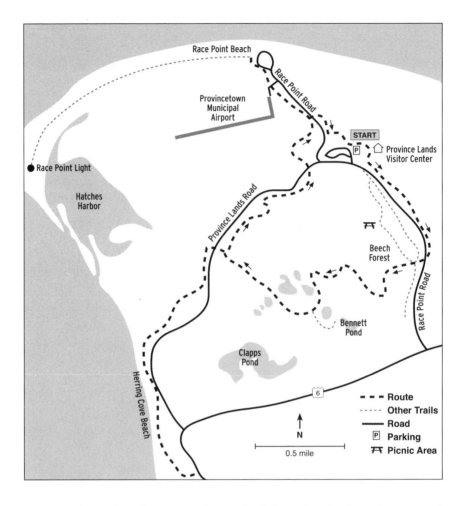

From the parking lot, turn right on the bike path, which can be accessed between the visitor center and the outdoor amphitheater. Descend a hill and you are pedaling parallel to Race Point Road, on your right. After 1.0 mile, the path turns right to cross the road. On the west side, you enter the parking lot for the Beech Forest, a lovely natural refuge home to some of the relatively few remaining hardwood trees in this outer region of the National Seashore. You find a picnic area here, as well as a loop trail skirting a pair of small ponds, well worth your consideration.

The bike trail continues southwest of the Beech Forest area and passes one of the ponds before moving deeper into the Province Lands. Just over a mile after departing the Beech Forest parking area, you find signs directing you left to Bennett Pond, about 0.25 mile away. I have taken this short spur to the pond and have been unimpressed each time. Great habitat for turtles and thick pond vegetation, but not much else, and the views are modest.

Save your energy for the 1.0 mile-long spur to Herring Cove Beach, which can be pedaled by taking a left at the next intersection. Herring Cove Beach is popular with bathers, anglers, and lovers of sunsets; at peak season the beach is swarming with people taking pictures as the sun sets beyond the western horizon. The beach also features a bathhouse and rest room complex.

Return northeast along the same spur and continue the loop that leads back to the visitor center. This stretch of the bike trail is the hilliest; prepare to use your brakes to control speed on the downhills, because the descents include turns and tight tunnels under the road. On the ascents, just imagine the views that await you at the crest of the hill: ocean, wild dune lands, the Pilgrim Monument in downtown Provincetown. (Walking your bike is also acceptable, of course.)

When you reach Race Point Road, you can see the visitor center on a rise just beyond, signaling you've almost completed the loop. You can take satisfaction in knowing you enjoyed some healthy exercise and got a close-up look at one of New England's most spectacular landscapes. But your journey doesn't have to be over just yet; rather than crossing the road for the short pedal back up to the parking area, continue north on the bike trail, keeping Race Point Road on your right.

This flat stretch leads to Race Point Beach, another popular destination for swimmers and sun lovers, but also the site of Old Harbor Life-Saving Station. Located a short walk east of the beach entrance, it was originally built in Chatham, but it was moved here in the 1970s to save it from washing into the Atlantic from its perch along Chatham's shoreline. It was once manned by hardy rescuers who would launch their heavy wooden surfboats (hauled from the station by horse and wagon) into frightful weather and waves to save sailors from ships wrecked on the Cape's infamous shoals. Today it serves as a museum dedicated to sharing the life-saving story. It's open most afternoons during the summer months, and is also the site of a popular historical reenactment of a rescue drill.

If you have time and energy, consider the 2.0 mile walk in the other direction along the beach or sand road to Race Point Lighthouse, located at the westernmost tip of the Cape, where the bay meets the Atlantic Ocean. If the weather is clear and the water is calm, you might spy whales spouting just

Be sure to wear the proper safety gear when cycling.

offshore; they come north each spring and summer with their young to feed in the rich waters of the bay and Stellwagen Bank, just to the north.

From the Race Point parking lot, take one last look around at the memorable panoramas before taking the 0.5 mile bike trail spur back to the cutoff (left) leading back to the visitor center. Along the way, notice the Provincetown airport on your right. If planes are taking off and landing, it's worth waiting a few minutes to watch one pass low overhead.

Consider stepping inside the visitor center, where the National Park Service presents lectures, films, and ecological demonstrations. You also find a worthy selection of books, offering works from Henry David Thoreau and Henry Beston, as well as more contemporary books on the region and the nature of the Cape by authors including John Hay, Robert Finch, and Annie Dillard.

3

Paddling Cape Cod

THE CAPE WAS CREATED FOR STRIPED BASS and horseshoe crabs, osprey and shorebirds—and paddlers. For generations, canoeists have been seen riding the tide up coastal streams, challenging the waves of windy bays, or placidly casting a line from the middle of a pond. Now that the public's recreation imagination has been captured by kayaks—lighter, faster, easier to maneuver than canoes—more paddlers than ever seem to migrate, shorebird-like, to Cape Cod during the warm months.

All paddlers must be able to swim, and you need to have some basic experience in a boat. Looking for paddling lessons? Kayak outfitters up and down the Cape rent boats, teach, and conduct tours (one source for outfitters can be found at www.capecodrec.com).

These trips range from leisurely paddles across serene ponds and along meandering tidal creeks to more ambitious coastal excursions. All are designed to have you back at your starting point within 4 hours or less.

But whether you go out for a half-hour or a half-day, the wildlife-viewing opportunities you encounter are magical. You might see great blue herons rising from a marsh, gray seals sunning on a beach, fish slapping the surface, and perhaps a deer or coyote watching from a woodland border. You might want to keep a waterproof camera handy to preserve those memories!

Safety and Etiquette

While paddling on Cape Cod is a fairly safe activity, cold and deep waters require certain safety precautions. To ensure a safe and comfortable paddling experience, consider the following safety tips:

- Know how to use your canoe or kayak. Small ponds and other protected waters are the perfect place for inexperienced paddlers to learn, but if you are new to the sport, have someone show you some basic tips on paddling strokes and how to enter and exit your boat.
- If you are going to paddle the coast, know the tides and currents. And never paddle in foggy conditions, hoping the sun will burn through.
- Turn around before the members of your party start feeling tired. Paddling a few miles after your arms are spent—especially against wind and current—can diminish a trip's enjoyment.
- Make sure everyone in your group is wearing a life jacket or personal flotation device (PFD) that fits properly and securely. By Massachusetts law, it's *mandatory* for children under 12. *It's also mandatory that all paddlers wear PFDs, except between May 15 and September 15.* Ocean and bay water remains cold well into early summer, and immersion can quickly result in hypothermia.
- Be cautious around powerboats and sailboats; do not assume they can see you. Turn your bow into the wakes of passing vessels to avoid swamping.
- Be aware of wind, current, and the rising waves they can trigger. Carry a waterproof windbreaker and avoid cotton clothing, which retains moisture and clings to the skin when wet.
- Always know the weather forecast for your trip's location and pay heed. If you hear or read the phrase *small craft warnings*, this means you. Stay off the water if thunderstorms are nearby. Lightning is a serious danger to boaters. If you hear a thunderstorm approaching, get off the water immediately and seek shelter.
- Bring the following supplies along with you to make the trip more comfortable:
  - ✓ Two quarts of water per person, depending on the weather and length of the trip
  - ✓ Sunblock (apply beforehand and during) and a broad-brimmed hat
  - ✓ Sunglasses
  - ✓ Even for a short trip, bring some high-energy snacks like nuts, dried fruit, or snack bars. For a longer one, pack a lunch.
  - ✓ Map and compass—and the ability to use them
  - ✓ Extra clothing—weatherproof windbreaker, fleece, extra hat
  - ✓ First-aid kit

✓ Pocketknife

✓ Binoculars

In addition to the Leave No Trace principles described earlier in this book, please keep the following things in mind while paddling:

- Give all wildlife a wide berth. Coastal environments leave fauna much more exposed, from wading birds and plodding horseshoe crabs to dozing seals. Numerous people are on the water during the summer months, and birds waste a good deal of energy just swimming or flying away from curious boaters. Do not walk up to groups of shorebirds and make them take flight to avoid you.

  Remember: Endangered piping plovers are a protected species and harassing them is a federal crime. If you spot wildlife, remain still and quiet and let the animals decide whether or not to approach you. Use binoculars if you want a closer view.

- Respect private property. Do not land your boat on private property, and speak quietly when paddling near homes and cottages.

- Respect the purity of the water. Some Cape Cod ponds and streams are part of watersheds that provide drinking and bathing water for residents. If you need to relieve yourself, find land at least 200 yards from the shoreline.

TRIP 38
WAQUOIT BAY AND WASHBURN ISLAND

Rating: Moderate
Distance: 5.0 miles
Estimated Time: 4 hours
Location: Mashpee and Falmouth

Paddle across a spectacular South Cape estuary to a barrier island where you can spend an hour or two—or stay overnight. Enter the placid world of a salt pond, and observe nature at its most profound.

Directions

From Route 6 east, take Exit 5, Route 149, and proceed south to its terminus with Route 28. Go right on Route 28 approximately 5.0 miles to the Mashpee rotary. Take the last right around the rotary onto Great Neck Road (which becomes Great Oak Road) for 4.5 miles. Look for a sign designating a boat landing on the right just beyond Tide Run Road. Access is at the tidal Great River.

Trip Description

This complex of coastal habitats, dominated by 825-acre Waquoit Bay, offers some of the best paddling and nature watching on Cape Cod. Many people, even in-the-know outdoors types, consider busy Route 28 and the southern stretch of the Cape it passes through to represent development sprawl, cheesy tourism, and vacation kitsch. But Waquoit Bay's serene environment and many similar oases of nature from Falmouth to Chatham put the lie to that uninformed notion.

It helps, of course, that the bay and much of its surrounding shore and uplands are part of the Waquoit Bay National Estuarine Research Reserve, managed by federal and state environmental agencies. This federally funded scientific and education center studies coastal flora and fauna, as well as the natural and human processes that affect coastal environments—including the Cape, of course. Without the Reserve, much of what we all enjoy here might have been lost to the public forever.

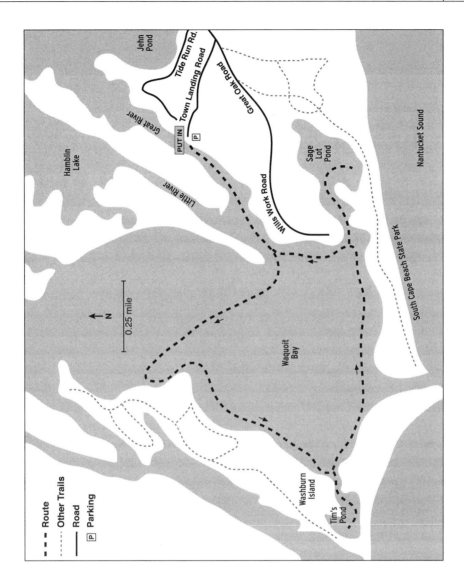

Launch into the Great River and head left toward open water. The Little River, a companion tidal stream, joins from the right almost immediately. Waquoit Bay opens before you where the blended river squeezes between two necks of land. Add a few strokes on the port (left) side and swing west, leaving the sandy finger on Seconset Island to starboard (right). Make your way straight across the broad sparkling bay, where Washburn Island looms about 1.0 mile distant.

The bay is wide but hardly deep, the result of shoal-creating sand that flows in on the tides from Nantucket Sound; the maximum depth is 8.9 feet. Washburn Island is a worthy destination, whether you are a first-time visitor, occasional explorer, or among those who consider its beaches, great swimming, and lovely vistas their own private deserted island (proprietary thoughts that are totally understandable, by the way).

In fact, the 335-acre island faced a resort development threat until the state stepped in to save it in the early 1980s. Upon reaching Washburn, haul up your boat(s) and go exploring. Follow trails and old government roads through a feisty woodland habitat of pitch pine and scrub oak, among the few trees species than can handle the harsh winds and salt spray of this exposed barrier beach. Better yet, if you're making this trip during the warm-weather months, go for a swim. These shallow waters of the sound, which heat up all summer, are some of the most welcoming on the Cape.

Feel free to be jealous of those who are enjoying the eleven shore-side campsites (reserve in advance through the Massachusetts Department of Conservation and Recreation). You find no facilities on Washburn—bring in and carry out everything you need—but if you appreciate rustic camping in a spectacular coastal location, this experience is hard to beat.

Return to your boats and paddle southwest, keeping the island to starboard. Washburn Island forms a "forearm" to encircle Waquoit Bay from the west and at the crease of the island's elbow, a tidal inlet beckons. Here at Tim's Pond, you see cordgrass waving in the breeze, and maybe see kingfishers or great blue herons. This habitat also attracts bluefish and striped bass, which corral small fish in the shallows of the pond and the bay.

Take time to enjoy fine views of Martha's Vineyard rising only 7.0 miles to the southwest. (The Vineyard can boast plenty of lovely beaches and secluded destinations, but from your vantage point on this island, you can't mistake who's in the lovelier spot.)

As you begin your return trip, watch for powerboat traffic zipping in and out of the channel that marks where the bay meets the sound; it can get pretty lively at this entry and exit point. A lot of water moves through the channel, especially at mid-tide, so mind the currents, winds, and other elements than can affect your paddling in such an exposed environment. (Do not turn right and pass through the channel: Nantucket Sound can turn mean without notice, and only experienced sea kayakers who know these waters should consider such an excursion.)

Waquoit Bay, with an area of approximately 825 acres, is the dominant feature of the Waquoit Bay National Estuarine Research Reserve.

After you reach the east side of the channel, you pass the tip of South Cape Beach, another large natural feature of the Reserve, popular with vacationers and locals alike—again, worth a stop, especially because at this far end of the beach, your only company might be a few other boaters or gulls. Back in your boat, continue east, keeping the long spit of South Cape beach to starboard. In about 0.5 mile, you spy the entrance to another salt pond. Follow a meandering channel that continues east before hooking south (right) into Sage Lot Pond. This pretty little salt pond does not see much traffic, except for wading birds and shorebirds, from egrets and herons to plovers and other sandpipers. They all feast on the bounty of small fish, shellfish, and wrackline organisms.

This pond, located so close to the channel at the sound, has a tendency to shoal up, so be sure the water will be deep enough (check a tide chart) to explore it and the tidal creek without scraping bottom. An exploration of Sage Lot Pond can provide a very enjoyable side trip toward the end of your Waquoit Bay excursion. Paddle back out to the bay, turn right, and then bear right again into Great River. Keep to starboard where the river splits, and the landing soon appears on the right.

Waquoit Bay National Estuarine Research Reserve

Waquoit Bay might best be recognized from the air. When you approach the Cape's south-facing shore from Nantucket Sound, look for the coastscape that resembles a pair of crab claws about to meet and that shelters a broad body of water. Welcome to the Waquoit Bay National Estuarine Research Reserve, which encompasses more than 2,500 acres of protected coastal waters and surrounding land in Falmouth and Mashpee.

The large arm reaching in from the east is South Cape Beach, a popular recreational destination for swimmers and saltwater anglers. The smaller appendage that forms the west border of the bay is Washburn Island, formerly a private island. It performs the neat trick of being both accessible and semi-remote. Located just a clam shell's toss off the mainland in East Falmouth, the 335-acre mix of sandy shore and dune, pine-and-oak woods, and salt can be reached only by boat, but plenty of powerboaters and paddlers do reach it this way.

The island is a worthy destination not only for hikers, picnickers, beachcombers and other day-trippers, but also for overnighters: 11 primitive (no flush toilets, showers, or fresh water) campsites, and almost 2 miles of trails.

What exactly is an estuary? It's the confluence of salt water and fresh water meeting in a semi-sheltered natural environment—such as a bay. An estuary is flushed and nourished by the tides, but it is protected from direct ocean impacts, thanks, in Waquoit's case, to the barriers of Washburn Island and South Cape Beach. Estuaries are remarkably rich and productive, serving as nurseries for hundreds of fish and shellfish species.

The Quashnet River, which enters the bay from Falmouth and provides much of the estuary's fresh water from the mainland Cape, is a part of the Reserve that shelters a special fish: sea-run trout. Known as "salters" these fish are an uncommon sub-species of brook trout that spend their lives in both the stream and the bay.

The public is welcome to many places within the Reserve, but you should know the Reserve's primary mission is scientific research, education, and preservation and that some areas might be off limits to visitors. My wife and I made this discovery when we sought to access the beach in front of Reserve headquarters, located right off Route 28 on a former private estate. Signs were up that specific scientific programs were taking place, and we were out of luck.

The Reserve headquarters is located in a former mansion that was home in the late nineteenth century to the Sargent family, whose spectacular seaside estate this was. A modern visitor center explains the Reserve's work through exhibits, brochures, and other displays. Designated a member of the National Estuarine Research Reserve System in 1988, Waquoit Bay is managed by the National Oceanic and Atmospheric Administration and the state Department of Conservation and Recreation. As development continues to pressure the Cape, chemicals and other impacts are showing up in coastal waters and in fish, birds, and mammals that depend on these habitats. The Reserve is working hard to understand and combat these and other threats to the Cape. A trip to the trails and the delightful places they take you to within the Reserve should be on the list of every visitor who values a connection to nature.

My wife and I did not leave without one especially vivid memory. A boisterous osprey chick in a nest near the parking lot kept both parents on a busy feeding schedule; it seemed as soon as one returned with a fish for the youngster, the other adult was hovering overhead, prepared to deliver its scaly offering. With the raptors' hunting grounds, the bay, located only a few flap of wings away, it was no surprise they were finding plenty of food for the next generation.

The bay itself is large for this part of Cape Cod—more than 800 acres—but shallow, averaging 6 feet or less in depth. Its shallowness might be the result of sand washing in from Nantucket Sound on the twice-daily tides. You can learn more about these natural processes and others by enrolling in family activities and community programs, seasonal education initiatives to better inform visitors and locals about just how critical places such as Waquoit Bay are to all of our lives.

TRIP 39
SCORTON CREEK AND MARSH

Rating: Easy to Moderate
Distance: 3.0 miles
Estimated Time: 3 hours
Location: Sandwich

Experience one of the Upper Cape's prettiest tidal streams, and paddle from uplands and woods south of Route 6A through broad marshes to Cape Cod Bay.

Directions
From Route 6 east, take Exit 3 and proceed north on Quaker Meetinghouse Road to Route 6A. Turn right and follow about 1.5 miles to a dirt-road entrance at a state wildlife management area, just before passing over Scorton Creek. Drive up the dirt road to parking at the creek.

Trip Description
From the easy access to the creek to the gentle current and the lovely salt marsh vistas, this section of Scorton Creek offers a fine experience for families and newer paddlers. Put in and paddle inland, away from the Route 6A bridge. You soon find yourself immersed in the massive salt marsh habitat extending eastward into Barnstable and its large harbor. You can no longer paddle through the bulk of the marsh to reach Barnstable Harbor—development has seen to that—but this upper stretch above your put-in point allows you and your party to practice strokes and get used to your boats while enjoying fine salt marsh scenery.

Toward your right is a trio of smaller waterways, including Mill Creek and Jenny's Dam River, where settlers utilized tidal currents to power early industries. Be sure to consult a tide chart when exploring these upper stretches of Scorton Creek and plan your trip for about an hour before high tide—you don't want to get caught without water. (This way, you can paddle these upper stretches and then turn around and ride the tide back out to Cape Cod Bay.)

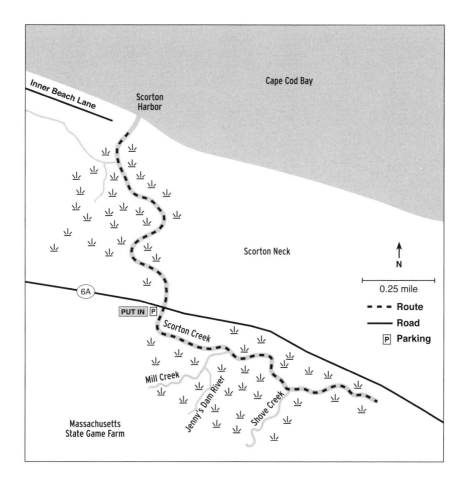

I've walked my dog on the right bank of this part of the property, called Talbot's Point, which sits between Jenny's Dam River and the last inlet a couple hundred yards farther east, Shove Creek. State and local conservation agencies have worked hard to keep this open space preserved; trails and cart paths lead you through an environment of resurgent woodlands, former pastures, and salt marsh. You can see the remains of old sluiceways and mill works, and other remnants of eighteenth- and nineteenth-century rural industry.

East of Shove Creek, the effects of twentieth-century development have impeded the water flow; don't get caught in the shallows. You might want to consider turning around after you pass Shove Creek. As you paddle west and

You will experience smooth paddling on this calm waterway.

then north toward the coast, you pass the put-in on your left (last chance to grab more supplies from your vehicle) and soon approach the Route 6A bridge. The creek broadens here and deepens; be alert for adventurous types (mostly teens) jumping from the bridge into the water. Paddling north of Route 6A, you again find yourself surrounded by cordgrass and the peat-like hummocks that compose the marsh. Look for great blue herons and bone-white egrets stalking small fish and crabs.

Spend some time in this broad estuarine environment, crucial to the health of so many species. Swallows dip and rise, plucking insects from the sky. Small fish jump, chased upstream by striped bass and other hungry predators. Horseshoe crabs slowly plow through the sand and mud, seeking mates, while fiddler crabs scurry about just above the water line, ready to duck into their holes at an approaching footfall—or shadow overhead.

The waterway makes a few twists and turns before smaller creeks enter from the left and the right. Straight ahead, the main artery meets Cape Cod Bay at Scorton Harbor. This is exposed water: Both wind and tide can play havoc with your boats, and the mouth has been known to shoal up with sand from the open bay.

TRIP 40
SWAN POND RIVER

Rating: Easy to Moderate
Distance: 2.0 miles
Estimated Time: 2 hours (depending on tide/wind)
Location: Dennis

**This striking mid-Cape tidal waterway wends through broad
salt marsh and past busy Route 28 on its way to Nantucket
Sound.**

Directions

From Route 6 east, take Exit 9A onto Route 134 in Dennis. Follow it south
0.75 mile to Searsville Road. Go left on Searsville, and then take a quick right
onto Upper County Road. Follow Upper County Road 1.0 mile to the bridge
over Swan Pond River and parking.

Trip Description

This quiet tidal river extending from Nantucket Sound to Swan Pond near
the Dennis-Harwich border offers a delightful introduction to the natural
attractions of the mid-Cape. Situated between the larger Bass River to the
west, the largest mid-Cape waterway, and Harwich's Herring River to the
east, less developed and more popular with birders and other nature lovers,
this modest waterway welcomes beginner and experienced paddlers alike.

The Swan Pond River also passes through some of the most striking
conservation land in the mid-Cape region. Look for gulls, cormorants, and
geese, but also more eye-appealing species including osprey, great blue herons, merganser ducks, and hovering high overhead, osprey.

What I most enjoy about this trip, however, is its length. From Route 28
north to Upper County Road is 1.0 mile (or less), including the meanders and
almost-oxbows of the river—truly ideal for newer paddlers and adults with
children. My wife's family kept a small cottage off Route 28 in Dennis for
some years, and the river became a familiar and favorite environment to me.
I learned a lot about Cape Cod ecology and coastal habitats from paddling

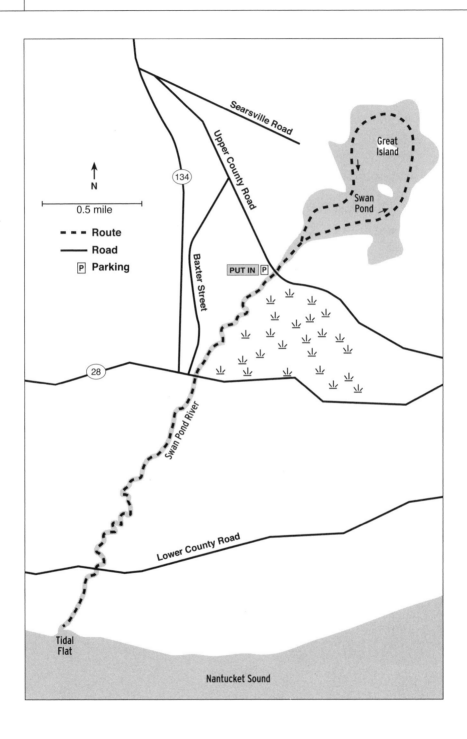

this river and noticing that the small streets ending at its banks bore names such as Scoter, Cygnet, and Mayflower, educating me and other paddlers about the native plant and bird species that are part of this rich coastal environment.

This trip description focuses on the stretch of river between Upper County Road and Route 28, but the waterway north and south of these roads also has much to recommend it. Paddling north beyond the restaurant, you pass through pretty uplands before Otter Creek enters from the right. You can explore this short inlet, but it grows narrow and shallow fairly quickly (the tidal action affects the river even this far north). After another 0.5 mile, you enter the stream's source Swan Pond. Paddle up the pond and around Great Island to extend your trip before returning to the Upper County Road Bridge.

Although fewer boats are encountered the closer you paddle to Swan Pond, making for a more serene experience, I've always preferred the southerly end of the river, which gently wends it way from Route 28 to Nantucket Sound. The scenery is much the same you enjoy when paddling north from Route 28, but the closer you get to the Sound, the stronger the action of the tidal current, especially as you near Lower County Road. Know when the tide is on this portion of the river, about 1.0 mile south of Route 28, so you can time your trip to take full advantage.

On a strong outgoing tide, you may find no paddling is necessary—you and your boat just go with the flow, the banks narrowing and forming a channel that turns your trip into an amusement park ride. But be aware of swimmers and youngsters on inflatables; you pass a popular beach that spreads to the right, as well as a breakwater. The sand shoals and the (sometimes) strong current can combine to present a tricky combination of shallows and deep spots. When you haul out your boat, make sure you're not over a hidden pool, or you'll be over your head before your feet touch bottom.

And if you have paddled as far as the Sound, hauling out is definitely recommended. As the tide recedes, a sandbar appears that's perfect for parking kayaks or canoes for an hour or two. This shoreline offers plenty of warm, shallow water on the beachfront. You encounter no surf to speak of, meaning the beach is very child friendly, although the wind can occasionally blow from across the sound. At low tide, you can walk out across the sandy shallows seemingly to the horizon. To your right, West Dennis Beach extends to

The Swan Pond River offers a delightful paddle all the way to Nantucket Sound.

Bass River, with the south Yarmouth shoreline beyond. Looking left, you can see a string of old-time Dennisport beach properties, a campground, small motels, and larger, ornate resort hotels.

And if you chose to paddle this southern-most stretch of the river when the tide is against you, you want to make sure to hop back into your boat(s) when the tide is moving strongly inland and enjoy a nifty push back up-stream, all the way to Route 28. As noted previously, the Swan Pond River offers an ideal paddling for newer boaters, but you might want to experience it over several trips. The Route 28-Upper County Road excursion is a great introduction.

TRIP 41
HERRING RIVER

Rating: Moderate
Distance: 7.0 miles
Estimated Time: 3 hours
Location: West Harwich

Paddle away from busy Route 28 on a winding tidal river, into a world of broad marshlands stalked by wading birds, tall grasses waving in the breeze, and uplands of woods and cranberry bogs.

Directions

From Route 6 east, take Exit 10 South (Route 124) to where it meets Route 139 at Harwich Center. Follow Route 139 south to the terminus with Route 28, and go right on Route 28 for 1.0 mile to the launch ramp on the left at the river.

Trip Description

This mid-Cape tidal river and marsh complex is one of the most beautiful in Massachusetts, nurturing myriad species of flora and fauna and protected by more than 200 acres of town conservation land. The main stem of the river is interrupted by two dirt roads and a dike, above which spread an expansive freshwater marsh and West Reservoir, itself a popular destination with birders, paddlers, and other outdoors enthusiasts.

From the launch site, put in and paddle right, under the Route 28 bridge and upstream. Launch a little before slack tide; you won't get much of an assist on your upstream passage, but you'll still have plenty of water—and a nice outgoing current—on the return. Pass a few docks and piers, some more rickety than others, some with handsome boats tied up, others looking a little lonely. Unlike most other villages of Harwich, the Route 28 stretch through town is fairly touristy and always busy, but the noise and bustle is left behind within minutes of paddling through a substantial salt marsh. Look for cordgrass growing tall where the tide nurtures this salt marsh plant

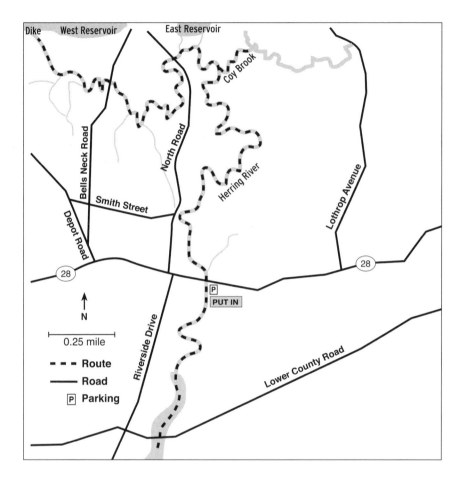

twice every 24 hours, as well as hardy marsh elder and salt meadow grass, where the tides reach less frequently.

Depending on the height of tide, you can see fiddler crabs skittering along the mud banks, chasing off rivals while being hunted by herons, egrets, and other formidable winged predators. To port, you begin to see North Road, a dirt roadway running parallel to the river. Almost immediately the stream forks, with the main stem continuing westward, under the bridge, where the river forms the south boundary of Bell's Neck, a popular birding area. Bear to starboard (right) and enter a smaller stream that is part of a large marsh habitat extending eastward to Lothrop Avenue.

This is Coy Brook, a classic tidal creek bounded by salt and brackish marsh on both sides. After about 0.5 mile, the brook gradually peters out

A paddle on Herring River will take you past cordgrass.

into a system of narrow shallows. Return to the main stem of the river, and continue west, upstream, past a small channel leading to East Reservoir. You're entering the heart of Harwich cranberry bog territory here—both East and West Reservoirs were designed to supply the bogs with water for cranberry production. The river snakes south and then east, as if to back on itself into an oxbow, but soon rights course and continues west to Bell's Neck Road. You pass through a brackish/freshwater marsh here, including a substantial colony of cattails. This is essentially a freshwater environment, several miles inland from the Sound. In addition to cattails, look for red (or swamp) maple, tupelo and other taller, stouter hardwoods, and grasses and smallish shrubs intolerant of salt water and tidal flow.

When paddling tidal waters, I always hope for sightings of great blue heron, great and snowy egrets, and other salt marsh waders. But this far upstream on the Herring River you can spot chattering kingfishers, swooping swallows, and even ivory-white mute swans, which have built nests along this portion of the river. Watch also for osprey crying and soaring overhead.

If you're fortunate, you might see one flutter above the water before pulling in its wings and diving for a hapless fish that has ventured too close to the surface. These fierce raptors are not the only hunters small fish need be wary about. Young striped bass, most of them shorter than the 28-inch size minimum for anglers and called "schoolies," chase herring and other baitfish up the river or else lie in wait for fish to come back down river on an ebbing tide.

You can paddle farther upriver to where you reach a dike, and from there continue with a portage into West Reservoir, but we suggest turning around here, if only to make sure you have good water for the return trip. (It should be noted the dike features a fish ladder to provide for the annual herring migration and an overflow culvert, making the crossing potentially difficult for newer paddlers and families.)

On the return trip to the Route 28 launch site, enjoy a leisurely paddle, aided by the ebbing tide. Indeed, when no breeze is coming off Nantucket Sound, at the Herring River's mouth, you can use your paddle solely as a tiller, to help steer your way around the bends and twists in the stream.

When you reach the put-in at Route 28, your trip still might not be over. Here, where the river broadens on its way to the Sound about 1.0 mile father south, paddlers find another fine excursion—depending on the tide and height of water. Pass south through much the same natural environment you did when you first paddled upstream, beyond the Route 28 bridge—salt marsh and meadow leading to homes on the river bank.

Pass under Lower County Road and approach the exposed mouth of the river, where wind and wave can create challenging conditions. Turn around before the river reaches the Sound. Paddle back upstream to Route 28 and offer congratulations all around for several hours well spent on a premier New England tidal stream. And because a couple of restaurants are within walking distance of the boat launch, you and your party can review the trip over a good meal.

TRIP 42
THE RIVER AND POCHET

$

Rating: Moderate
Distance: 4.0 miles
Estimated Time: 4 hours
Location: Orleans

From its source at Meeting House Pond, the tidal waterway known as The River widens and narrows as it flows southward to meet Little Pleasant Bay. Be sure to explore the tide creeks of Pochet on the return trip.

Directions
From Route 6 east, take Exit 12. Turn right onto Route 6A and then right again at the first set of lights onto Eldredge Parkway. Continue through intersection with Route 28 and then turn right onto Main Street. Bear right onto River Road and proceed a 0.5 mile to the landing just below the mouth of Meeting House Pond.

Trip Description
From the River Road launch, paddle downstream a short distance to where it merges with Meeting House Pond on the left. You might want to explore this small, relatively shallow basin first, to settle into your boat and get in some warm-up strokes (if you've launched at the pond, mission accomplished). Beyond the pond, Lucy's Point snubs out from port and leads to a small salt marsh, home to shellfish and wading birds. (A point about the tide: It reaches high tide here about two hours later than it does on the ocean front, so note the conditions. If you're hoping for an easy ride down The River and are not planning on spending several hours, you'll probably be fighting the ebb on the return trip. But if you begin when the tide has half retreated, you might be on the water long enough to pick up the returning tide on the way back. It's nice to have it both ways.)

Frostfish Cove soon appears to starboard. The name is connected to the tomcod fish that would appear in autumn, just around the time of the year's

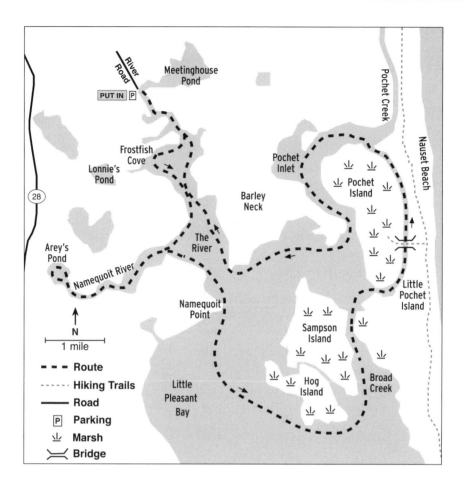

first frost. The cove is situated near an Orleans conservation area, Kent's Point, and well worth a pullout and walk-around. A trail system extends from the cove south to the entrance of Lonnie's Pond (also called Kescayogansett). It's a nice view from land, but better by sea. Return to your boat and paddle down the small inlet leading to Lonnie's Pond. At the far end is another public launch ramp, but with very limited parking.

Back on The River, you pass through a narrows marked by Jackknife Point to port and Lickey's Point to starboard. At Lickey's Point, the Namequoit River leads about 0.5 mile into Arey's Pond, a scenic little cove that's home to a marina and the famed Arey's Pond boatyard, which turns out beautiful catboats, most from 12 to 20 feet in length. You see them making their way down The River into Little Pleasant Bay. Paddle up the Namequoit River, but be prepared for a bit of a breeze funneling through the relatively narrow passage. On both banks, piers and docks are festooned with every sort of vessel, from kayaks and catboats to rowboats and cabin cruisers. The boats belong to the owners of all manner of waterside homes, from small, traditional cottages to Martha Stewart-style enclaves.

Just before entering the pond, look to the starboard shore for a pathway running parallel to the river. You can pull out here and explore another, hillier town conservation area, one which was home to a very active pair of red-tailed hawks when we last paddled here. Smallish Arey's Pond is worth a quick circumnavigation, if only to admire the floating handiwork of boatyard owner Tony Davis, who has been building these broad-beamed cats since 1990.

Paddle out of the pond and back down the inlet to The River. Continue south and Namequoit Point gradually appears on the right. This extension of land forms the unofficial entry into Little Pleasant Bay. It's all private property, but some owners are more generous than others when it comes to determining the tide line. As the tide continues to fall, a sand spit begins to appear at the easternmost tip of the point, providing a scenic resting spot with panoramic views. As you apply more sunscreen and take a drink of water, gaze southward into the bay, with Sipson Island in the distance. Those two islands just a short paddle to port are Sampson and Hog. The very shallow Hog Island Channel runs between them and beyond it, separated by Broad Creek, is the long spit of Nauset Beach.

Paddle over to these islands (privately owned but welcoming of day visitors), and leave them to port. Enter Broad Creek, heading north, with the marshes and flats of Nauset Beach on your right. Pochet (pronounced "po-chee") looms ahead. Paddle east into the small passage between Pochet Island to your left and Little Pochet Island (now an upland hillock that's part of the Nauset barrier) to starboard. You can pull out here, make your way to the beach sand road, and follow the road to the next access point to the beach. Do not cross the dunes, which are fragile and support vulnerable bird species. A jeep trail provides access to Little Pochet, and here you might see northern harriers wafting low over the beach grass; motionless deer staring at you, reluctant to bolt until your impatient movement triggers flight; and songbirds in the pitch pine and scrub oak. You're also likely to find poison ivy, ubiquitous at these upland portions of the sand spit. So always be aware of the oily leaves and berries of this green-red annoyance.

You may see a variety of boats on this trip.

Return to your boat and paddle back around Pochet Island, leaving it to starboard, and proceed into Pochet Inlet. When the tide is in, you can paddle deep along Pochet Creek into East Orleans to a small footbridge at the edge of the Nauset Beach barrier. Watch fiddler crabs mine the mud and green crabs move along with the tidal current. Make sure you have enough water to navigate your way back out! You can use any of several landings on the mainland, if you need to bail out, but they offer limited parking and are surrounded by private property.

If you're planning a full River-Pochet excursion, you want to be paddling this latter portion on an incoming tide, both to assure good water for the salt creeks of the deeper reaches, but also to help propel you back up The River at a time when your body is going to be understandably tired. A sea breeze often develops in the afternoon, so to have the wind at your stern is an added treat.

Be sure to leave Barley Neck on your right and Sampson Island on your left as you briefly re-enter upper Little Pleasant Bay. Continue in a clockwise direction, from south to west to northwest, which puts you on a heading for Namequoit Point (this time on your left) and the gradually narrowing waters of The River.

TRIP 43
MILL POND, STAGE HARBOR

Rating: Moderate
Distance: 4.0 miles
Estimated Time: 4 hours
Location: Chatham

**From a salt pond located within walking distance of Chatham
village, paddle along a tidal creek into a small bay and from
there to a lovely beach on Nantucket Sound.**

Directions
From Route 6 east, take Exit 11. Turn left off the ramp onto Route 137 south
and proceed 2.5 miles to the terminus at Route 28. Take a left on Route 28
and proceed to the rotary, taking a right onto Stage Harbor Road. Proceed
1.5 miles and turn left onto Bridge Street. Cross bridge and park off the
road.

Trip Description
This trip offers an ideal mix of Cape Cod environments, and all on a paddling
excursion that leaves you plenty of time for other activities. With its classic
Cape houses and quaint cottages and lively Main Street bracketed by narrow
lanes, Chatham is a postcard coastal community. The fog that visits each
summer (a result of warmer Nantucket Sound waters meeting those of the
colder Atlantic) adds to the town's maritime authenticity.

Launching on the Mitchell River, paddle northeast toward town on this
short and scenic tidal channel that links Mill Pond and Stage Harbor. The
blades and tower of an old windmill, now the dominant feature of a small
town park, appear on a hill off to the left as you enter the pond; the windmill was constructed here, of course, to take advantage of the same breezes
that might confront you. Circle the pond and return to the river, now on a
southwest heading.

As you proceed down the river, the number of houses and other buildings
on either shore grow fewer, and the salt marsh, eel grass, and diverse marine life come to the fore. Soon, you return to Bridge Street, which connects

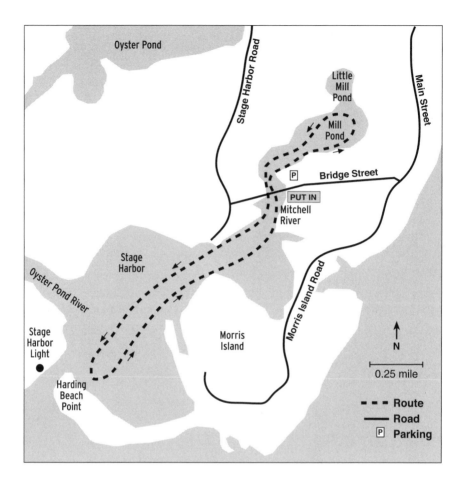

mainland Chatham to Tom's Neck and Morris Island, which form the eastern
arm cradling Stage Harbor. Stage Harbor Marine is located here, an active
marina and boatyard. Numerous boats, from elegant catboats and cabin
cruisers to scallop draggers, are moored at and near the marina, so be aware
of traffic. Anglers also favor these tidal waters, especially when the tide is
running, so keep clear of lines and baited hooks.

South of the bridge, the river widens into Stage Harbor, one of the most
scenic embayments on the south side of the Cape. Point your bow straight
ahead toward the sand barrier of Harding Beach Point. This sand neck forms
the southwesternmost feature of the mainland section of the Monomoy National Wildlife Refuge (the greater part of which comprises North and South
Monomoy Islands to the southeast.)

Off to your right, the Oyster Pond River flows in from Oyster Pond and a town beach, 2.0 miles upstream (a substantial trip in itself). As you continue the paddle across the harbor, you spy Stage Harbor Light ahead on the right-hand shore. The decommissioned navigational guide might no longer play the crucial role it did for mariners it generations ago, but it remains one of the most handsome on the southern New England coast. The lighthouse is located at the tip of Harding's Beach, one of Chatham's prettiest beaches, and at the height of summer one of the most crowded. But you might want to haul out here nonetheless, if only to check out the noble lighthouse. Wind and current can be strong where the harbor meets the open sound, so be sure to find a safe landing spot.

You might be better off steering for the port (east) side of Stage Harbor, which puts you comfortably against the leeward shore of Harding Beach Point. Here you find good shelter from the wind and current, and you enjoy a wide choice of take-out places. This side of the harbor backs up against the Monomoy National Wildlife Refuge at Morris Island. You see many fewer people here than you do on the Harding's Beach side, and the wading, swimming, and beachcombing might even be better. And, if you've packed some sandwiches and cold drinks, this is a perfect spot to enjoy a picnic.

Sit back and enjoy the shore-side show: boat anglers patrolling the channel and shoal water for striped bass, which are plentiful here, and slow-moving, prehistoric horseshoe crabs, covered with barnacles and seaweed, emerging from the water onto the beach.

If you are in a sea kayak, you might consider heading beyond the mouth of Stage Harbor into the sound; consider winds, wave conditions, and current first. If you are paddling an open-cockpit or sit-on-top kayak, stay inside the protected waters, and haul out your boat well in the lee of Harding's Beach or Harding Beach Point.

When you're planning an out-and-back trip on a coastal inlet, deciding how to play the tides is always a challenge, even a puzzle. It is best to launch on an incoming tide; when you are ready to return, you'll have plenty of water. The tide might be slack high or have just turned; any breeze at your back helps send you on your way.

With the wind and sun at your back, watch for great blue heron standing erect, then hunched, as they target small fish and crabs in the marshes. You might also witness more substantial splashes, bluefish corralling bait against shoals and shallows and then launching a feeding frenzy.

A boat is anchored at a dock near Mill Pond.

As you once again approach the marina at Bridge Street, keep an eye on anglers and other boat traffic, but take time to admire the scenic environment that surrounds you on all sides: lovely tidal water bordered by woods and uplands, family boaters and fishers, a working marina. After hauling and securing your boat, you are free to ponder the immediate possibilities: Yes, you can head home or back to your vacation accommodation. Or you can head up into town for shopping, dining, and drinking. From the downtown public parking lot just south of Main Street, you can even zigzag your way along pretty side streets out to Shore Road and to Chatham Lighthouse, where a spectacular view of the ever-changing sand barrier just offshore awaits.

TRIP 44
MONOMOY NATIONAL WILDLIFE REFUGE, MORRIS ISLAND

Rating: Moderate to Difficult
Distance: 10.0 miles
Estimated Time: 5 hours
Location: South Chatham

Explore some of the finest coastal waters of Cape Cod on your way to a pair of islands that comprise the heart of a spectacular national wildlife refuge.

Directions

Follow Main Street east in Chatham to where it intersects with Shore Road. Turn right and continue past the U.S. Coast Guard Station and lighthouse (right) and the public beach (left). Where Bridge Street intersects from the right, descend straight onto what becomes Morris Island Road. The road bears right then meanders left, before crossing a causeway. As you enter the private residential area of Morris Island, look for U.S. Fish and Wildlife Refuge signs; the entrance to the refuge is on the left.

Trip Description

Monomoy, situated on the very tip of the elbow of Cape Cod at the southernmost corner of Chatham, is a National Wildlife Refuge maintained by the U.S. Fish and Wildlife Service. Comprising North and South Monomoy Islands and Morris Island, the refuge totals more than 7,600 acres—two-thirds of it water.

The region was formed by the last ice sheet as it retreated from what is now New England about 18,000 years ago; the islands are estimated to be about 6,000 years old. The area today is home to endangered terns, piping plovers, and an array of other shorebirds. It also supports a large rookery of gray seals.

Launch from refuge headquarters on Morris Island and paddle due east across the Southway to South Beach (an extension of Nauset Beach in

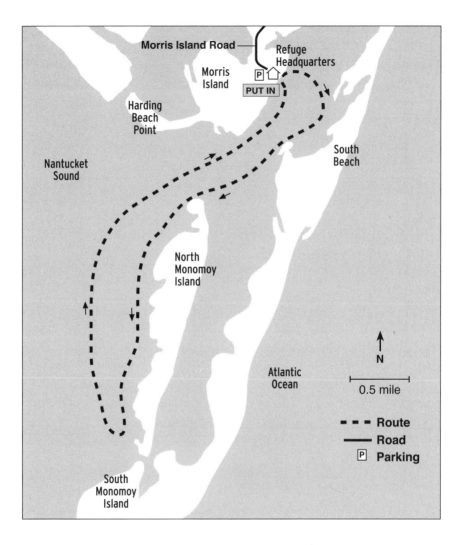

Orleans, but extending below the break across from Chatham Lighthouse). The 0.5-mile paddle is within protected waters—Morris Island, now at your stern, blocks the big breeze—but you should be aware of steady powerboat traffic running perpendicular to your direction here.

This part of the Cape also is subject to some of the most dramatic coastal re-shaping on the East Coast. It was not so long ago that there was no land bridge to South Beach. But nor'easters and other storms have triggered erosional forces that have yet to play out.

Cormorants and seals are just two of the coastal species visitors might spot here.

Constant shoaling caused by ocean storms has altered the coastal geography from year to year, sometimes season to season. In fact, Monomoy and the mainland were linked until a storm cut them off in 1958. The Blizzard of 1978 caused more dramatic changes, as did storms over the next three decades, and today one can walk from Chatham beaches south to the islands again. Over the past few years the Southway, a water artery stretching between the islands and the mainland popular with boaters and saltwater anglers, has continued to fill with sand to the point of impassability in some areas. Local harbor officials, working with state and federal agencies, have been hard-pressed to mark workable, if short-lived channels. For kayakers, however, navigation remains less problematic, even as the age-old challenges remain: wind, current, and fog.

Poet T.S. Eliot, who described fog as moving about "on little cat feet," could never have spent time in Chatham, where the sea-level cloud drops like a dank, stone curtain, and does not lift for days. The town is situated where the shallower and warmer waters of Nantucket Sound meet those of the cold Atlantic, creating ideal conditions for salty condensation.

So, always know the local weather and forecast beforehand. If you en-counter fog, don't paddle; if the forecast calls for fog, be prepared to turn around or have a responsible backup plan.

You must also consider tide and currents (particularly given the capri-cious re-arranging of channels and bars), but the wind—a fairly dependable southwesterly in the warm-weather months—can prove a challenge. A 15-knot breeze on the nose as you're pushing hard for South Monomoy Island can dishearten even the strongest paddler. The challenge is more intense when you venture a bit westward into open Nantucket Sound, where a lively chop can set up.

Pull your boat above the wrack line and enjoy some of the best sunning, swimming, and/or surfcasting on the eastern seaboard. Look for "horse-heads" as the gray seals are called. You can be staring across the water, and suddenly a seal will surface, only its elongated head visible, its dark eyes watching you curiously. You also find this area is prime striped bass and bluefish water. Fishing from kayaks is becoming more popular, and you might want to be part of the trend.

You are going to find it a hard slog along the sand to Monomoy proper, so you might want to re-launch from South Beach and paddle southward across the flats to North Monomoy Island, the 2.5-mile arm of sand and dune that's about half the size of its larger sister. All but 300 acres of the Monomoy refuge is a national wilderness area, so tread lightly. The islands support nesting colonies of endangered least and roseate terns and piping plovers. You also stand a good chance of seeing the dark-bodied, bright-orange-billed oystercatcher, so named because it uses its outsized bill as a tool to open the shells of oysters, clams, and other tasty bivalves.

South Monomoy Island, a short paddle farther, is a more substantial des-tination, home to freshwater ponds, woodsy uplands, a lighthouse, and rem-nants of fishing camps and a nineteenth-century settlement called "White-wash Village." This island is a day trip in itself, recommended for fit paddlers and hikers. (For those not interested in providing all the muscle power, pri-vate charters and tours offer daily trips to the island in season.)

Returning to Morris Island, you might want to linger a bit longer before disembarking. The south tip of Morris is a haven for many marine species, including horseshoe crabs, which patrol these waters by the thousands, feed-ing and resting, mating and dying. Take a leisurely paddle west to Morris

Island Point (yes, a bit into the breeze) for a panoramic view of the mainland stretching west toward Hyannis on Nantucket Sound, the flats approaching the Monomoy Islands, and the southward-extending South Beach.

Return northeast to the stretch of shoreline leading back to the refuge headquarters parking lot and look farther north, to where one of the largest osprey nests in this part of the Cape sits on a tall pole.

Listen for the osprey's cry and then watch for it to appear, the fish in its talons a meal for its mate and young. Having returned from your journey into the wild heart of Monomoy, you may feel a deeper kinship with this being and the other creatures of the coast.

Striped Bass

Cape Cod was named for a fish that sustained indigenous people, colonists, and their descendants. But contemporary residents, vacationers, and, especially, saltwater anglers associate the Cape not with the cod but with *Morone saxatilus*, the striped bass.

Explorer Bartholomew Gosnold, who named Cape Cod in 1602 for the fish he and his crew found in countless numbers, might have just as easily chosen the striper; it, too, was extremely populous and easy to catch. Its Latin genus name, *Morone*, has roots in the Greek *moros*, which means among other things "stupid." But anyone knowledgeable in fishing can quickly reject this historical insult: colonists, and for centuries before them, Americans Indians, found bass numerous precisely because the fish were skilled at hunting, efficient at breeding, and smart enough at avoiding death to safeguard their populations. Bass fishing on the Cape continued for many centuries.

However, in the 1970s stocks began to plunge, as too much commercial fishing, too many recreational anglers, and ignorance about natural pressures on the striper wreaked havoc on the population. What followed were a federal moratorium, state controls, and longer minimum-length restrictions for catching these fish. Many longtime anglers, who grew up catching as many bass as they wanted, found these measures draconian. Nevertheless, ultimately the fishery recovered, and now the moratorium is considered to have been a great success.

Today in Massachusetts, recreational anglers can keep two fish per day that are each a minimum of 28 inches long. Bass can grow to longer than 5 feet. Unlike freshwater fishing, no license is required at present to fish in salt water. Stripers do not put up the same fight as bluefish (the other popular sport fish in these waters), but their meat is sweeter, and more can be done with bass on the grill than with the more oily flesh from a bluefish.

Named for the series of elongated lines running along its body, the striped bass is a popular sport fish along the Northeast coast, Rhode Island to Maine, spring through fall. Stripers are anadromous, meaning they spawn in fresh water and spend most of their lives in salt water. The bass that so enthrall anglers on Cape Cod begin their lives farther down the Atlantic seaboard, primarily in the rivers and feeder streams that enter into Chesapeake Bay. (Stripers that emerge from New York's Hudson River tend to stay closer to home, ranging from New Jersey to Long Island.)

In spring, large schools of stripers descend Chesapeake Bay, reach the Atlantic, and hang a left. They make their way northeast along the coast, skirting the Delaware and Jersey coasts, bearing right to trace the southern shorelines of New York's Long Island. By early June the bass have settled into familiar haunts such as Block Island, Martha's Vineyard, and Nantucket—and Cape Cod.

The powerful currents of the Cape Cod Canal, which is affected by tides at either end, draw stripers from both Cape Cod Bay (east) and Buzzards Bay (west). Anglers line its banks—because the canal is such a busy waterway, fishing from boats is prohibited—especially in late spring and early summer, when bass are chasing herring up local rivers.

Boat anglers do well in Cape Cod Bay, especially above deeper "holes" leading up toward Billingsgate Shoal and Wellfleet. Some of these boats belong to a small charter fleet out of Rock Harbor, on the Orleans/Eastham line.

From mid-September into November, bass are returning south to their wintering and spawning grounds in the Chesapeake. As the water turns colder and the days grow shorter, a primal mechanism triggers this homing instinct, and vast schools of stripers begin to move down the National Seashore. In their need to fatten up for the long trip down the Atlantic coast, stripers are in full feed mode; some of the best fishing of the season takes place when most of the Cape crowds are long gone.

TRIP 45
LITTLE PLEASANT BAY

$ 🏊

Rating: Moderate
Distance: 3.0 miles
Estimated Time: 3 hours
Location: Orleans

Explore this scenic embayment and its islands, salt marshes, and barrier beach, which link sprawling Pleasant Bay in Chatham and The River, which extends into the center of Orleans.

Directions

From Route 6 east, take Exit 11. Turn left onto Route 137 and then take another immediate left onto Pleasant Bay Road. Continue 1.0 mile to a stop-sign intersection with Route 39. Take a left, and proceed 2.0 miles to a stop-sign intersection with Route 28. Proceed through the intersection onto Quanset Road. The town landing is located at the end of the road, about 1.5 miles ahead on the left.

Trip Description

When you emerge from one of the several tidal rivers that wind through the eastern and southern Orleans into Little Pleasant Bay, the paddling possibilities suddenly seem infinite. Begin your trip by paddling east toward the Horseshoe and Sipson Island. This short, scenic stretch of water is The Narrows, one of the gateways to Little Pleasant Bay. As you head north, you will be leaving behind Pleasant Bay to your south. The largest embayment on Cape Cod, Pleasant Bay spreads between the mainland and the 7.0-mile barrier of sand, dune, and marsh that is Nauset Beach, one of the most popular summer destinations in New England.

When you paddle into Little Pleasant Bay, this lovely piece of semi-open water reveals its true charms and attractions. The wide, blue plain of the water, interrupted only by an island once owned by a Middle Eastern prince, beckons canoeists and kayakers. To port, the undulating shore demands

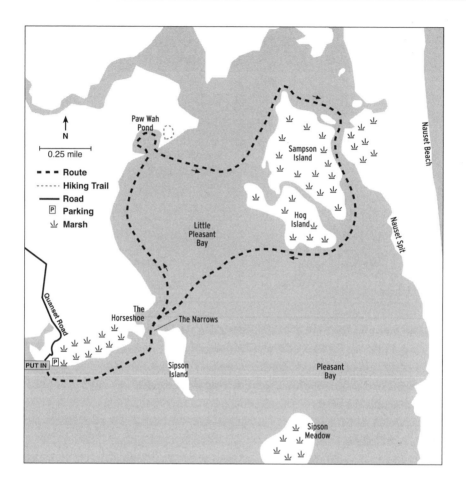

exploration. The Paw Wah Point Conservation Area, managed by the Orleans Conservation Commission, offers a delightful pullout spot. Direct your boat toward Paw Wah Pond, an intimate, sheltered cove that features a small public launch. A quick trip around the pond provides a worthwhile diversion. The swimming in the warm and shallow water of the pond is great, and a loop trail wends through pine, scrub oak, and larger hardwoods and past benches and picnic tables. The view into larger Pleasant Bay is sublime.

As you return to Little Pleasant Bay, watch for osprey circling above a marsh fed by a small tidal creek. What is now a private beach once held piers fronting on an asparagus farm (this part of the Cape was a major asparagus-growing center a century ago). Stalks still spout around the cottages and homes that have been built over the intervening decades. Cross Little Pleasant Bay, bound for the backside of Nauset, where you might still find quiet and solitude even on the busiest weekend of the season. (You might also find greenhead flies for a good part of July.)

On the way, be sure to check out Sampson and Hog Islands, a two-isle archipelago separated by the thinnest of channels. You also find osprey here, as well as herring and black-back gulls, terns, and the full gamut of shorebirds, especially during spring and fall migration seasons. You might also spy a coyote, which can reach the islands from the nearby Nauset spit, where the opportunistic critters have done quite well on birds, washed-up fish, and unsuspecting young seals.

However, remember where you are: looking skyward and waterward is not enough. Little Pleasant Bay attracts plenty of boaters, some more accomplished, experienced, and responsible than others. I have never seen a paddler get tangled up with one of the elegant, broad-beamed catboats that ply these waters (cats were originally a workboat design, steady, sturdy, and shallow-drafted for these waters). But powerboats and personal watercraft are another matter, especially when they're bouncing across the water at full throttle. Keep an eye out at all times for other traffic.

Also, Little Pleasant Bay can present challenges in terms of both wind and tide. Through much of the summer, be prepared for a prevailing southwesterly wind that moves on a diagonal northeastward along this part of the Cape coast; if you are paddling down bay, the pressure is going to be on your starboard bow. Tidal currents affect all boaters in these waters. Little Pleasant Bay emerges into Pleasant Bay, which empties into the Atlantic at Chatham, just south of Orleans. Chatham has had to confront several cracks in the Nauset bar over the past two decades; a breakthrough in spring 2008 has brought a stronger tidal flow into Little Pleasant Bay (where high tide can take place two hours later than at the entrance to Chatham harbor).

Paddlers can take some satisfaction in realizing they have a lot more knowledge than Samuel de Champlain, one of the world's great sea explorers. Of course, Champlain was sailing up and down the New England coast, including what is now Orleans, at the beginning of the seventeenth century. Reportedly, the captain determined the town was too crowded (with local Indians) and chose to establish a settlement instead in what is now Canada.

Little Pleasant Bay features a number of protected coves worthy of exploration.

Returning from Nauset to the mainland, you often find a nice easterly breeze providing a generous push off the beach. The reason is that as the air on the mainland heats up under the summer sun, it rises into the atmosphere, and cooler air off the ocean rushes in to replace it. The extra power provided by nature is a welcome surprise on the trip back.

TRIP 46
NAUSET MARSH

Rating: Moderate
Distance: 5.0 miles
Estimated Time: 3 hours
Location: Eastham

Explore one of the Cape's largest estuaries and see why this spectacular inlet on the Atlantic shore inspired the author of an environmental classic.

Directions
At the Route 6 Orleans-Eastham rotary, continue north on Route 6 into Eastham about 1.5 miles and then turn right onto Hemenway Road, which leads to a town landing on the marsh front.

Trip Description
When you first dip a paddle into the water of Skiff Hill Creek, the tidal stream that introduces you to Nauset Marsh, your inclination might be to explore every backwater and corner in a single day. But you can find so much to see here you may want to split your Nauset Marsh experience into several days, depending on tide and if you want to spend time on the oceanfront.

This trip is ideal when you embark about an hour to 90 minutes before high tide. Slip into the creek and almost immediately you paddle left into Salt Pond Bay. At the northwest corner of the bay you reach a short connector creek leading to Salt Pond, its northern shoreline running just below the Salt Pond Visitor Center. (The center's ranger/educators can fill you in on the history and ecology of the marsh—and they offer plenty of printed material to choose from—but you might want to save this on-land visit for another day.) Shell fishing has a long legacy at Salt Pond, and you might see "farmers" tending their beds.

Paddling back into Salt Pond Bay, continue to port and into Cedar Bank Creek. On your left rise uplands where a bike trail connects the visitor center to Coast Guard Beach. On your right, the marsh extends in a mix of salt grass

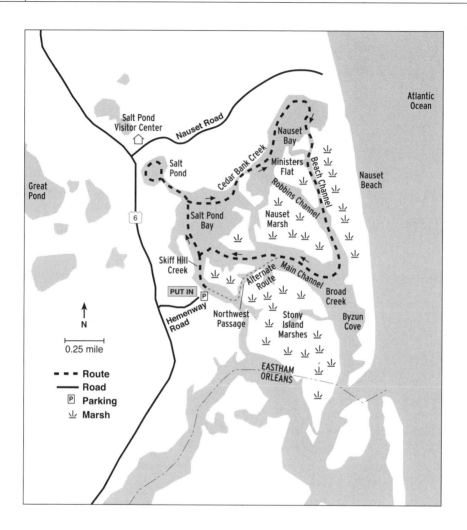

and sand-bottomed channels to the ocean. Especially on a rising tide, you have plenty of water. You can either remain in the main channel (keeping the Eastham mainland on your left) or dart through smaller creeks that define the marsh "islands." Just keep the sun on your right as you make your way into Nauset Bay at the northernmost corner of the marsh.

Now head south across Nauset Bay. Hug the east side (with the long stretch of beach and dunes on your left) and approach Ministers Flat, which you leave to starboard. You now enter Beach Channel, a tidal corridor that is soon joined by Robbins Channel from the right. Beach Channel broad-

You may encounter small boats when paddling Nauset Marsh.

ens here, and the water grows more bay-like as you enter Main Channel. In this stretch, you are the most exposed to natural conditions: the prevailing southwesterlies of summer or sometimes stronger breezes off the ocean.

Where Broad Creek emerges from the Stony Island marshes on your right, bear off to port and haul out on the back side of the ocean beach at semi-protected Byzun Cove. Take a break here (remember: carry two quarts of drinking water and sunscreen on all trips and be prepared for marsh-loving greenhead flies in July). After you are back in your boats, point the bows northwestward (sun on your left, now) and paddle up the Main Channel, leaving Beach Channel to starboard. The tide will probably have turned by this time on your trip, but in the first 90 minutes or so, the currents run only gently against you.

Continue west until a series of creeks enter the marsh on your left. This is the entrance to Northwest Passage, hardly as imposing or challenging as its name might suggest. You have a couple of choices here: Continue along the Main Channel to where it empties into Salt Pond Bay and turn left into Skiff Hill Creek where your launch site awaits a short distance up on your right or paddle into Northwest Passage.

Depending on the water level and your own energy reserves, I recommend this one final exploration in Northwest Passage, with its thick waves of salt marsh grass and their peat underpinnings flanking you on both starboard and port. This narrow tidal waterway also intersects with Skiff Hill Creek. Turn right, and your launch site/starting point looms just ahead.

Before you haul out, take an appreciative glance backward. Estuaries and salt marshes are the world's richest nurseries for marine life and might rival rain forests for overall ecological importance. Much of the finfish and most of the shellfish we consume spend critical periods of their lives in this environment, feeding and growing while (relatively) safe from predators. And given the fact that the desire for water views continues to spur residential development on our coastlines, it's amazing as much salt marsh remains as there is. Once again, we must be grateful for the oversight of the Cape Cod National Seashore.

TRIP 47
WELLFLEET HARBOR AND GREAT ISLAND $ · ≥

Rating: Moderate
Distance: 3.0 miles
Estimated Time: 2 hours
Location: Wellfleet

Paddle across this lovely embayment—explored by Captain John Smith in 1614—then head north to the mouth of the Herring River, and return along the shore of spectacular Great Island.

Directions
From Route 6 east, take a left at the sign for Wellfleet Center (at a traffic light). Bear left onto Commercial Street and follow it to the town pier and parking lot on the left. Launch from the town pier or from adjacent Mayo Beach where Commercial Street turns sharply right to become Kendrick Avenue.

Trip Description
The harbor of this picturesque Outer Cape town of Wellfleet is a recreational enthusiast's delight: You can swim, fish, sail, hike, dig for shellfish, and reserve space on a charter boat bound for Cape Cod Bay practically all in the same day. Kayaking has become an increasingly popular addition to the list; during the summer, especially, it's a rare day that you don't see single paddlers, or more often, multiple boats in small flotillas on the water.

Some kayakers can be spied paddling purposefully across the harbor to Great Island, where they spend an hour or three on this impressive barrier beach. Others leave the pier, hook to the right around Mayo Beach, and explore the upper reaches of the harbor to where it meets the mouth of the Herring River.

This trip combines both routes; upon launching (heed the currents), follow the shoreline on your right, but make sure not to drift into the shallows where commercial aquaculture takes place—stay away from the shellfish

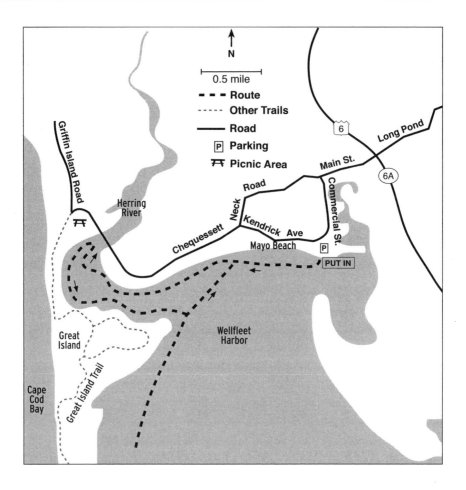

beds! Leaving Mayo Beach off your right stern, proceed up the harbor, and set out one hour before high tide. You pass houses on a bluff as you round Chequessett Neck and the yacht club. The shoreline along the upper harbor veers northwest and soon the bridge separating the harbor from the Herring River appears.

The Herring River, like other tidal waterways along Cape Cod with the same name, earned its moniker from the million of migrating alewives and other anadromous fish that spend most of their lives in salt water but spawn in freshwater streams and inland ponds. Wellfleet's Herring River was once a wide-open artery pushing east 4.0 miles across the Cape to ponds located so close to the ocean side you can hear the surf. The ponds and river mouth remain, but most everything else in between has been altered by a combination of human and natural processes.

Much of the upland stream was hemmed in by plant growth, including dominating shrubs and invasive species such as common reed (phragmites), and pressured by residential development. Mud and other sediment have also had negative effects. But the biggest factor has been the series of dikes built at what is now Chequessett Neck Road, which is as far as you can paddle. The present dike allows for a healthier tidal flow, offering more nourishment to the river habitat inland of the road, which spans the dike on its way to Great Island and Duck Harbor, at the northwest corner of the town.

From your vantage point in the upper harbor, imagine a more ambitious restoration of the tidal river environment: It's going to happen. Local, state, and federal natural resource agencies have produced a plan to restore the Herring River and its watershed to healthy status and thus save one of the largest coastal wetland systems in the nation.

Turning back down the harbor, paddle due west, and the uplands of the Great Island's National Park Service parking and entrance point appear to starboard (on your right). Look for a trail leading down through the pine woods. If you've brought a picnic but prefer eating off the sand, haul out your boat here. Follow the footpath uphill and across the parking lot to where you find picnic tables nestled among the woodlands. Check out the bulletin boards and kiosks that provide additional information about the history and ecology of this intriguing landscape. If picnic tables (which attract more people) are not your thing, continue paddling east and then south and follow the long spit of barrier beach that is Great Island.

This peninsula, which forms the western arm of the harbor and has protected the town from storms for centuries, extends for more than 4.0 miles southward into Cape Cod Bay. Unless you are very experienced and comfortable with potentially ornery wind, wave, and current, remain within the more protected waters of the upper harbor.

After a short paddle south of the picnic area, the spit to your right immediately grows thin; from your boat you can spy small routes off the main trail that lead up and over the dune. They lead to the long bayside beach—and to terrific swimming. If you're looking for a quick dip, this is your chance. Because the prevailing winds of the warm-weather months blow from the southwest and west, hugging the shoreline is advisable. The proximity to land also allows you to see other haul-out places; this lee shore comprises sand, gravel, or shallow marsh and is welcoming to boats along most of its length.

Directly across from a breakwater on the mainland called Indian Neck Jetty, you can pull your boat and explore a short spur of the main Great Island Trail, one that leads to the site of an eighteenth-century tavern. A rough village of seafarers, whalers, and (legend has it) pirates populated this wild coast, and the tavern was the center of social "activity." Storms and civilization eventually brought the demise of this semi-lawless outpost, but its spirit can still be felt by visitors when the wind is up and the skies turn threatening. From this site, situated on a point that juts back toward the mainland, you are afforded terrific views of the harbor, its bobbing boats, and the village rising behind.

Return to your boat, and point your bow to the jetty, the starboard entrance to the harbor. Remember to watch for other boat traffic entering and exiting the harbor/pier area and be especially careful if you are crossing the inner harbor entrance to reach Mayo Beach. If the southwesterly wind is up, as it frequently is by afternoon, you can enjoy a wind-powered ride back to the mainland and your vehicle.

TRIP 48
WELLFLEET PONDS

Rating: Easy to Moderate
Distance: 1.0 mile
Estimated Time: 1.5 hours
Location: Wellfleet

Experience Gull Pond, one of Wellfleet's legendary kettle holes, and the smaller and semi-remote Higgins and Williams Ponds.

Directions

From Route 6 east in Wellfleet, turn right on Gull Pond Road, across from Moby Dick's Restaurant. Follow 1.5 miles to School House Road and the stone marker for Gull Pond on the left. Follow School House Road (dirt) a couple hundred yards to parking on the right.

Trip Description

Plenty of kettle hole ponds can be found on Cape Cod, created in the wake of the retreating ice sheet from melting glacier water left behind in geologic indentations. But Wellfleet's ponds seem special, in terms of both "swimability" and general beauty. The largest, Gull Pond, has been refreshing swimmers and replenishing parched souls (often one and the same) since local Nauset and Payomet Indians were on this landscape many centuries ago. Today, Gull attracts enthusiastic crowds of vacationers, especially families eager to swim, boat, fish, or enjoy all three. (Beach stickers are required from third week in June through Labor Day.)

Anglers and homeowners have kept small dinghies, rowboats, and canoes on the pond for generations, and in recent years, kayakers have discovered this special body of water: a boat livery operates here in season, so visitors can rent boats if they haven't brought their own.

Because this and other Wellfleet ponds tend to be busiest at midday, I recommend paddling either early or late in the day. Like many of these ponds, Gull Pond is round like a kettle. Paddle straight out into the middle

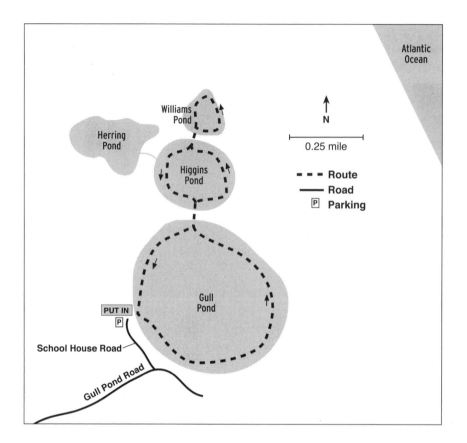

and see how deeply you can see into its extremely clear waters, or follow the shoreline in a lazy circle.

I suggest a counterclockwise paddle, keeping close to shore for a couple of reasons. You are protected from the prevailing breezes out of the southwest, and you can more closely observe shore-side wildlife. Look for frogs among the reed grass and sedges. Ospreys settle on tree branches, waiting for gulls and crows to get out of the sky over the pond and give these fish hawks some hunting room.

Two-thirds of the way around the pond, you pass a small connector channel into much smaller Higgins Pond on your right. Note the remnants of a wood rail system which long ago eased the way for boats moving from one pond to another, when ice harvesting was an important industry and the herring were more plentiful.

Prepare to enter the second stage of your tour of this trio of northern Wellfleet ponds. When the water table is especially high you can probably make it from Gull into Higgins without leaving your boat, but because the passage is only about 30 feet, it's an easy haul when the water is low. Entering Higgins Pond is like passing through a portal to the past; it's quiet, with few or no other boats to disturb the scene. The few homes on its shores provide a study in contrasts—and construction eras. Across the small pond on the northeast shore, an old, classic, Cape-style farmhouse is the picture of simple elegance. Hidden off on the northwest shore is a low, flat, single-story, Modernist home that reflects the architectural aesthetics of a Boston/Cambridge/New York design influence dating to the 1930s.

The shore vegetation grows thicker in Higgins Pond, but another channel leads to Williams Pond, the smallest of this three-pond complex. In making our way into Williams Pond one autumn morning, my wife and I came upon several young Green herons; rather than take flight, they simply stepped through the shallows ahead of us, as if leading the way. Williams Pond is a beautiful, intimate body of water, ringed by water lilies, thick grasses, and red maples. (And high on a shore sits another iconic Modernist house.) It is also the least sandy, marshiest of the three; in fact, the pond is slowly transforming into a swamp—a not-so-rare Cape wetlands phenomenon.

Emerging back into Higgins Pond, look to your immediate right: Deep within the floating-plant habitat hides a small outlet to Herring Pond, which feeds the Herring River, which meanders all the way to Cape Cod Bay by way of upper Wellfleet harbor. Currently, this entire coastal corridor is being restored by local, state, and federal agencies in an effort to preserve the herring fishery.

Continue across Higgins Pond and again cross the short sand bar into Gull Pond. In summer, the activity and sound of people enjoying active recreation seem either reassuring or overwhelming, depending on your personality. Either way, back at the Gull Pond launch site, it's always nice to have people around to help haul out the boats and lift them back onto your vehicle.

TRIP 49
PAMET RIVER

Rating: Easy to Moderate
Distance: 4.0 miles
Estimated Time: 4 hours (depending on take-outs)
Location: Truro

Ride the tide through an attractive salt marsh and enjoy a swim on the Cape Cod Bay.

Directions
From Route 6 east in Truro, take the "Pamet Roads" exit and continue right to the immediate junction with South Pamet Road. Take another quick right and proceed under the highway to the intersection with Truro Center Road. Turn right and then take a quick left into the parking lot between the Jams store and U.S. Post Office. River access is behind the post office, down a short embankment.

Trip Description
This picturesque tidal stream meanders like few others, almost to the point of creating oxbows; you often feel you're moving north-south as often as east-west on this watercourse that nourishes a broad salt marsh. Of course, the tide can work for you: If you launch a couple hours after slack high, you can enjoy a pretty sweet ride out to the bay, with only occasional paddling required.

Not far from the put in, a few inlets snake away to port. Be careful here. These fingers can lead you into a maze of false starts and dead ends, and if the tide is retreating, you can find yourself at low water, too shallow for even a kayak.

What I most enjoy about this trip is the broad vistas that spread before you; the salt marsh is almost 0.5 mile wide for much of the journey to the bay. The sun runs along your left shoulder and, by the time you reach the harbor, is glistening across the bay from the southwest. As you meander westward, watch for great blue herons poking their heads out of the salt

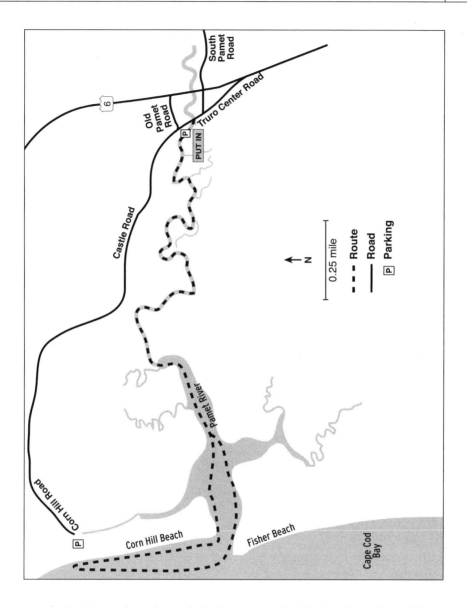

marsh. By September, this rich feeding ground, full of crabs and small fish, attracts the graceful wading birds in substantial numbers; they're bulking up before migrating south for the winter.

Approaching the harbor, you pass the remains of a rail bed and trestle on your right; on the left it has been replaced by part of the town landing parking lot. In the 1870s, the Old Colony line finally reached Provincetown and its substantial fishing industry. The train ran all the way to a pier on Provincetown harbor, where freight cars would be loaded with fish before heading back to Boston, New York, and points west.

Just west of the rail bed, watch for signs designating shallows and barely submerged rock piles. Also keep an eye on boat traffic emerging from the yacht club located just beyond the town landing (which also is home to the office of the Truro harbormaster, who can answer plenty of questions about the river, tides, and weather).

Continue through a small mooring field of boats ranging from rowing dinghies and day sailors to larger motor vessels and sport fishing boats. Because of continued shoaling of the harbor (which effectively ended the town's whaling industry after the American Revolution, allowing Nantucket to claim title as whaling capital by the early nineteenth century), most recreational vessels must negotiate the harbor entrance within two hours on either side of high tide. But kayaks face no such restrictions.

Note that the conditions on the open bay, exposed to the summer months' prevailing southwesterly wind, can be more challenging than those of the sheltered river. Depending on the combination of wind and tide, you can face a chop as you emerge at the river mouth, a stiff breeze, or both.

Those opting to remain inside the harbor but looking for a place to take out and maybe take a swim have some nice options. Bear off to port and land on the back side of what is the northernmost stretch of Fisher Beach. Haul your boats above the high-water mark and walk around a small dune structure to the beach front. Walk south along the beach and find yourself in "Hopper country." Look left to see where renowned American artist Edward Hopper lived in a Cape-style house nestled within a coastal moorland overlooking the dunes.

Or paddle to starboard and land where a small tide pool laps against a protective sand spit that's part of the backside of Corn Hill Beach. My wife and I call this take-out spot "Labrador Point," in honor of our kayak-riding Labrador retriever, Oban, who digs himself a sand hole here to rest up between plunges into the tide pool. Those paddlers looking for a more robust and scenic trip can continue between the breakwaters into the bay. You are going to be gazing into the sun (unless you're on dawn patrol), so wear a hat and sunglasses to cut down on the glare off the water and be prepared for one of the finest views the Cape has to offer. The curve of the shore grows increasingly concave here; you can look to port and see all the way beyond Wellfleet to Eastham or to starboard for views of North Truro's Beach Point, downtown Provincetown, and curling back southeast toward you, the sandy finger of Long Point at the Cape's slowly elongating tip.

Point your bow northwestward, so that the shoreline of Corn Hill Beach is on your right. The hill is located a few hundred yards ahead and is home to a former colony of quaint artist cottages and other, more recent—and much larger—vacations homes, all taking advantage of the fabulous bay views. (Because it faces west, the beach and hillside are prime vantage points for enjoying sunsets.)

At the north end of the town beach parking lot, look for a historical plaque at the base of Corn Hill that explains the name. Famished explorers from the Mayflower reportedly discovered a cache of corn that local Payomet people had buried. The Pilgrims consumed the corn and supposedly invited the Indians to dine with them to make amends. The feast took place in the fall of 1621: the first Thanksgiving.

Return to the harbor entrance and make your way carefully into the harbor, again keeping an eye out for boat traffic. If you haven't spent a few hours exploring, you might find yourself pushing against the still-outgoing tide. If you've planned well, you again have the tide at your stern, providing a nice assist all the way back to the post office parking lot.

TRIP 50
PROVINCETOWN HARBOR/LONG POINT

Rating: Moderate
Distance: 4.0 miles
Estimated Time: 4 hours
Location: Provincetown

Paddle across an historic harbor to a scenic beach that serves as a natural protective barrier for this legendary community.

Directions
From Route 6 in Provincetown, take a left at a traffic light onto Conwell Street and follow it to the terminus at Bradford Street. Take a right on Bradford Street for 0.75 mile to Franklin Street, which joins Commercial Street. Follow Commercial Street as it jogs right a couple hundred yards to a municipal, metered parking lot on the left, adjacent to the boat launch and harborside beach.

Trip Description
Provincetown Harbor can be a lively place at peak paddling season in summer, so I don't recommend launching from the main piers and parking areas in the center of town. Instead, head for this quieter spot in the lovely West End, just beyond the U.S. Coast Guard station. At this far end of the harbor, the water at low tide gets pretty thin indeed, so heed your tide chart.

To your right is a series of shore-side cottages and private homes, and the Red Inn, which offers some of the finest dining on the Cape with an unparalleled view of the harbor and Long Point. At the farthest end is a dike built to protect a salt marsh farther west and, beyond, Herring Cove Beach. The fact that this upper part of Provincetown Harbor is so protected is partially why the Pilgrims decided to make landfall here in 1620.

After crossing the open ocean in the Mayflower (which must have seemed smaller and more cramped by the day) and being rebuffed by the unbroken wall of dune cliffs that are now the foundation of the National Seashore, this hardy band was certainly relieved to round the hook of Race Point and find a large inlet generally protected from wave and wind.

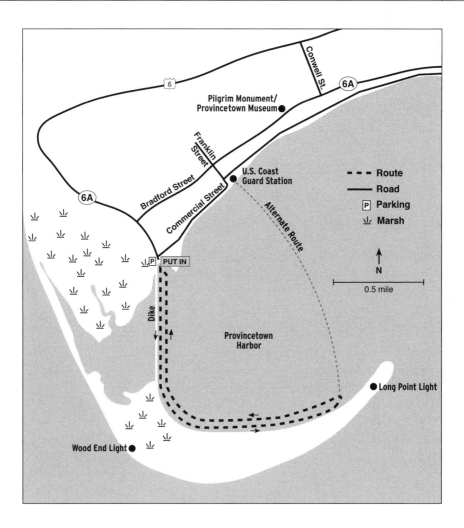

This inlet is where you find yourselves now. Keep the boulder dike (by which walkers can reach the peninsula) well on your right; sand flats appear as the tide falls, and you want to make sure you have good water for the crossing. Gaze over at the far terminus of the dike, and you can see Wood End Light, one of two mariner aids on the sand barrier that forms the outermost tip of Provincetown. Long Point Light is the other beacon and is situated at the far end of the barrier, where the spit is pointing like a crooked finger back northeast toward the Truro-Provincetown border. Both lights, Wood End blinking red and Long Point green, have been automated for many years.

Well into the nineteenth century, men, women, and children lived and worked in a thriving fishing station on Long Point. The community gradually declined, and many of its houses were transported by barge across the water to the West End, where they stand today, marked by blue-and-white tiles denoting their history and origin.

Keep your bow headed for the middle of Long Point, roughly south from the long pier of the U.S. Coast Guard station you are leaving over your left shoulder. You approach a network of tidal inlets and small embayments, marked by cordgrass and sheltering everything from shorebirds to fiddler crabs. You can explore these habitats and pull your boat onto a sandy area or reverse course and continue farther east and northeast along the inside shore.

If you're in the mood for a hike, secure your boats among the far edges of this marshy area. Walk south, be careful not to disturb the beach grass, and cross the sand road that traces the beach on the bay side. Here, you have the chance to encounter more iconic wildlife, including gray seals near the shore and, in the mid-distance on a clear, calm day, whales. Each spring, Cape Cod Bay welcomes back several species of whales that have traveled up the East Coast from the Caribbean to feed in the warm, rich waters off Provincetown. You might see minke, finback, humpback, or the rare right whale.

With your kayak or canoe secure from an incoming tide, you can continue exploring this spectacular barrier all the way to the tip of Long Point (about a 0.5-mile walk). But paddling along the shore can be even more memorable. Return to the inlet entrance and paddle to starboard, keeping the barrier on your right. As you make your way down the inside shore, boat traffic grows. Keep an eye out for power boaters also headed for Long Point; commercial fishing boats, both those bound for the open ocean and others returning to port; and whale-watch cruises. Whale-watching has grown into a major tourism industry for the state, and Provincetown is its epicenter. Several companies offer tours to thousands of tourists each season; you stand a good chance that you and your boat wind up as part of someone's photo collection of their trip to Cape Cod.

All the larger vessels give the inner harbor a wide berth and rarely pose a threat. But as you pass Long Point Light and approach the coarse-sand tip of the barrier, you want to be extra careful. I've seen kayakers round Long Point and paddle along its outer shore. But extending your trip in this way leaves

Provincetown Harbor is home to many types of boats.

you exposed to wind, wave, and current, which can provide substantial challenges when the prevailing southwesterly wind is up.

I recommend leaving such adventures to experienced sea kayakers, those who possess the appropriate knowledge, experience, and equipment. When you've decided to head back, either again hug the shore (now on your left) and then bear off to starboard when the U.S. Coast Guard pier looms off to your right, across the harbor. Or if you've gained confidence after your successful outward passage, just paddle in a straight shot northwest across the harbor, using the U.S. Coast Guard Station pier as your navigational point. Then bear off slightly to port to reach the beach and launch area by the parking lot.

Appendix A:
Outfitters

Biking

Brewster
Brewster Bike (adjacent to the Cape Cod Rail Trail)
442 Underpass Rd.
Brewster, MA 02631
508-896-8149
www.brewsterbike.com

Chatham
Chatham Cycle (near the Harwich-Chatham spur bike path)
193 Depot Rd.
Chatham, MA 02633
508-945-8981
www.brewsterbike.com/chatham.html

Eastham
Little Capistrano Bike Shop (between the Cape Cod Rail Trail and Nauset
Marsh Bike Trail)
30 Salt Pond Rd.
Eastham, MA 02642
508-255-6515
www.capecodbike.com

Idle Times Bike Shop (adjacent to the Cape Cod Rail Trail)
4550 Rte. 6
North Eastham, MA 02651
508-255-8281
www.idletimesbikes.com

Falmouth
Corner Cycle (near Shining Sea Bikeway)
115 Palmer Ave.
Falmouth, MA 02540
508-540-4195
www.cornercycle.com

Provincetown
Ptown Bikes (near Province Lands Bike Trail)
42 Bradford St.
Provincetown, MA 02657
508- 487-8735
www.ptownbikes.com

Paddling

Bourne
Cape Cod Kayak
1270 Rte. 28A
Bourne, MA 02532
508-563-9377
www.capecodkayak.com

Dennis
Bass River Cruises/Howie's Kayaks (on Bass River)
Rte. 28
West Dennis, MA 02670
508-362-5555

Cape Cod Waterways (on Swan Pond River)
16 Rte. 28
Dennis Port, MA 02639
508- 398-0080
www.capecodwaterways.org

Hyannis
Sea Sports
195 Ridgewood Ave.
Hyannis, MA 02601
508-790-1217
www.capecodseasports.com

Orleans
Goose Hummock Shop
Rte. 6A (at rotary)
Orleans, MA 02653
508-255-0455
www.goose.com

Provincetown
Flyer's Boat Rental Inc.
131A Commercial St. (on Provincetown Harbor)
Provincetown, MA 02657
508-487-0898, ext. 205

Appendix B: Conservation and Recreation Organizations

Appalachian Mountain Club
5 Joy St.
Boston, MA 02108
Tel: 617-523-0636
www.outdoors.org

Cape Cod National Seashore
99 Marconi Site Rd.
Wellfleet, MA 02667
Tel: 508-771-2144
www.nps.gov/caco

The Compact of Cape Cod Conservation Trusts, Inc.
3239 Main St.
P.O. Box 443
Barnstable, MA 02630
Tel: 508-362-2565
www.compact.cape.com

Massachusetts Audubon Society
208 South Great Rd.
Lincoln, MA 01773
Tel: 781-259-9500
www.massaudubon.org

Monomoy National Wildlife Refuge
Wikis Way, Morris Island
Chatham, MA 02633
Tel: 508-945-0594
www.fws.gov/northeast/monomoy

The Nature Conservancy of Massachusetts
205 Portland St.
Suite 400
Boston, MA 02114
Tel: 617-227-7017
www.nature.org/massachusetts

The Trustees of Reservations
Long Hill
572 Essex St.
Beverly, MA 01915
Tel: 978-921-1944
www.thetrustees.org

U.S. Army Corps of Engineers
Cape Cod Canal Visitor Center
60 Ed Moffitt Dr.
Sandwich, MA 02563
Tel: 508-833-9678
www.nae.usace.army.mil

Index

About the Author

MICHAEL O'CONNOR is a writer and editor for The Trustees of Reservations. Previously, he was the *Boston Herald* outdoors and recreation writer for 20 years.

For more than three decades, he has hiked throughout New England, from the mountains of Maine to the trails of Cape Cod. O'Connor has paddled on Maine's whitewater rivers, the quiet rivers of eastern Massachusetts, and along many of Cape Cod's bays, harbors, and tidal streams. He is often accompanied by his wife, Jackie, in her kayak, and by their dog, Oban, who sits nobly in the front of the author's open-cockpit model.

O'Connor has been riding mountain bikes on both single track and rail trails since 1986. Before that, his most challenging cycling adventure was a frantic loop around the Arc de Triomphe in Paris at rush hour.

The Appalachian Mountain Club

Founded in 1876, the AMC is the nation's oldest outdoor recreation and conservation organization. The AMC promotes the protection, enjoyment, and wise use of the mountains, rivers, and trails of the Northeast outdoors.

People

We are nearly 90,000 members in 12 chapters, 16,000 volunteers, and more than 450 full time and seasonal staff. Our chapters reach from Maine to Washington, D.C.

Outdoor Adventure and Fun

We offer more than 8,000 trips each year, from local chapter activities to major excursions worldwide, for every ability level and outdoor interest—from hiking and climbing to paddling, snowshoeing, and skiing.

Great Places to Stay

We host more than 150,000 guest nights each year at our AMC lodges, huts, camps, shelters, and campgrounds. Each AMC Destination is a model for environmental education and stewardship.

Opportunities for Learning

We teach people the skills to be safe outdoors and to care for the natural world around us through programs for children, teens, and adults, as well as outdoor leadership training.

Caring for Trails

We maintain more than 1,700 miles of trails throughout the Northeast, including nearly 350 miles of the Appalachian Trail in five states.

Protecting Wild Places

We advocate for land and riverway conservation, monitor air quality, and work to protect alpine and forest ecosystems throughout the Northern Forest and Highlands regions.

Engaging the Public

We seek to educate and inform our own members and an additional 2 million people annually through AMC Books, our website, our White Mountain visitor centers, and AMC Destinations.

Join Us!

Members support our mission while enjoying great AMC programs, our award-winning *AMC Outdoors* magazine, and special discounts. Visit www.outdoors.org or call 617-523-0636 for more information.

THE APPALACHIAN MOUNTAIN CLUB
Recreation • Education • Conservation
www.outdoors.org

AMC Southeastern Massachusetts Chapter

The Appalachian Mountain Club's Southeastern Massachusetts Chapter offers outdoor activities, conducts trail work, and addresses local conservation issues south of Boston and on Cape Cod and the Islands. Programs range from hiking and cycling to skiing, paddling, and backpacking.

To view a list of AMC activities in Southeastern Massachusetts and other parts of the Northeast, visit trips.outdoors.org

AMC Book Updates

AMC Books strives to keep our guidebooks as up-to-date as possible to help you plan safe and enjoyable adventures. If after publishing a book we learn that trails are relocated or route or contact information has changed, we will post the updated information online. Before you hit the trail, check for updates at www.outdoors.org/publications/books/updates.

While hiking or paddling, if you notice discrepancies with the trail description or map, or if you find any other errors in the book, please let us know by submitting them to amcbookupdates@outdoors.org or in writing to Books Editor, c/o AMC, 5 Joy Street, Boston, MA 02108. We will verify all submissions and post key updates each month.

AMC Books is dedicated to being a recognized leader in outdoor publishing. Thank you for your participation.

AMC BOOKS & MAPS

EXPLORE THE POSSIBILITIES

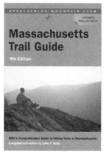

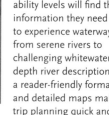